CULTURAL REVOLUTIONS

CULTURAL REVOLUTIONS

reason versus culture
in philosophy,
politics, and *jihad*

lawrence e. cahoone

**the pennsylvania state university press
university park, pennsylvania**

Lyrics excerpted from Bob Dylan's "All Along the
Watchtower." Copyright © 1968 by Dwarf Music.
All rights reserved. International copyright secured.
Reprinted by permission.

Library of Congress Cataloging-in-Publication Data

Cahoone, Lawrence E., 1954–
    Cultural revolutions : reason versus culture in
    philosophy, politics, and jihad / Lawrence E. Cahoone.
       p.   cm.
Includes bibliographical references and index.
ISBN 978-0-271-02525-4 (alk. paper)
1. Social history—20th century.
2. Social history—21st century.
3. Cognition and culture.
4. Culture conflict.
5. Cultural relativism.
6. Multiculturalism.
I. Title.

HN17.5.C314 2005
306'.09—dc22
2004020481

First paperback printing, 2006

Copyright © 2005 The Pennsylvania State University
All rights reserved
Printed in the United States of America
Published by The Pennsylvania State University Press,
University Park, PA 16802-1003

The Pennsylvania State University Press is a member of the
Association of American University Presses.

It is the policy of The Pennsylvania State University Press
to use acid-free paper. Publications on uncoated stock
satisfy the minimum requirements of American National
Standard for Information Sciences—Permanence of Paper
for Printed Library Material, ANSI Z39.48–1992.

CONTENTS

For the New York,
and the New Yorkers,
I have loved

ACKNOWLEDGMENTS

I would like to thank Anthony Appiah, Elizabeth Baeten, Peter Berger, Glenn Loury, Bhikhu Parekh, and David Wong for helpful discussions and encouragement over the years regarding the issues discussed in this book. I am especially grateful to Ibrahim Kalin, Robert Neville, and Lorenzo Simpson for critical comments on parts or all of the text. Of course none of the above ought to be tarred by my tribute; like most sensible people they can be presumed to disagree with my views. I assert my claim to sole discredit. Last, I thank Sandy Thatcher of Penn State Press for bringing my work to print.

Rationalization has thus far been successful because it has
not been completely successful.

—EDWARD SHILS

INTRODUCTION: THE RETURN OF THE REPRESSED

When I graduated from college in the American bicentennial year of 1976 preparing to vote for Jimmy Carter, the most important geopolitical distinction on Earth was clear to everyone. It was the opposition between the democratic, capitalist West (plus Japan) and the Soviet Union (with China and other communist allies). Of course there was a "third world" and there were "nonaligned" countries. From today's standpoint those very terms were a Eurocentric conceit expressing the priority that the developed North granted itself over the concerns of the developing-and-undeveloped South (or to be more precise, the Not-So-North, populations living entirely below thirty-eight degrees north). But whatever its indigenous issues, the South had always to be conscious of the third rail of international relations, that bipolar Northern line, where every step toward/away from the "West" meant a step away from/toward the "East." The complexities of the Soviet-China relationship and Richard Nixon's deft manipulations had rendered "monolithic" communism a fantasy, but had done nothing to defang the conflict of two globe-straddling political economies sporting globe-annihilating nuclear overkill. As long as it dominated, this geopolitical paradigm gave credence to the modern European philosophy of Economic Man, common to the capitalist West and the communist East, for which secular prosperity, privately held or publicly owned, unequally accumulated or equally distributed, is the great determinant of social reality. After all, nationalistic and racist mysticism, the assumed remnants of a premodern world of superstition and jingoism, had been defeated on the battlefield in 1945. And if the greatest domestic struggle of postwar America was an analogous fight against a "primitive" racism, its resolution was understood by black activists, white liberals, and even its white opponents to be the transcendence of race by political-economic equality. Power and prosperity were the shared languages of the Cold War era, internationally and domestically; any problem was caused by their absence, any solution by their provision.

For progressives and economic conservatives, welfare state liberals and minimal state libertarians, John Rawls and Robert Nozick, money, jobs, taxes, and economic opportunity were the coin of the political realm. On these grounds, in 1976 Carter, who hedged toward the former, defeated Gerald Ford, who hedged toward the latter.

But not so four years later, when Carter ran against Ronald Reagan, but was defeated by the Ayatollah Khomeini. Ronald Reagan won the election, of course, but it was arguably the Khomeini-led Iranian revolution, whose Islamists painted America as "the Great Satan" and held American embassy hostages in Teheran for more than a year that finished Carter's chances. It was the first major shock to the triumphant liberal paradigm. Suddenly it appeared that some people were willing to trade economic development for religious identity, to—in the paradigm's terms—go backward. Still, the modern economic framework's greatest success was yet to come, for after an intensification of the Cold War in the next decade, 1989 brought the fall of the Berlin Wall, inspiring Francis Fukuyama's famous essay, "The End of History." His argument that liberal democratic capitalism was the final and universal form of world history captured the mood, and seemed confirmed by the end of communism in Central Europe, the collapse of the USSR, and China's experiments with the free market. After the first war in the Persian Gulf reshuffled the deck in the Middle East, setting the stage for the Oslo Accords, and a possible Israeli-Palestinian settlement, it seemed that without the prospect of Soviet backing a number of apparently intransigent international and sectarian conflicts might simply burn out. Peace seemed to be breaking out all over.

But the Pax Fukuyama didn't last long. By the mid-1990s a general renewal of nationalism and ethnic politics became apparent, most notably in the Balkans, but most horribly in Rwanda. All over the world there seemed to be a rebirth of tribal, ethnonationalist aspirations and intolerance. Religious fundamentalism, or as Giles Keppel put it, "the revenge of God," was in full swing: Christian fundamentalism in domestic American politics; Jewish, Buddhist, and Hindu fundamentalisms in Israel and south Asia; and of course the ever widening hit-and-run conflict with Islamic militancy (Keppel 1994). Samuel Huntington's announcement of the coming "clash of civilizations" in a 1993 essay gave a name to this dawning reality. But in America under the Clinton administration the rising din of ethnic and religious revivalism was drowned out by the louder sounds of happy cash registers and less-than-happy presidential depositions. Meanwhile, officials and pundits seemed almost nostalgically to reimpose a bipolar world in their concern over the fate of Russian missiles and the likelihood of China as the threat of the new century, the latter encouraged by the Chinese holding of an American military jet and crew, a "crisis" now barely remembered. Roughly, this is how things stood at eight in the morning, EDT, on September 11, 2001.

But not an hour later. The events of that morning did not "change everything." Islamic fundamentalism, American terror casualties, even the attempted destruction of the World Trade Center were already old hat. But September 11 did complete the shift in our priorities, putting the final nail in the coffin of the economistic paradigm. It was now apparent that globalization meant not the end of Old World politics but their magnification, ancient rickety joints now greased by an open, technological, mass media environment. The irony is deep. Precisely when the most advanced societies were rushing to trade in the Grand Narratives of history, and perhaps even the nation-state, for an exploding network of information markets in a borderless space of free trade—globalization meets the postmodern condition—they came face to face with an apparently premodern fundamentalism as their main enemy, the thin edge of a world environment suddenly brimming with fights over blood, soil, and God. Who would have thought as Bill Gates and other computer cowboys rode their bulls down Wall Street in the mid-1990s into the Brave New World of nonideological capital circulating the world as electronic data, that in half a decade we would be discussing the *Crusades* as a significant predisposing event for international relations! Or that the most devastating military attack on American soil in history, a security undented by two World Wars and a forty-year nuclear stand-off, never breached by German planes, Japanese *kamikazes,* or Soviet missiles, would be accomplished by nineteen religious zealots with plastic box-cutters during "peacetime."

For, as a recent book title has it, we have now to admit that *culture matters.* From our concern for toleration and diversity in an increasingly multicultural America to the global rise in ethnic-cultural violence, from the creation of new fields like "cultural studies" to the cultural-religious clash of Islam with the West, the things labeled "cultural" seem to be at the forefront of our time. As Huntington argued, after being driven by political and economic ideology for seventy years, international conflict now is re-forming along civilizational or cultural axes. Not that economics has left center stage; it is one of the perennial house players. But we no longer imagine that all human motivation, all conflict, all serious debates, are ultimately about money, or money-and-power. Man does not kill for bread alone. Our world's most deadly struggles are about blood and soil and language and who your grandparents were. Along a series of political issues, *identity* has trumped *class*. Today the furors of domestic politics are more likely to concern the complaints of disenfranchised ethnic, sexual, and gender groups than the poor. Cultures themselves are being rewritten because of the new recognition of culture, long-standing historical narratives revised by the incorporation of indigenous and non-Western viewpoints: it is now a canonical piece of grade school learning that Columbus did *not* discover America. The left attacks cultural imperialism, the right attacks cultural relativism. Clashing cultures, recognizing cultures, fearing cultures: these now take up a large part of our attention.

The sea change goes beyond the task of dealing with the legacy of racism or colonialism, beyond the issue of "inclusiveness." It reveals a new notion of self and equality. A half-century ago the equality sought by most disenfranchised Americans was moral, civic, and economic, an equality that was supposed to ignore ethnic or cultural differences in favor of the common humanity beneath. The figure of the "melting pot" that Israel Zangwill used to title his 1908 play was pleasantly warm, not oppressively hot, as long as sameness meant educational, economic, and political opportunity. Minority Americans wanted to be recognized as equals *despite* their ethnicity. Lyndon Johnson, champion of the welfare state, who did more for the civil rights of African-Americans than any president since Lincoln, understood himself to be voicing the ultimate respect for Martin Luther King Jr. by saying that King "is a credit to his race — the *human* race." In 1965 that saying was progressive and liberal; now it is viewed as an unattractive compromise. Minorities today want to be recognized as equals *not despite* but *through* their distinctive identities, as fully encultured agents. They want admittance to the forum and the market in their own skins and traditional clothing. During a speech Colin Powell noted the tendency of some people to cease identifying him as black once he became successful, to grant him a kind of ethnic-racial neutrality. To which Powell rhetorically objected, "Don't stop now!"

All this troubles the very heart of our understanding of the modern age and its direction. From the 1950s through the early 1970s, despite the widespread prejudices of the day, the "enlightened" or official progressive view held that culture and religion are private matters, that public policy, domestic and international, should focus on the pragmatic issues of economic development. The future would be one of mutually respectful individuals pursuing the benefits of culture-neutral technology and science within a framework of universally recognized political rights. If not now, then soon, the world's peoples would stop worrying about silly things like ethnic conflicts and religious wars and recognize that deep down they are all modern liberal materialists at heart, primarily interested in education, economic security, modern health care, and Colonel Sanders. This was not a bad or amoral vision. Conflicts over money, taxes and welfare, unions and big business, however troublesome and even bloody, do seem more tractable for rational argument than questions over identity. If primordial issues of religion and ethnicity could be taken off the agenda, then, however rancorously, we could at least *do business* with each other.

A marvelous sample of our old thinking comes, again, from that Texan who bestrode the 1960s like, well, a Texan. In April 1965 Johnson, who had made his early political career fighting for rural electrification, tried to entice the North Vietnamese to the bargaining table with a promise of American help in building a hydroelectric grid for the Mekong Delta, modeled on the Tennessee Valley Authority. LBJ wanted to build a TVA for the NLF. We can almost hear him now: "If Ho Chi Minh wants to do some bargaining, we'll God damn well show him some bargaining!" As Bill Moyers later commented, "If Ho had been [then AFL-CIO president] George Meaney, Johnson would have had a deal." But Ho wasn't a jowly, clean-shaven union leader, he was a thin Vietnamese nationalist and communist with a long beard and a longer memory of grievances against the West. Whatever we may think of him, he could not be bought off with light bulbs.

Today Johnson's proposal may seem more lovable than loathsome, but in either case, laughable. The list of sobering experiences we have graduated from is long: Ho's introductory course in Third World nationalism and ideological tenacity heads the list, of course, followed by the intermediate course in Teheran, advanced study in the Persian Gulf, the never-ending Israeli-Palestinian seminar, and finally our graduation exercises on September 11. But even if we are less naive today, I suspect that deep down we contemporary Americans still find it no easier than did LBJ to understand people who are willing to sacrifice their children's lives to avenge their parents, or to ensure that their rulers pray in the right language or with the right book. But many *are* willing. "It's the economy, stupid" may work in some U.S. presidential elections, but it most emphatically has not worked in Bosnia or Jerusalem or Rwanda or Afghanistan. Or lower Manhattan.

Philosophy and political theory have not ignored the new salience of culture. Many writers have come to question the "classical" liberal theorists of the 1970s—John Rawls, Robert Nozick, Thomas Nagel, Ronald Dworkin, Bruce Ackerman, and others—for imagining systems of political rights that hold universally regardless of cultural differences and which, although concerned with social justice, allow no role whatsoever for cultural identity. In response, a new generation of political theorists has sought to find a place for "group" identity and a "right to culture" within liberal democracy, even if this requires that such will sometimes trump strict legal equality or individual liberty. While echoing the critique of rights-based liberalism developed by the communitarians in the 1980s and early 1990s, most of these "new culturalists" follow the progressive-liberal tradition—famously expressed by historian Richard Hofstadter—in fearing local community as a source of jingoistic antipathy to minorities. Nor was this new cultural turn limited to political theory. Recent ethicists have reacted against the rationalist-theoretical project of establishing universal moral principles on the basis of an individually accessed Reason. Stuart Hampshire, Alasdair MacIntyre, Bernard Williams, and Martha Nussbaum have all argued that the complexity of moral life, dependent as it is on the ethical significance of manners, social customs, moral "luck," and inherited cultural narratives, cannot be reduced to a few abstract and universal principles.

A cultural turn can be identified in even the more abstruse areas of philosophical thought. Recent attacks on realism, the claim that our knowledge is made true by its relation to objective facts, have invoked the cognitive role of culture, proposing "solidarity" rather than "objectivity" as the court of last resort for the legitimation of belief (Rorty 1991b). The retreat from transcendental and foundationalist theories of meaning, common to both Anglo-American and European philosophy in the middle of the last century, has in effect *opened epistemology to culture.* In Anglo-American philosophy the early twentieth-century dominance of logical positivism had been eclipsed in midcentury by Wittgenstein's ordinary-language philosophy, which made meaning emergent from social practice. "Social constructivism" became a major contributor to, and problem in, the philosophy of science after the ground-breaking work of Thomas Kuhn. Eventually Richard Rorty declared that the commitment to rights and reason, lacking any noncircular justification, should simply be accepted as the "frankly ethnocentric" orientation of the West. Meanwhile, in European thought a parallel development took place. The early and mid-twentieth-century "philosophies of the subject"—

phenomenology, psychoanalysis, existentialism, and "Western" Marxism—
had shared the view that an inner self, alienated by the social forces of capitalism, religion, science, and mass culture, was the real source of meaning,
truth, and society. These philosophies were eclipsed in the century's second
half by hermeneutics, structuralism, and eventually poststructuralism, for
which historicized networks of signs form the background from which
meaning and self emerge. On both sides of the North Atlantic, language,
understood now as social, contingent, and practical, became the dominant
topic of twentieth-century philosophy and, through a remarkable inver-
sion, came to be understood as the *source of* logic, truth, and the self, rather
than their product.

Unfortunately, all this attention to the trees failed to reveal the forest.
While ethics, epistemology, metaphilosophy, and political philosophy embraced intersubjectivity, dialogue, and signs, their authors rarely achieved
the revelation of Monsieur Jourdain in Molière's *The Bourgeois Gentleman,*
who discovers that he has been speaking prose all his life. They failed to
recognize that the collective name for the diverse phenomena they were
examining is "culture." So while social and political philosophy, philosophy
of language, philosophy of art, philosophy of religion, and philosophy of
history sailed happily along, the philosophy of that domain of human existence that overlaps all of them, *culture,* remained a kind of backwater. Its
greatest twentieth-century practitioner, Ernst Cassirer, is a largely neglected
figure. When philosophers do speak of "culture," they typically use it as a
synonym for "high culture," that is to say, artistic and intellectual history.
And where they employ the adjective "cultural" to refer to something more
basic and distinctive, it mainly functions as a prefix to that feared but widely
courted term "relativism."

Arguably this neglect of culture is an Enlightenment legacy, culture being
a casualty of the rising power of an ideal of knowledge that viewed contingent, historical, socially specific ways of practice and thought as mere tradition, the repository of myth and superstition, hence an obstacle to progress. What after all was the antonym of the Enlightenment ideal of *Reason?*
Not *Nature,* certainly. It was *Culture,* inherited social beliefs about God,
nature, authority, and inequality. For early twentieth-century philosophy, if
society was a superstructure covering up the infrastructure of authentic
subjectivity or objective reality or sense data, then, as Plato held of art's
imitation of mere sensory appearances, culture seemed *twice* removed from
the real, a collection of self-deceptions promoted by a mendacious super-

structure. Even today, among thinkers who make the cultural turn away from transcendentalism, foundationalism, and universalism, culture still tends to appear as a background *surd,* the name of a dimension of reality in terms of which any topic under discussion will be explained, but which itself goes largely unexamined. Exotic cultural practices are cited to make a point, a paragraph or page gives an uncritical definition of culture on the way to hunt for bigger game. One searches in vain for a fundamental philosophical exploration of what culture is.

But let's not be too hard on contemporary philosophers, or on the Enlightenment for that matter. Both have had good reason to fear or dismiss culture. For once we decide to remedy their deficit, we discover the real problem: *culture is trouble.* Defining it is first of all a complex and controversial chore. Even once, or if, we can tentatively say what culture is, we are faced with the even more daunting task of saying what *a* culture is, where one ends and another begins. Then comes a succession of troubling terms often attached to the social groups that have cultures: peoples, ethnicities, nations, and races. What are they? In each case we struggle under the burden of recognizing that their shifting meanings threaten to make historiographical hash of the whole business. All of this comes *before we even begin* to confront the philosophical problems that led us to investigate culture in the first place: what is culture's social and cognitive role? Are human living-together and human knowing inherently cultural? If so, what happens to our view of knowledge and political life, what happens to truth, knowledge, reason, equality, universal rights, and freedom? Wouldn't relativism and historicism be unavoidable, and truth and right reduced to true and right *for* some particular culture? The stakes are high. For if the Enlightenment attempted to forge norms that transcend culture precisely in order to defend science and rights and equality, then will the return to culture undermine our Enlightenment heritage? Dig far enough into the "postmodern condition," into contemporary worries about the meaning and legitimacy of the intellectual scaffolding of the modern world, and there, in its now fractured foundations, you find two old snakes, Reason and Culture, lying coiled together in a hostile embrace. How did they get there, what are they doing, and what should *we* do about *them?*

The theme of this book's approach to these conundrums will be, *not around but through.* I will argue that there is nothing we do or say that is beyond or outside culture, including reason itself. Knowing, moral action, and all human norms operate through culture. But the cultural embeddedness of cognition does *not* imply a troubling relativism. Cultural differences there are, but the complexity both of the cultures involved, and the cultural relations among them, make the identification of incommensurable cultures impossible. Reason can learn to live with culture. It had better, since it has no choice in the matter. It is, after all, culture's creation.

Modernity is in part *about* culture. For that collection of beliefs, practices, and institutions which set contemporary life apart from the rest of human history defined itself by a new relation to culture. Not a new culture—although that is also true—but a new relation to culture *per se.* The very idea of culture, as we understand it, is a product of the Enlightenment. It had to be. We could only conceive culture at the point that we imagined we could see beyond it, which is precisely what Western modernity claimed to do. *Modernity is the first age to constitute "culture" as a problem.* Indeed, the current problems of modern society that we call postmodern—here understood as the advanced course in modernity, where modernity's implications are more completely revealed—largely hang on the role of culture in social and cognitive life. Just as a new relation of reason and culture defined the break of the modern from the premodern, so our postmodern present is defined by a further change in the status of culture. Culture ain't what it used to be, for better and for worse. How we understand *that* is central to how we understand ourselves.

At the same time, the seemingly antimodern character of the various revivals of fundamentalism, ethnocentrism, and nationalism, conflicts among and with which define global politics at the outset of our new century, is an artifact of our vision, not fact. For these revivals are characteristically *modernist,* not reversions to a primordial, premodern past. Their conflicts *with* modernity are fought with weapons *from* modernity—and not only weapons made of steel and silicon, but of ideas and practices too. This does not gainsay the fact that we are entering an era of renewed cultural conflict (which is true). Nor does it imply that we have reached the "end of history" where all ways are the West's ways (which is false). It means rather that we are forced to recognize that there are many ways to be modern.

Inevitably this discussion provokes the question: where is this train we call modernization going? In a marvelous series of essays, each the basis for a subsequent book, Huntington, Fukuyama, and Benjamin Barber set out three hypotheses for our global future. As we saw, Fukuyama's 1989 "The End of History?" argued that liberal capitalist democracy is the final form of political maturity, the only legitimate answer to the universal human desire for recognition and freedom. Barber's 1992 "Jihad vs. McWorld" saw the Cold War bipolarity of capitalism and communism being replaced by a new global dualism between a superficial postmodern consumer culture and a reactionary primordial authoritarianism. And Huntington's 1993 "The Clash of Civilizations" predicted a multipolar conflict of cultural families whose modernization pushes them further apart, not closer together. Fukuyama's thesis may seem dated by the rise of cultural and nationalist conflicts of the last decade, but it remains the case today that the most technically and economically advanced countries on Earth are liberal capitalist democracies. So which of these numerical hypotheses about the postmodern era is right: will the world of our new century be One, Two, or Many?

There is no possibility of a systematic world tour of these issues. We must be content with a tourist package of brief encounters with key locales. Fortunately, we will not be completely alone on our journey. Some few thinkers of the last century have shined their light into culture and its place in knowledge and social life, most prominently Ernst Cassirer, but also Edward Shils and Hans-Georg Gadamer. More recently, Elizabeth Baeten, Samuel Fleischacker, Alasdair MacIntyre, Bhikhu Parekh, Lorenzo Simpson, and the late Ernest Gellner have separately probed these depths, trying to give an adequate account of the cultural nature of human thought while at the same time avoiding relativism. The following chapters attempt merely to push their frontier of exploration forward by a few kilometers. We will not reach the pole. Culture is a realm that can be explored, but never exhausted. We will lug our interrogative baggage through the following inquiry, to be reorganized and repacked as we go, but never ditched. Our present aim is not to reach a destination, so we can stop traveling, but to become better travelers, to see more, experience more, and discriminate better than your average tourist. We hope to develop a finer appreciation for culture's role, to get some sense of the vast terrain it implicates, by the time our strength and money are used up. But as for completing our journey, that is out of the question. For culture is not only endlessly complex, each whole exhibiting parts that are themselves equally complex wholes, it is always changing and growing. If not in the olden days, at least in our contemporary world, we cannot step into the same culture twice. For the volcanic depths spew ever more and expanding terrain as we walk.

LIBERALISM AND *LA REVANCHE DE LA CULTURE*

Liberalism has always distinguished the political sphere from the rest of culture. John Locke's attempt in the his 1689 *Second Treatise on Government* to separate the magistrate-citizen relationship from all other social relations, and his simultaneous separation of "private" salvation from "public" political matters in the *Letter Concerning Toleration,* inaugurated that strategy. For only thus, liberals have ever since thought, can the public realm of political coercion be kept away from matters of nonpolitical belief. But the privacy to which nonpolitical culture was thereby banished often seemed a rather public nuisance. By the mid-nineteenth century, J. S. Mill could refer to "custom" as a "despot," cultural tradition as the source of anti-individualist conformity. Natural rights liberals sought rights not dependent on culture; utilitarians and, by the twentieth century, progressives found inherited culture the chief obstacle to social progress. Whether the goal was individual liberty or prosperity or egalitarian justice, custom stood in the way. Then fascism, the Holocaust, and the American civil rights struggle provided liberals a new lesson: *culture kills!* Cultural identity, in nationalism or racism or anti-Semitism, is the greatest of evils. Fortunately, Cold War history seemed to confirm the anachronism of cultural identity in a modernizing world whose major issues revolved around political economy. Liberal theory then evolved the view that government is to be "neutral" regarding substantive accounts of the Good. Since whatever culture is, an individual culture *cannot* be neutral with respect to what it considers good, it follows that government must be neutral with respect to culture. The pursuit of neutrality reached its apotheosis in John Rawls's *Political Liberalism* (1993) by denying any political role to "comprehensive doctrines," hence cultural narratives.

But today we can say that reports of the death of culture were greatly exaggerated. Theoretically, neutralism has been under attack since the advent of "communitarianism" in the 1980s; "perfectionist" liberals have arisen who, like Stephen Macedo and William Galston, accept that liberalism intrinsically endorses a set of liberal "virtues" or "purposes." Brian Barry himself, a classical rights–based opponent of multiculturalism if ever there was one, argued that liberal politics presupposes a liberal outlook, or as Dewey long ago insisted, a liberal culture (Barry 1990; Dewey 1979). And in the real world cultural membership has renewed its claim to political legitimacy. Multiculturalism and the politics of "identity," "recognition," or "presence" have arisen in liberal societies, condemning the "assimilationist ideal" with its "melting pot" metaphor, aspiring to *sighted,* not *blind,* justice, to recognition through, not despite, *somatic-cultural* particularity ("somatic" referring not only to racial morphology but also to gender and sexual orientation). Thus the neutralist and secular tendencies of recent liberal theory today face, not only that global religious revival that Giles Keppel calls *la revanche de Dieu,* the revenge of God, but also a broader *la revanche de la culture.*

In response, a number of liberal theorists have opened their political anthropologies to cultural membership. We may call them the new culturalists. Some include among liberal individual rights the *right to culture.* Others eschew the foundational concern with individual rights for a "postliberal" theory while still arguing for typically liberal institutions and practices. I suggest that neither adequately conceptualizes a free society's relation to culture. Instead of weaving liberal republican values out of a culturally embedded conception of self and politics, they cut culture to fit liberal anthropology and egalitarian policy, thereby minimizing the problems culture causes liberalism. My aim will be, not to roll back the new culturalism, nor to answer the important issues attendant on a culturally informed liberalism (such as, for example, cultural rights, proportional representation, minority legal exemptions, and so on), but to address the conceptual implications of a liberal recognition of culture. Ultimately, I believe, such requires a rejection of dominant forms of liberal *theory,* although not of *liberalism,* it being fully possible to endorse many liberal institutions, practices, and values while objecting to their common justifications (Cahoone 2002a). But here we can only recognize some of the complexities raised by opening liberal theory to culture.

The New Culturalism

Not that all historical strains of liberalism have ignored or opposed cultural identity. The political theorists Yael Tamir and Will Kymlicka rightly point out that nineteenth- and early twentieth-century liberalism was pleasantly disposed toward nationalism. Woodrow Wilson led the movement that in the Treaty of Versailles made national determination a watchword of liberal democracy. Recognition of the rights of culturally defined groups has long been accepted in liberal states—e.g., Native American communities in the United States and Canada. Indeed, liberalism covertly depends on nationalism and the recognition of culture, not only in the historical formation of liberal states, but in the acquisition of citizenship by birth, both of which liberals accept without comment. For Tamir and Kymlicka, only hegemonic and "particularist" nationalism, the self-determination of one people at the expense of others and of individual rights, is antiliberal.

In *Liberal Nationalism* Tamir agrees with mainstream liberals that nationalism defined by "blood and soil" is wrong and dangerous. But national identity based in *culture* is not. Echoing Benedict Anderson's *Imagined Communities,* she stipulates that "nations are communities imagined though culture" (Tamir 1993: 64). Tamir gives communitarian justifications for the primacy of national "associative obligations," claiming that a polity requires a sense of belonging rooted in "identity and relatedness." Liberals must recognize a right to culture, a right to live in a "meaningful environment." This is an individual, not a group, right, and thus can fit into the liberal list of individually borne rights, to be balanced with the others. She claims, however, that culture is something we *choose,* a "constitutive choice." We are "contextual individuals," but every aspect of our cultural or contextual identification is subject to our free affirmation or disavowal. She cautions that since culture is a personal choice, individuals may not only switch cultures but reform their culture. Cultures have no immunity from internal critique.

Tamir rejects state prohibition of minority cultural expression. For "refusing individuals the right to express their culture in the public sphere in compliance with the ruling culture compels them to forgo their identity" (Tamir 1993: 54). Liberal equality demands that the state not favor any culture over another. Every individual deserves an equal share of governmental resources ("cultural vouchers") for making possible his or her cultural life. If its small numbers means that a minority's cultural activities are in market terms more expensive than others, then "we may wish to supplement the funds granted to members of the [minority] community" (Tamir 1994: 55). Since Tamir allows that what is claimed by the liberal state to be "neutral" may in fact be a covert support of its dominant culture, her position implies that all minority cultures may be actively and disproportionately supported by tax dollars.

Tamir endorses national "self-determination" with two caveats. As noted, choice, not genes, determines membership, and there are no rights to particular plots of turf. Presumably this is an anti-Zionist claim directed at least partly to her fellow Israelis. Second, the institutional form taken by self-determination rightly depends on circumstances. The right to culture is not the right to a state. Because self-determination of one culture must be compatible with the same right for others groups, a liberal nationalism renounces the strict nationalist claim of "one people, one state." Even on prudential grounds the best way to preserve one's culture is not always a nation-state. Tamir's aim is to dissociate cultural expression from political self-rule; she hopes to strengthen borders between cultures while weakening those between states. For nations are only dangerous if combined with states. What is often preferable, she suggests, are regional state-like associations, like the European Union, within which self-determining cultures can have a home.

Will Kymlicka is distinctively concerned with national minorities, like Native Americans, rather than immigrant minorities. In a series of books he has argued that liberal freedom requires a "societal culture," a meaningful cultural environment in which members can make their choices. Cultural membership is a "primary good" in the Rawlsian sense, hence must be distributed justly, like income and opportunity. Applying Ronald Dworkin's concept of equality of resources to cultural traditions, he notes that cultural majorities in liberal states enjoy an undeserved advantage by accident of birth, while minorities must often bargain away cultural identity for success or income. Indeed, he leaves no doubt that he feels the majority has its culture secured by the state, despite liberal claims to neutrality (Kymlicka 1995a: 189). Special support is justified where a minority suffers from unequal "unchosen" circumstances, as is the case with national minorities, as opposed to suffering from the consequences of their unique choices, as do voluntary immigrants. Thus, while rejecting the proceduralist liberal notion that "the right is prior to the good," Kymlicka employs standard egalitarian liberal redistributive arguments. This expansion of rights-based liberalism is required if liberalism is "to ensure that no one is penalized or disadvantaged by their natural or social endowment, but allow that people's fates vary with their choices" (Kymlicka 1995a: 190).

Kymlicka occasionally implies that cultural identity is unchosen, but like Tamir he seeks to defuse the implications of his apparently communitarian notion of the self as constituted by, and inheriting values and ends from, community or tradition. He clarifies that liberalism requires, not that the self be "prior" to its communally inculcated ends, but merely that "no end or goal is exempt from possible re-examination." Ends, while communally bequeathed, are all "reversible" by the individual's choice. Each can be distributively, that is, piecemeal, subjected to critical revision. Hence the liberal "desires a society that is transparently intelligible—where nothing works behind the backs of its members," determining their actions without their self-aware approval (Kymlicka 1995a: 63). This conforms to his view, shared by Tamir, that the source of affinity among a people is culture, not ethnicity. For "descent-based approaches to national membership have obvious racial overtones, and are manifestly unjust" (Kymlicka 1995a: 23).

Kymlicka maintains individual rights for the members of minority cultures against their own cultural communities. He denies that self-ruling, democratic cultural minorities will often need to restrict the freedom of members, although he admits temporary restrictions on members' liberty to ensure cultural survival: "If certain liberties really would undermine the very existence of the community, then we should allow what would otherwise be illiberal measures" (Kymlicka 1989: 170). Such measures may be "wrong," but the state may not prohibit them. "Peaceful negotiation, not force," should carry the day, even though this may involve "exempting the national minority from federal bills of rights and judicial review" (Kymlicka 1989: 167–68). But, he continues, "Obviously intervention is justified in the case of gross and systematic violation of human rights...just as these are grounds for intervention in foreign countries" (Kymlicka 1989: 169). Here, as elsewhere, Kymlicka models the rights of national minorities on those of sovereign states.

Other thinkers, whom we might call postliberals, are heir to a more radical approach, finding that difference cuts deeper into the fabric of liberal thought. Iris Marion Young's influential *Justice and the Politics of Difference* is not specifically concerned with ethnic or national groups, but more broadly with social groups "differentiated from at least one other group by cultural forms, practices, or way of life" (Young 1990: 43). Such groups "constitute individuals... [in their] sense of history, affinity and separateness, even the person's mode of reasoning, evaluating, and expressing feeling." Denying that group identity is chosen, she evokes a Heideggerian notion that "group affiliation has the character of... 'thrownness': one *finds oneself* as a member of a group." The majority's oppression of such groups inhibits group members' "ability to develop and exercise their capacities and express their needs, thoughts, and feelings" (Young 1990: 40). What grounds oppression is the ascription of a "unified, orderly identity" which must "essentialize" otherness so as to deny any sameness between self and other. This reflects majoritarian fear of particularity or "specificity," or in Julia Kristeva's term, the *abject* in oneself, which is represented by the other. In contrast, the nonoppressive use of difference conceives it as relational and circumstantial, hence variable, thereby avoiding exclusion. Young writes, "Difference no longer implies that groups lie outside one another... that there are no overlapping experiences... nothing in common. Different groups are always similar in some respects" (Young 1990: 171).

Of the allegedly impartial liberal state, Young claims that "the idea of impartiality legitimates hierarchical decision making and allows the standpoint for the privileged to appear as universal" (Young 1990: 116). Against this oppressive "depoliticization," Young insists that "all aspects of institutional structure, public action, social practices and habits, and cultural meanings" are to be politicized, "potentially subject to collective discussion and decision making." A *cultural politics* that critically examines all forms of group oppression will contribute to achieving the "democratic cultural pluralism" of "city life." City dwellers do not, like rural people and suburbanites, stick to their own. Their lives are lived in public space, in the "being together of strangers" who belong to the city without unity or commonness, an "infinite... network" that encourages risky encounters, difference "without exclusion."

In a series of essays, culminating in his *Rethinking Multiculturalism: Cultural Diversity and Political Theory,* Lord Bhikhu Parekh has pushed the confrontation of liberal theory with culture the furthest of all (Parekh 2000). Like Young, he accepts that cultural identity is un-chosen. He explicitly qualifies liberalism with multiculturalism, endorsing group rights and refusing to grant unqualified priority to individual rights. Parekh distinguishes several models for handling cultural diversity in a modern state (Parekh 1998). "Cultural assimilation" takes the state to be underwritten by a common culture into which immigrants and minorities must be assimilated. "Proceduralism" or neutralism demands that the state have no cultural predilections. "Civic assimilation" bifurcates a common political or civic culture, to which immigrants and minorities must be assimilated, from "private" culture with respect to which the state must be neutral. The bifurcationist and neutralist approaches in the end suffer from a version of the

MoMA PS1

THE MUSEUM OF MODERN ART'S CONTEMPORARY ART AFFILIATE

Located in Queens, NY, just two subway stops away.

assimilationist model: they effectively leave the inherited civic or majority culture as an unalterable given.

The multicultural model, on the other hand, opens civic and supracivic majority culture to transformation. Minorities are to receive not only toleration but support *qua* minorities, guaranteeing a robust pluralism. The dominant culture is then liable to ongoing negotiation with minorities regarding what it means to be a member of society. Not only can the majority change the minority, the minority can change the majority. The Indian or Pakistani can change England for the better; the constitution of English identity is "negotiable." Parekh admirably foresees a relationship of reciprocity that obligates the minority as well; thus in Britain, "minorities can hardly expect to be taken seriously and play their part unless they accept the full obligations of British citizenship . . . and sensitivity to [British society's] values, fears and dilemmas. . . . they must master English and acquire detailed knowledge of British history" (Parekh 1991: 200). *Rethinking Multiculturalism* is a mediator's handbook, arguing above all for intercultural dialogue within a just "community of communities." Like Kymlicka, he accepts a differentiated or pluralistic conception of citizenship, by which individuals and groups may exhibit different ties to the state. Social unity is then to be "grounded in a multiculturally constituted public realm which both sustains, and is in turn sustained by, a multiculturally constituted private realm" (Parekh 1998: 10). Parekh writes that "a politics of citizenship which both promotes the *rights* of communities with regard to each other, as well as the *obligations* of communities to each other is an essential precondition of this pluralist vision" (Parekh 1991: 199). What is needed between minority and majority communities is "what the Romans called civic friendship."

Culture Without Tears

These thinkers perform the needed service of opening our understanding of the politics of a free society to cultural group differences. Nevertheless, they share three problems: their conclusions differ less from the standard liberal approach than they suggest; they fail to credit the antiliberal troubles caused by the new culturalism; and they offer a conception of cultural group identity that has already been predigested by notions of liberal freedom and equality, mitigating their claimed *rapprochement* with the realities of culture.

First, a preliminary question whose homely answer will become more significant later: is what distinguishes the Quebecois or the Native American or the Israeli Palestinian from fellow citizens entirely cultural? Is "a culture" the right name for the unity of these groups? As Anthony Appiah has warned, recent critics tend to expand the application of "cultural" to what is merely "social" (Appiah 1997). Exhibiting a culture, without mutual social obligations and interactions, might not be sufficient to the kind of associational identity the new culturalists are after. The objection is not solely terminological. For the expansion of "culture" is motivated, since group identity hanging on culture seems furthest removed from descent, race, and biology generally. The move also presupposes a central feature of modern, polyethnic societies, namely, their acceptance of the distinction between society and culture, which permits social members to be culturally distinct. However attractive that feature may be, we ought not to build it into our very concept of the polity (on pain of disqualifying most states in history). I would rather say that the groupings in question are *socio*cultural; if their group identities matter, they matter in a social network of expectations, both of members and nonmembers.

Tamir's conclusion that we can draw a line between state and nation, leaving national groups their right to cultural self-determination while avoiding *staatlich* consequences, is very important. She is surely right that in most cases cultural self-determination can and ought to be achieved without a state. All that is required to reach this conclusion is to do the math: as Ernest Gellner notes, by any reasonable count the numbers of peoples far exceeds any plausible number of states the world could accommodate. But Tamir's approach does not actually dissociate state from nation: it multiplies the *levels of state,* associating nation with a lower or subsovereign level of state. After all, cultural self-determination must have *some* political-legal-governmental expression, some political borders and special rules. If not, if state and culture are utterly dissociated, then we have returned to the standard liberal model in which culturally distinctive groups are supposed to go unrecognized at the state level.

Likewise, the kind of polity Parekh and Young endorse cannot differ greatly from the standard liberal one. For what would the political forum of the multicultural polity, or of "city life," sound like? If it is *a* forum, that is, an inclusive public discourse among equals that constitutes or influences power, then it must have *a* grammar, a set of rules that excludes and, in our theorists' view, privileges none. This may not be old-style assimilation to a supposedly neutral forum that in fact privileged the Anglo-Saxon, not a store selling only white bread. Granted, it is an eclectic supermarket in which loaves of wheat, rye, and pumpernickel, not to mention bagels, proudly sport distinctive wrappings. But such a supermarket must still have rules; customers must relate to the clerks in a linguistic or behavioral Esperanto, accepting universal if minimal standards of propriety. In other words, *this is assimilation at a higher level.* The authors remain at least second-order egalitarian liberals, revisited at that level by many of the problems they raise against liberalism.

For in the end there are only three options regarding diversity, even if these can be recursively applied. The political environment in which cultures and culturally identified individuals interact must be understood *either* as culturally neutral (as the standard liberal view claimed), or as *somebody's* culture (hence an openly proclaimed liberal nationalism or a liberally hidden assimilationism), or as a capacious and tolerant megaculture produced by the merging of cultural elements, which itself must be either noncultural or one of the cultures in question. Note that the third option empties into the first or, if neutrality is a ruse, the second. That is, any megaculture would still be derived from some cultural traditions and not others, excluding or disadvantaging minorities who either find its capaciousness limited or who are offended by capaciousness (namely, ethnic or religious purists). Tolerating every cultural identity is after all a specific way of life, one that makes *pluralism* a chief good. Parekh is right that liberal autonomy is not an inescapable or universally acclaimed virtue, but neither is the creative tension he values so highly. As such, this megaculture is still a particular culture (option two), albeit at a higher level, to which assimilation would be required. As a particular culture it bears important similarities with a way of life that encourages people publicly to disregard cultural identity as private (option one), for it would be inconceivable without rules that are up to some point neutral among members' cultures. Parekh himself argues that "from a multicultural perspective the good society does not commit itself to a particular political doctrine or vision of the good life," it "privileges no particular cultural perspective, be it liberal or otherwise" (Parekh 2000: 340). But this is just a higher neutralism.

Moving to the question of the nature of the self, liberals have been criticized by communitarians for accepting an impossible anthropology, in which the self is entirely constituted by its own free choices, rather than by community or tradition. Tamir and Kymlicka assert a middle ground: even if the self is constituted by community, all liberalism requires is that *every element* of the self be open to piecemeal, critical self-revision. Now, they are certainly right that many, maybe most, humans can critically revise aspects of their selves. But is there any evidence that *all* people have the capacity to revise *every* aspect of self, piecemeal or otherwise? Or even to *know* every aspect? No doubt virtually all people can raise some aspects of self to critical reflection, but the vast majority seem to do a very limited job of it. Presumably the ability to critically revise oneself is, like other human capacities, variable, contingent, and limited: most have a moderate dose, a few have a lot, and a few have almost none. True, we cannot say in advance which traits of which persons are incapable of revision, or which are *a priori* beneath awareness, but that ignorance does not justify the claim that all traits are revisable, any more than the fact that I don't know *when* I will die justifies me in doubting *that* I will die. The claim of universal, even if distributive, revisability is a remnant of the metaphysics of transcendent freedom that has become anachronistic in almost every other area of contemporary philosophy.

Parekh and Young try to avoid this form of transcendence, but they retain an analogous version. For theirs is an *interculturalism,* a multiculturalism of interaction, creative tension, and personal transformation. All citizens must accept the merely partial validity of their own culture. But like other liberals, the overcoming of fate, limitation, and ethnocentricity is still their social and cultural ideal. Parekh writes that education in a multicultural society should enable individuals to "see the contingency of their culture and relate to it freely rather than as a fate or a predicament" (Parekh 2000: 167). This is an analogue of the notion of liberal freedom as the capacity to transcend any particular set of constitutive bounds. Young and Parekh thus inherit the tradition of *romantic* liberalism, albeit one with strong egalitarian commitments. They share the Socratic ideal evident in John Stuart Mill's diatribe against conformity, John Dewey's justification of democracy as endless growth, and George Kateb's evocation of the transcendental experience fostered by liberal democracy (Mill 1978; Dewey 1944; Kateb 1992). All the writers mentioned maintain the liberal commitment to self-reflection, the ideal of a life in which all self-constituents are either chosen or freely affirmed.

Self-reflection may generally be an admirable quality, but is it the best quality, or good in every case? Would Mother Theresa have lived a better life if one morning she awoke to the realization that religious service had been foisted on her by family and church, that she had never questioned whether it suited her deepest self, and so opted instead to read philosophy in a left-bank Parisian café and let the lepers die? Were there no young Germans in the 1930s who came to Nazism via a sincere critique of their childhood acceptance of bourgeois Weimar liberalism? Is the examined life more likely to lead to a commitment to human rights than skepticism regarding such rights? My point is neither to reject nor to ridicule the Socratic ideal, but to deny that it has a necessary relation to the good life, or any obvious superiority over a number of other moral ideals. Not only is it the case that, as William Galston wrote, people have "the right to live unexamined lives," but in some cases an unexamined life may be better than an examined one (Galston 1991). From a practical or political point of view, with the exception of professional philosophers, for whom "the examined life" *is* their practical life, it is presumably in the results, *not the examination itself,* that moral value lies.

All the thinkers in question seriously underestimate the threat of cultural identity and cultural membership to individual liberties. Regarding one putative example of intracultural conflict, Kymlicka insists, "But there needn't be any conflict here, for the kind of commonality involved—i.e. commonality of language and history, shared membership in a cultural community—doesn't constrain individuality. On the contrary, membership in a cultural structure is what enables individual freedom" (Kymlicka 1989: 208). Here we see the tendency to conceive ethnic culture as a language that grants ability but has no substantive, choice-restricting content. Parekh likewise defines culture at one point as a grammar. But culture is not only a *how;* it is also a *what* and a *who.* Cultures are not mere languages. We know cases of rare individuals who speak ten languages. Can anybody belong to ten cultures?

This attempt to have identity without tears leads Kymlicka to a strange distinction between membership in a cultural community and adherence to the content of its traditions. He insists that cultural identity does not require fealty to tradition. While of course cultures change, being a member of a cultural community cannot be wholly independent of inherited content. Such a community cannot even be defined without reference to inherited content, lest membership become indistinct from that of any voluntary association. Erasing the substance of cultural tradition makes being Armenian and Rotarian equal in political significance, undermining the new culturalism altogether. Similarly, Parekh accepts the inherited nature of culture, then compensates by making it utterly flexible, insisting that "every tradition can be read in different ways, none of them definitive and final" (Parekh 2000: 175–77). His case studies make it clear that for him *virtually no* modern, liberal, egalitarian policy—such as, for example, gender equality—is incompatible with *any* cultural tradition; under his hand, every tradition has the resources to adapt to liberal and egalitarian views. If that were true, there would be little need for cultural rights in the first place.

This connects to the broader question of intercultural judgment, regarding which, ironically, multiculturalists typically find identification with one's culture a liability. The issue was famously addressed by Amy Gutmann's popular 1992 collection, *Multiculturalism and the Politics of Recognition,* featuring an essay by the philosopher Charles Taylor, which sparked much of the philosophical debate over cultural identity and liberalism. In his essay Taylor defends a moderately communitarian liberalism, arguing for liberal rights but acknowledging that identity and self-recognition crucially arise only in dialogue or communally. He accepts that attempts to protect a culture from withering away may justify some relaxation of normal liberal rules of equality, like allowing Quebec to limit the property rights of shopkeepers to prohibit the proliferation of English-language signs. At the same time, Taylor criticizes the limits on our freedom of cultural judgment that would be imposed by any stridently multicultural claim that we must recognize the "equal value" of different cultures. To grant foreign cultures the benefit of the doubt, to respect them politically, to accept the obligation to learn about them is one thing; but to deny that one culture's literature or art or politics can be *better* than another's would be tantamount to a critical self-lobotomy.

It is a bit unfortunate that Taylor did not extend similar recognition to American novelist Saul Bellow. Taylor reproduces a remark that Bellow is "famously quoted" as having said—although Taylor adds in a footnote that he has "no idea whether this statement was actually made in this form by Saul Bellow, or by anyone else"—to wit: "When the Zulus produce a Tolstoi, we will read him" (Gutmann 1994: 42). Taylor and another contributor to the volume differed on just how repugnant this insult was supposed to be, but here as elsewhere it came to be regarded as a paradigmatic case of ethnocentrism, or worse. The rumored insult seems to have been passed around intellectual circles for years without proper documentation. The issue became heated enough that Bellow eventually responded in a *New York Times* op-ed essay, claiming that he *had* read a Zulu novel in college

(*Chaka* by Thomas Mofolo), but had forgotten it. We now know that the actual remark, as recorded by James Atlas during a 1987 interview with Bellow, was "Who is the Zulu Tolstoy? The Proust of the Papuans? I'd be glad to read him!" (Atlas 2000: 572–76). It is odd that no one seems upset that the Papuans have been neglected in the retelling.*

Putting aside the mild nature of Bellow's actual remark, those upset by the apocryphal comment seem to have been exercised by the presupposition that Zulu culture had not produced literature comparable to Western in quality, and by the very act of negative evaluation across cultures. Both reactions seem exaggerated. By all means such comparisons ought to be based on knowledge, not ignorance. The most knowledgeable person in the current case would be someone deeply familiar with Tolstoi and the literary world in which he has a place, and equally familiar with Zulu contemporary literature and traditions. There is probably a very good chance that, if I were a Zulu bilingual in either Russian or a West European language, I might still say that my Zulu culture has not produced a Tolstoi, if only because of the relatively short history of writing in Zulu. That judgment would not thereby declare the *wholesale* superiority of Western culture—if Tolstoi is "Western" in the first place—to Zulu culture, not only because literature is not the whole of anybody's culture, but because the novel arguably does not have an analogous place in Southern African and European culture. A more sensible comparison with Tolstoi as creative wordsmith might be instead to some great speaker or interpreter of Zulu traditional stories, although admittedly the more different the projects are, the more tenuous such comparison becomes. All this aside, Taylor's rejection of *de jure* cultural egalitarianism is surely right. To declare all cultures' products of equal value would not only inhibit Western cultural judgments, but those of non-Western peoples as well. It would have been rather bizarre to demand that an Egyptian visiting Northern Europe in the second millennium B.C.E. acknowledge that, in their own way, those European mud huts and piles of manure were just as impressive as the pyramids. What does belonging to a cultural tradition mean if it does not entail the judgment that one's culture is superior in some respects to others? One would be a rather poor Zulu if she did not regard Zulu culture as superior to Western, at least in some respects. Why expect more from Bellow, unless one already has made a tacit judgment that Westerners are supposed to "know better"?

---

*I thank Dr. Christopher Walsh for his research on this matter.

In this connection, Anthony K. Appiah cites the marvelous example of the selection committee for a New York exhibit of African art, whose curator sought a diverse group to pick out "authentic" pieces, even including one plausibly authentic practitioner, a traditional Baule artist from Ivory Coast. But while the European, American, and African curators, academics, and collectors comprising the rest of the group were shown photographs of all potential selections, the Baule artist was allowed only to select among the Baule pieces, because, the exhibition curator remarked, "African informants will criticize sculptures from other ethnic groups in terms of their own traditional criteria," hence reject them. As Appiah summarizes, "This Baule diviner, this authentically African villager, the [curator's] message is, does not know what we, authentic postmodernists, now know: that the first and last mistake is to judge the Other on one's own terms. And so, in the name of this, the relativist insight, we impose our judgment that [the Baule] may not judge sculpture from beyond the Baule culture zone" (Appiah 1992: 139). For the curator, cultural diversity is *de rigeur,* but only as long as the cultural "member" has thinned her membership so much that she no longer identifies with it completely. But the inevitable fact is that cultural membership shapes judgment, whether one's culture is that of a former colonizer repentantly gone relativist, or a former colonized who remains identified with her ethnic group. It is not *a priori* clear which perspective is in any particular case the more insightful or the more jingoist.

The new culturalists seem unwilling to acknowledge that culture *limits.* If it empowers, it also disempowers; if it enables, it disables too. A few current writers have accepted the constraining reality of culture. Allen Buchanan points out that it is culture's job to provide limits. Human existence needs a "structure" of what is intelligible, proper, and rightly desirable (Buchanan 1995: 356). Even if my culture is a smorgasbord of elements drawn from diverse societal cultures, it is still *a* culture, and a culture that does not limit cannot perform its job. Chandran Kukathas, a rare libertarian in a discussion dominated by egalitarian liberals, proposes that a minimal-state policy toward cultural minorities, built on a negative conception of liberty as mere "acquiescence," would be *more* tolerant of non-Western minority communities inside the liberal polity than "progressive" policies which promote the values of individual autonomy and equality (for example, gender equality) that many of the aforementioned communities *reject,* thereby undermining them (Kukathas 2003). In classical (not progressive) liberal style, Kukathas argues that the state's legitimate concern about individuals inside an illiberal minority community is to guarantee their right to exit, not their right to legislate community reform. He is willing to recognize that his kind of libertarian toleration means *tolerating what progressives consider coercion,* because that is what cultural diversity often entails. Likewise, Appiah points out the downside to a politics that recognizes cultural identity: "The politics of recognition requires that one's skin color, one's sexual body, should be acknowledged politically in ways that make it hard for those who want to treat their skin and sexual body as personal . . . [where] personal means . . . not too tightly scripted" (Appiah 1994: 163). Moral-political recognition of such identity makes it inevitable that there will be "proper ways of being black and gay, there will be expectations to be met, demands will be made." There is no cultural or associational identity without scripting. Absence of scripts would mean absence of identity, just as absence of exclusion means absence of membership. Appiah concludes, "Between the politics of recognition and the politics of compulsion, there is no bright line." Most cultures are pluralistic, but not utterly so. If *a* culture is not *all* cultures—if it is one thing and not another—it must be limited, hence impose limits.

Analogously, to allow culture into the center of our politics is not merely to empower minority affiliations, but to render majority cultural power unobjectionable. It is to turn the allegedly *de facto* promotion of the majority culture by the liberal state into an explicit promotion. Multiculturalists go to remarkable lengths to avoid this consequence. While Parekh admirably accepts that the majority culture has rightful claims against minorities, he consistently denies its coercive power. Thus in calling for a differentiated citizenship he writes, "A white Briton who does not understand the cultural accents of his Muslim or Afro-Caribbean fellow-citizen is just as incompletely British as the Indian ignorant of the way his white fellow-citizens speak. . . . Only he is fully British who can honestly say that no British citizen, black or white, Christian or Hindu, is a cultural stranger to him" (Parekh 1991: 203). Well, do the Chinese suddenly fail to be fully Chinese if I move to Beijing, obtain citizenship, and they fail to understand my "cultural accents"? This sets the bar so high that the concept of cultural membership lapses into uselessness. Once culture matters, *some* cultures will matter *more* than others, and some may matter very little. Parekh is right that culture must be "negotiated," but to be open to negotiation is to be open to the relative power of different groups, hence to the likelihood of unequal outcomes.

The new culturalists have cooked the books. They have forced cultural identity onto a diet, making it thin enough to be compatible with their politics. They follow the classical liberals they criticize in their fear of biology, that is, race, ethnicity, or any descent-based affinity, which they link automatically with racism and anti-Semitism. For them, as for most liberals, the mention of blood and soil always brings Birmingham and Auschwitz to mind. At the same time, of course, they motivate their work by claiming to accommodate liberalism to ethnic, racial, and cultural identity. But despite that motivation, their analyses and proposals are justified—through what we might call *argument creep*—by reference to lighter, thinner, liberal identities, often freely chosen, unburdened by objective criteria, for which blood, soil, and birthright are irrelevant. As in the old joke about the man who loses his keys in the grass, but searches for them under a streetlight, they look for answers where the light is better. They should have tested their reformed liberalism against a thicker notion of culture, one not predigested by liberal values. If thin and elective associations adequately described cultural identity, then there would be no problem to address in the first place.

A Culture-Based Liberalism?

I agree with the new culturalists that cultural identity is compatible with liberal society, not because cultural identity is thin and nonethnic, but because even moderately thick, descent- hence blood-and-soil-based ethnicity is not a problem for liberal institutions and practices. To see this, however, requires work on the political end of their view, their concept of a liberal polity. For, despite their openness to culture, they derive their concept of a free society from the neutralism they claim to transcend. They continue to insist that government's handling of cultural identity must be neutral with respect to all cultural identities and associations, hence such groups must be treated equally in all respects. If these theorists made their lives easier by short-weighting culture, they made them harder by staying too close to the neutralist, and especially Rawlsian, version of liberalism. A less dogmatic liberalism would have been easier to combine with thicker and thornier cultural differences. To see this we must examine the forms of identity liberals fear most (which will be explored more fully in Chapter 3).

We may begin with the blood and soil. Blood does not mean race, but descent, the relation to parentage. To say that blood matters is merely to say that *who my parents were* plays a role in constituting my associational identity. Minimally, soil is locale. Their salience is a consequence of the front-loaded character of human biography. Blood and the soil that surrounds it are markers for the *natal-maturational world of personal origin,* which plays a disproportionate role in the constitution of identity. Descent and locale are thus virtually ubiquitous as the first determinants of social and cultural membership, because almost everyone in every society descends from some other social members. As Edward Shils writes, kin loyalty cathects a social environment, not because all social members are related—which would make society a clan—but because virtually everyone in a society *has kin in* that society. Put it this way: where is there a political society which does not regard the offspring of members automatically as members? Being born and growing up in a place inevitably tie one to that place and its residents, even if they are civic and liberal in their conception of membership.

Contrary to Tamir and Kymlicka, racial, ethnic, national, and cultural memberships cannot be solely personal choices because they logically entail *public and social* criteria. Their meanings are no more under personal control than the meanings of words in a natural language are. The culture sets its membership criteria, and often they cannot be acquired through choice. Must the Sioux accept me, with no Sioux blood, if I learn Lakota and give up my credentials in the outside world? Of course not. Some cultures set criteria that are easier to meet than others; the point is that the criteria are not under the individual's control. The "right to culture" is thus more like the right of association than, for example, the right to self-expression. My right to speak in Hyde Park is actualized whether or not anyone listens, but I cannot associate with others if they walk away. If cultural membership is a right, it is a right to *seek* such membership, not to have it.

Simply, for the vast majority of human beings, including those in contemporary liberal societies, culture and cultural identity are largely found or inherited, not created or selected. Most of us lack a self that could gain the "distance" required critically to examine and "revise" our cultural repertoire and exchange our identity. Even in the most liberal case of all, the highly modern, immigrant society that is the United States, such freedom there is mostly means the freedom to avoid affirming the group identity we were bequeathed via descent, or to prioritize one of several cultural identities my genealogy and maturation offer me. Even this degree of freedom is rare, and more rare as we go back in time, arising historically only in those cases where people occupy a "boundary situation" where they happen to meet the criteria of two different societal cultures, often after conquest or dislocation (MacIntyre 1989). Tiger Woods could indeed identify himself as African-, Thai-, or European-American. But Arab-American?

As Michael Walzer rightly argues in *On Toleration,* political history exhibits a variety of "regimes of toleration" (Walzer 1997). For example, the liberal nation-state, where there is a dominant yet tolerant cultural majority and guaranteed civic rights for all as individuals, takes a different approach to polyethnicity than do liberal immigrant societies, where no ethnicity is officially dominant. France exemplifies the first, and the United States the second. Thus, as I write, the French continue to face a basic controversy over whether Islamic public school girls should be allowed to wear religious veils in school. The French understood the veil not as an issue of religious liberty but as a denial of a public religious neutrality that is synonymous with secular French culture and the guarantor of its equality and liberty. The girls were seen not as asserting individual freedom but as *rejecting* that freedom, and the French culture that provides it, by absorbing themselves into an anti-French, antisecular *faction.* In the United States of today it is hard to imagine the issue arising, even given the American wariness of Islamic dress since September 11, 2001. We are legally and culturally committed to the notion that religious expression is *not* in conflict with our notion of citizenship, which we structure differently than the French. For us, individual identity is outside the civic realm; wearing the marker of an ethnic or religious community does not imply civic disloyalty (as long as the wearers pay their taxes and respond to draft notices). For the French, civic liberties are based in identification with a French-speaking, secular tradition.

Kymlicka is right that citizenship can be "differentiated," various citizens being tied to the polity in various ways. But it is differentiated both in the sense of permitting different ties to the polity and in the sense of differentiating or narrowing the requirements of citizenship. The traits which constitute liberal citizenship are indeed more limited or thin than ethnicity, hence the former is compatible with, "civil" or tolerant of, a variety of other group memberships and identifications on the part of its citizens. The kind of cultural identity the theorists *want* their work to concern is actually best termed *ethnic,* not merely cultural, identity (although the two overlap, as we shall see in Chapter 3). For present purposes, we may say that such identity is acquired by *descent,* from what is understood by members to be a present or past *culturally homogeneous society;* and is *thick,* meaning that it significantly determines the meaning of the bearer's life across institutional roles (thin identities being role- and institution-specific), hence is relatively *exclusive* of others (thickness being proportional to exclusivity). Liberal citizenship then requires of domestic associational groups an inversely proportional narrowing of associational identity to permit civic membership; the group identity must leave open whatever space is required by the thin civic identity. My point is that what violates liberal civility is not blood or soil or unchosen history; it is a matter not of identity's *source* but rather of its *thickness,* hence dominance over the rest of identity and the degree of exclusion of others.

We can see this in application to American cases. Clearly some Americans identify with no ethnic or national group except what they regard as "American." They may regard that identity, and the association it implicates, as purely civic, the endorsement of a political form of life; or they may regard it as relatively thick and descent-based, investing "American" with supracivic traits. Still other citizens affirm their citizenship while nevertheless identifying themselves with an ethnic (or other) group understood to be relatively thick—so-called hyphenated Americans. Concomitantly, they must regard their American-ness as relatively thinner. Their ethnicity has a significant meaning-constituting role in their lives; they may prioritize it in mundane circumstances over their American-ness, although they must limit its demands to make room for citizenship. American civic identity is *thin enough* to be compatible with these moderately thick group identities; in fact, probably most Americans fall in this category. It remains the case that the differences between the unhyphenated and the hyphenated, or all the various particular hyphenations, can lead to conflicting notions of who is a "real" American. But no stronger or thicker American unity is required; what I have described is for America the normal ongoing negotiation over the meaning of American identity.

What is more troublesome are the very thick, hence highly exclusive, forms of associational identity, which are at home only in homogeneous societies in which citizenship, social membership, and cultural identity are *fused,* that is to say, where to be a member of society also means being a citizen and having a single thick cultural identity. The American who invests American-ness with ethnic or descent-based meaning can reach this point— thinking, for example, that only American-born white English-speakers are "real" Americans. The same is true of a resident alien, or a hyphenated American, whose "offshore" identity thickens to the point of reducing the "American" component below its minimal, civic threshold. It is these forms of thick association and identity which, when writ large, are sacralized by the highly modern technologies of an authoritarian-nationalist state, which are indeed at odds with civil society. But unlike some other liberal societies (such as France), *even these* forms of association and identity can be tolerated in America if they remain largely *private,* hence make minimal demands on fellow citizens. Members of the Aryan nation who stay on their compound in Idaho and Islamic fundamentalists who stay in their neighborhood are acceptable. It is only when they become a force in the public—not only in acts of intolerance or violence, but as a political movements—that they threaten civil society.

Thus I agree with the new culturalists that liberal society is *not* violated by cultural memberships or identities. But this is so whether the latter are thin or moderately thick, inherited, fixed or unchangeable, perceived as "primordial," tied to blood and soil or even race. Those characteristics by themselves need not imply the exclusivity that either prevents or is in direct conflict with the conditions of citizenship.

The Dialectic of Civility and Culture

But to claim such compatibility we must move beyond the concept of liberalism that the new culturalists take over from neutralist liberals with little modification. We must accept that liberal society—or better, civil society—obtains only *in and through cultural tradition.* (Cahoone 2002a). This implies, among other things, that political norms cannot be wholly independent of other sociocultural norms and values, thus liberal politics must be undergirded by extrapolitical commitments; that liberalism may be incompatible with some cultures; and that individual liberty cannot mean independence from communal inheritance. The issue is not one of fleshing out a "liberal culture," but of recognizing our political form as part of a cultural tradition sufficiently complex that it qualifies, and is qualified by, its civility or civic rules. This means breaking with the neutralist ideal. It means accepting that liberal or civil society, in its politics, law, and government, can *never be neutral with respect to cultures.* It cannot treat all cultures equally, cannot avoid differentially advantaging and disadvantaging particular cultural identities and group associations. Neither its "official," civically implicated culture, nor its mass culture can fail to script, or valorize, cultural identities differently. Its polity cannot avoid cultural exclusion or discrimination. All it can do is coerce as little as possible, exclude least often, permit in privacy what is publicly excluded, and treat a wider, rather than a narrower, set of cultural identities as officially, publicly equal. The toleration of civil society is a matter of degree.

Civility, which for present purposes we may take to be the rules of citizenship in a liberal society, needs cultural tradition. For civility must be interpreted, and the transmission across generations of the store of interpretive resources that form the background against which individuals make their unique selections and contributions *is* culture. The rules of citizen relations and behavior, including an account of membership, rights, obligations, and liberty, must be culturally represented and valorized across generations. Edward Shils was one of the few to articulate the complex relation of civil structures and culture. He reminds us that "civility requires respect for tradition because the sense of affinity on which it rests is not momentary only but reaches into the past and the future" (Shils 1997: 51). If civil rules are to be upheld as more than a *modus vivendi* or means of avoiding conflict (as Rawls agreed they must), then the cultures of society must endorse them as valuable in themselves. Loyalty to the sovereign society and fellow citizens, which is required as much by redistributive justice as by military service, implies that under culturally inherited accounts of the Good, the *polity is good*. Tradition thus provides the "largely unreflective acceptance" of the ultimate rightness of "rules of the game of the free society" (Shils 1997: 110).

But even while civility is culturally informed, it must also *restrain* cultural tradition. Culturally transmitted civility can limit and oppose other parts of the cultural tradition, thereby promoting toleration and liberty. There is nothing strange about this once we accept the complex and agonistic constitution of what Alasdair MacIntyre called living traditions (MacIntyre 1981). Civility exists in tension with other elements of our culture. And why not? Civility is, after all, all about limitation; as Shils claimed, it "permits neither the single individual nor the total community the complete realization of their essential potentialities" (Shils 1997: 49). Civility inhibits tendencies within a culture toward what he called ideology. Endorsing a pluralism represented in contemporary political theory by Michael Walzer, Shils wrote, "What is so malign in ideology is the elevation of one value, such as equality or national or ethnic solidarity, to supremacy over all others, and the insistence on its exclusive dominion in every sphere of life" (Shils 1997: 59). Thus the culture of a liberal society must distinguish between the rules of association—culturally interpreted—and its supracivil cultural aims, in order to tolerate wider deviance in the latter than in the former. Cultures often designate subspheres as quasi-independent, that is, as operating by distinctive rules that differentiate them from other cultural spheres. The cultures of modern civil societies grant such quasi-independence to civic life. If we say that American culture currently valorizes both the civil good of individual liberty and commitment to the supracivic goods of work, family, and religion (if inconsistently), then the former must sometimes lead our culture to restrict its promotion of the latter. The culture of liberal society thus engages in self-deformation or self-limitation, itself restraining its reproduction of supracivil values by a valorization of civility, hence of the liberty and dignity of each member. That is the real basis of toleration.

An Overlapping Cultural Consensus

This opposition appears analogous to the neutralist distinction between the political and the cultural. That is true. But it is only "analogous," and this makes, in my view, all the difference. First, here the line is drawn *within* the realm of culture, between the culturally valorized civic tradition and other cultural strains. Second, the line is *porous,* not rigid. As Shils rightly argued, there can be no "pure" civility, utterly procedural norms unconnected with cultural sources of legitimacy or theories of the Good. The problem with neutralism was not that it drew a line, but that it drew a *rigid* line and drew it in the wrong place, or better, in a *place that does not exist*—a "noncultural" place. Consequently, minority cultures can come fully dressed to the forum to negotiate their interests and impact political norms. But this also means, as neutralist liberals quickly point out, that cultural majorities would likewise be empowered, hence may be able to "establish" their dominant cultures and hence sanction intolerance of cultural minorities and individuals. To this a cultured liberalism must make a complex response.

First, a negative point. Critics of neutralism must admit the truth of the neutralists' underlying fear: *any step away from neutrality permits greater limits on individual and minority liberty.* Yet, we retort, there has never been nor will ever be a culturally neutral polity, hence the kind of individual liberty neutralists hope for. Thus, the neutralist and I agree that any reasonable interpretation of American civil rules through its legitimately dominant cultural tradition must outlaw ritual genital mutilation of underage females.

The neutralist must argue that this prohibition is based on a culturally neutral principle of individual liberty. I suggest there is no such principle, that our prohibition is as inevitably cultured as our notion of liberty, and nevertheless acceptable as such.

More positively, in a diverse liberal society the "cultural majority" takes a rather special form. Here a Rawlsian concept is helpful, albeit for a purpose not shared by its author. In *Political Liberalism* Rawls introduced the notion of an "overlapping consensus" of reasonable, that is, fair or tolerant, comprehensive doctrines (Rawls 1993). Distinctive comprehensive meta-narratives overlap, or jointly endorse, political liberalism, each on a distinctive basis. The overlap for Rawls is solely political—it is a set of political values, procedures, and institutions. But arguably liberal societies require as well an overlapping *cultural* consensus, the joint endorsement of an account of the human Good and key social practices and institutions by distinctive cultural traditions. This consensus is likely to be *thick but vague,* in Martha Nussbaum's phrase, substantive but formulated in nonsectarian terms (Nussbaum 1990). It can include goods or institutions jointly valued but differentially instantiated by prominent cultural groups, such as, for example, the promotion of family-friendly economic policies. The consensus around liberal or civil political practices, institutions, and values is then a subset of this broader, nonpolitical consensus. So the cultural majority of a pluralistic liberal society is already culturally pluralistic.

Still, the empowerment of an overlapping cultural consensus would authorize the depriviliging of those minority cultural values and practices which fall outside the overlapping consensus. In short, some people's cultures will be more fully reflected in public policy than others. It is the function of a culturally valorized *civility* to provide the limit on what the consensus may encourage or require of all members. Civility requires tolerance of those who do not share the dominant cultural values and practices, since it requires the liberty and dignity of all members be respected. This is why civility is in occasional conflict with other cultural values. Civil society's repertoire of strategies for reproducing its dominant cultural values is complex, ranging from legal requirement or prohibition, to government promotion or discouragement, to extralegal social approbation and disapprobation. What makes society liberal is, as Galston argues, not the absence of officially promoted or required notions of the Good, but that the strategy of coercion be held to a minimum (Galston 1991). And what constitutes the minimum is itself a matter of cultural interpretation. All societies, including

civil or liberal ones, have texts and margins, norms and exceptions, dominant and subdominant narratives. Marginalized cultures can demand neither a social declaration of their cultural normativity nor that their vision
be uncluttered by the dominant consensus. I might be comfortable with a
subculture in which adults ride their motorcycles naked while swilling
beer, but while I can hope to do so on private land, I cannot expect others
to endure such a vision in public space. The cultural majority has a right to
promote its supracivil cultural aims via the *civitas,* as long as this promotion
does not threaten to undermine civility, membership, and liberty—again,
as interpreted—for any members. And the consensus is open to change
through minority negotiation and promotion of their cultural aims within
the civil space.

Arguably the political force of an overlapping cultural consensus *is a fact*
in any liberal democratic society. What else ought we call that set of social
meanings which interprets the requirements of civility, liberty, and membership, which teaches social members how to be civil, tolerant and respectful of others, other than the intersection and accommodation of a finite set
of cultural traditions varying in pervasiveness and dominance? This affects
even policies of distributive justice, which cannot ignore the cultural meanings of the goods that need to be distributed; as Michael Walzer writes,
"Every substantive account of distributive justice is a local account" (Walzer
1983: 314). Culturally diverse Americans constantly negotiate these matters,
striking a shifting balance in national politics, mass culture, and local publics.
As in all negotiations, the outcome at any moment will tend to be closer
to the intersection of the interests or traits of the most dominant groups.
There is nothing profound or unusual in these observations; the point is simply that the political-legal-governmental sphere cannot be understood as
devoid of cultural partiality.

In sum, the relation of civil society and culture is a *dialectical* one. Civil
life cannot mean and be valued in itself without culture, and culture cannot be the culture of citizens unless it restrains itself from treading on civility, itself part of the complex of cultural values that gives life in the *civitas*
meaning. Society as civil is society understood as a moral association of free
members. Culture is the interpretive inheritance of those members. Thus
cultural reproduction must not be allowed to overwhelm civility, and civil
rules must not be allowed to eviscerate its own cultural cathexis. Neither
side can win, each must support the other while struggling against it, each
must limit its prevalence in order to survive.

KINGDOMS OF ENDS

Nobody makes the concept of culture more dubious than the practitioners of the discipline that defines itself in terms of culture. In their 1952 book, *Culture: A Critical Review of Concepts and Definitions,* the anthropologists Kroeber and Kluckhohn found 164 distinct meanings of the term in the literature, no doubt chilling further attempts at definition. Other anthropologists have lately been questioning whether there are any cultures at all. Thus Robert Brightman suggests that we "forget culture" (Brightman 1995). Perhaps this is not so odd. While we have made "culture" our favorite name for what it is about groups of "Others" we ought to tolerate, it is the anthropologists who have had to make methodological sense out of what is for many of us a bumper sticker.

Their worries are multiple. We cannot find in human societies anything answering to Emile Durkheim's *conscience collectif.* There is no reason to assume "holism" across very diverse social contexts, to expect a society's way of cooking, its literature, public health, sports, manners, religion, and military technology to express common meanings. Certainly in almost all societies social meanings are contested: rich and poor, high-status and low-status, employed and unemployed members may each give the anthropologist a different account of "shared" meanings depending on their position in the intramural competition. If the degree of diversity within a society rivals the degree of diversity between it and others, what does the ascription to that society of one shared culture explain? And last, even if it makes sense to speak of culture, it may not make sense to speak of *cultures,* bounded packets of meaning. Is "culture" then merely a simplifying construction meant to harness the exoticism of the native, the "other" for the Western anthropologist?

Our response can be simple, although working it out will be complex. Calling aspects of a social group's behavior cultural is an empirical claim that two conditions hold. The first is that explanations of the behavior of social members are not exhausted by class, occupation, legal status or citizenship, social status, clan, and gender differences or by species-wide characteristics. The second is that we can observe commonalities holding across distinctive behavioral zones in group members' lives, such that purely intracontextual explanations of their sports or business or religious rituals or kinship arrangements miss something. The tolerably adequate adjective for the commonalities missed by such explanations is "cultural." Would it really make sense to say that class, occupational, status, clan, and gender descriptions exhaust group dynamics, or that manners, religious belief, ritual, kinship rules, art, sport, and literature *never* exhibit overlapping meanings? Of course not. Likewise the fact that discrete, rigid boundaries defining a culture are not discoverable indicates only the continuous and stochastic (statistical) nature of the phenomena. That we cannot see a nonarbitrary point on the color spectrum where red turns into orange does not mean that red *is* orange, or that there are no distinct colors. The same is true of distinct cultures.

But there is another problem. Our understanding of culture is arguably modern, which means that we may be imposing on the historical record what culture means for us today. Of course, most of what we refer to with the term "culture"—distinctive peoples and their folkways—is not modern. But it would be right to say that the eighteenth century for the first time made culture *philosophically and politically important,* albeit ambivalently as a boon and threat. As Samuel Fleischacker recounts, it is the Enlightenment that distinguished the artificial cultivation of human faculties and manners beyond what is universally given by nature as a vehicle of progress (Fleischacker 1994). When in his 1765 *The Philosophy of History* Voltaire referred to "culture" as the higher values, the cultivation, of the Enlightened era, he reflected that modern usage. But it was the German philosopher Gottfried Herder who set out to provide a systematic account of culture. In his *Ideas on the Philosophy of the History of Mankind* (four volumes, 1784–91) Herder argued that the world's peoples embodied distinctive worldviews, virtues, and interpretive habits, ordered by God to fully reveal the totality of spirit. Thus for the first time in Western philosophical history, the differences between peoples were claimed to matter *philosophically.* For the Greco-Roman and Christian traditions, Goodness and Truth entailed approximation to a universal human standard, from which ethnic differences are at best a distraction. Likewise for the mainstream of the Enlightenment, the evolving ideal of universal scientific knowledge required abstraction from descent group, local origins, languages, and above all religious traditions and superstitions. Cosmopolitan cultivation was good; local acculturation created barriers to the universals of Reason and Science and Nature. In the classical, medieval, and dominant modern views, a difference in virtue or cognition between individuals or peoples just indicates that *somebody is wrong;* uniqueness is only valuable in so far as it is a unique approximation to the universal norm. To be sure, as recent critics of Eurocentrism have pointed out, this supposed universalism was at the same time regarded as the unique achievement of a particular continent, civilization, and race, in comparison to which others were viewed as backward, or worse.

The nineteenth century, led by Romanticism's love of the particular, embraced Herder's position. Anthropology emerged in 1843 as Gustav Klem first used "culture" to label the complex of customs, beliefs, and political forms that characterize a society, and was taken up in English by E. B. Tylor's influential *Primitive Culture* in 1871. Herder influenced Adolf Bastian, and through him Franz Boas, one of the earliest and most influential ethnographers, teacher of Ruth Benedict and Margaret Mead. But nothing could have enhanced the role of the concept of culture more than the political expression of Romanticism, *nationalism,* most famously formulated by Germans in response to Napoleonic France's threat to dominate Europe. We are familiar with nationalism's later checkered history, from the liberal nationalism of Mazzini to the fascism of Mussolini and Hitler. But as Ernest Gellner and Liah Greenfeld separately argue, nationalism played a crucial role throughout the modern West in forging the modern egalitarian notion of the citizen (Gellner 1983; Greenfeld 1992). Only nationalism was able to break the *ancien régime* separation of society into isonomic castes—a hierarchy of unequal classes with rough equality *within* each—making the German-speaking peasant and German-speaking aristocrat equal *as Germans.*

At any rate, the problem raised by this historical development is that when we use the term "culture" today we may be presupposing a particularly modern Western view of social behavior and meaning as resting on a fundamental hermeneutic web possessed by sovereign nations or "countries" that does not easily apply to world history or prehistory. We must especially be on guard against the canard that cultural politics or nationalism is something traditional, premodern, or primitive. For thousands of years, the great agricultural empires that created what we call civilization were certainly *not* organized around national or linguistic solidarity. If in ancient, hunter-gatherer societies *clan* trumped culture, in civilization *caste* trumped culture. The triumph of cultural identity has been made possible by the modernity that, with its other hand, dismissed culture as the great obstacle to progress.

Preliminary Considerations

William James liked to say that "experience" is a double-barreled term, being a name both for a process (experien*cing*) and for the contents or data revealed by that process (experien*ces*). Following his analogy beyond the possibilities of the shotgun, culture is a *triple*-barreled word. It is in one sense a *how,* a medium through which the world, society, and the self are interpreted and represented, in this sense like a language. But culture is not merely a process or medium, it is also a *what,* or a large collection of *whats* including physical things: buildings, symbols, rituals, artifacts, paintings, clothing, literary works, and so on. Cultures are repertoires, inventories. Indeed, cultures can be destroyed, or deeply harmed, through the destruction of key icons or buildings, or the prohibitions of key practices and discourses. Lastly, a culture is also a *who.* It belongs to or characterizes a group of people. As such it comes in collections or networks that differ from one another, even if, as noted, their borders are elusive. Thus an adequate view of culture must show how the what, the how, and the who of culture qualify one another. We may begin with some basic points attendant on the fact that cultures are social phenomena.

Culture is *collective,* not individual or private. There can no more be a "private" culture than a private language. So we may say that culture is public. But in saying so we must recognize that culture is *also* private in that people carry their cultures with them as individuals wherever they go, even in solitude. Culture is not solely public, nor public in the sense that, for example, politics is public. Robinson Crusoe remained a child of his culture (no doubt to Friday's dismay).

Some inquirers, especially in ethology and anthropology, mean by "culture" the intersection of two things: the totality of what any living group learns and passes on to the next generation, and what distinguishes one population of a species from another. The effect and conceptual purpose of such a definition is to make the antonym of culture whatever is genetic. For genes neither learn nor carry anything acquired or devised in the process of experience. Whatever else it is, then, a culture is learned. The term's Latin root *colere* means tending, as in agricultural husbandry, or more broadly "cultivation." In the nature-nurture debate culture is thus on the side of nurture and so, in this sense, against nature. Such learning is accomplished by a local population, a subgroup of the species. The tokens or instances of the term "culture" are *particular* and *historical*. Like persons, each culture *is* a history and cannot be understood independent of it. If there were only one culture among humans on Earth, there would be little point in giving an account of culture distinct from an account of human being *per se*. Discussing culture as distinct from human nature only makes sense because there is more than one. Further, each is, we would say today, "contingent," that is, a product of largely undesigned, collectively acting forces whose effects accumulate over time. Each culture could have been different if other things, like its physical environment, had been different.

Cultures in the primary sense of the term belong to whole societies or what Avishai Margalit and Joseph Raz call "encompassing groups" (Margalit and Raz 1995). To modify Will Kymlicka's term, we are here concerned with *societal cultures,* cultures of relatively independent, self-reproducing societies within which members can live their whole lives, and not the "cultures" of corporations, voluntary associations, or professions, in which people live only part of their days. Those things may be *cultural,* but they are not *cultures.* Neither are "subcultures," such as communes, monasteries, or bohemias, which depend on a larger encompassing society for all manner of sustenance. Likewise, cultures are almost never local or brief; they hold usually over at least a region and last many generations.

Culture represents a form of human grouping that must be distinctive; labeling the difference between two groups "cultural" must be different from labeling it "social," "economic," or "religious." A culture is not a family, tribe, class, caste, status, or occupational group. Those distinctions must range *within* the kind of grouping we are after. As seen earlier, this also implies that the functional spheres of a society's life—its sports, economy, politics, and so on—are not distinctive cultures. What the term "culture" refers to must be interdisciplinary, must include different kinds of phenomena, different zones or areas of social life. While particular activities within a culture can be regarded as valid in terms of distinctive norms—scientific claims are supposed to be true, art aesthetically compelling, and political action right—a culture spans all these activities, hence is *omnivalent,* responsible to several norms, not one. Culture cannot be understood as a disciplinary sphere *within* social life. We can speak of a society's economy, its politics, its art, its religion, its sports, as differing from each other, but culture cannot be on that list. That would be a category mistake. None of this implies, of course, that the various spheres of a culture's social life must all cohere or express a single pattern. Cultures are not monolithic; they do not even need to be coherent. They are always conflicted. Nevertheless, there is a kind of unity a culture must have: its various important components must be capable of functioning together, capable of being lived and belonged to by social members.

We could say that culture functions in part to provide sociocultural expectations and norms, so that signaling or being marked as a member activates the proper set of judgmental rules. We could call this *judgmental endogamy,* implying that under "normal" circumstances exogamous judgments carry little or no normative force. In this sense a culture is something in terms of which social members make their judgments (although culture is not the only thing of which that is true). Hence we might employ a criterion which applies to all human associational identities, cultural or not: ye shall know them by what they *exclude.* As argued by Fredrick Barth and his school, groups define themselves through boundary maintenance (Barth 1969). The kind of group a culture is will be evident in what other memberships or identities cannot be exhibited by its members, identities which render the individual's cultural membership suspect or marginal.

Finally, we ought to distinguish culture from *civilization,* a word that has its own long etymology. Without troubling ourselves with the fine points separating recent students of the term (c.f. Toynbee 1961, Hodgson 1974, Quigley 1979, and Huntington 1996), we can simply say that civilizations are the broadest cultural groupings, *families* of cultures related along some cultural axis. Thus it makes perfect sense to distinguish, for example, the West—that is to say, Western Christendom dating to the eighth century C.E.—as tied together by overlapping cultural themes, from Islamic civilization, a family of cultures from the Maghreb to Indonesia, tied together by religion above all.

Culture and Society

Having milked the dependence of culture upon society for what it's worth, we must, nevertheless, *not* identify society and culture. If we ascribe culture to any species that exhibits social behavior, then we must also assert that ants have cultures. But they don't. Perhaps some primates or cetaceans do, but it is very difficult to argue for culture much lower on the phylogenetic scale. Even staying with humans, the identification of society and culture muddies the waters. Is every social fact a cultural fact? The computer-generated list of courses for the next semester at my college is socially created and produced, full of signs meant to communicate, but is it a part of my culture? Using a distinction that will be important later, evolutionary anthropologists have argued for the distinction of social from cultural communication, or the social, communicative use of symbols from their cultural, ritual use (Chase 1999; Watts 1999). The distinction of society from culture is required if we are ever to notice that a society can change while its culture remains the same, or its culture may change while society stagnates. Suppose a society of hunter-gatherers is forced by lack of game to turn to rudimentary slash-and-burn agriculture. Which would illuminate their predicament more, to say that they have a "slash-and-burn culture" or that they are a hunter-gatherer culture that has recently and perhaps temporarily adopted a new social practice that they consider distinct from their culture? If there are culturally pluralistic societies, then it must be possible for two people to belong to the same society but different cultures. And finally, the distinction of society from culture also makes it at least logically possible for a society not to have a culture. This is useful to contemplate. The vaunted social contract theory of modern political philosophy precisely imagines a group of people coming out of the wild to form an interdependent socioeconomic group, arguably a society, but without any shared cultural resources. In the real world social groups under intense pressure to survive might in effect lose their cultures; we might want to say that refugees, residents of a concentration camp, or plane crash survivors constitute a "society" or social group, capable of cooperation, but share no culture. In *The Mountain People* Colin Turnbull described the Ik as so close to starvation that all long-term cooperation, rituals of marriage and death, all mediately significant human behavior, had fallen away (Turnbull 1972). The "high" end of culture—meaning not only fine art, music, and literature, but all symbolic practices—can be absent and yet a kind of rudimentary society exist, retaining predictable patterns of interaction and accepted forms of communication.

For these reasons we will throughout this study regard culture as a subset of the domain of social facts. We will reserve the term "society" for geographically continuous associations whose members are open to regular interaction in the tasks that constitute living, hence responsible to one continuous politics (note that members are "open to" such interaction, not actually interacting all the time). A society is a *horizon of interaction and interdependence.* Such social interaction entails a *grammar of intelligibility and propriety.* Culture extends, contextualizes, and legitimates that grammar. It thus has something to do with how and what a society thinks, means, understands, interprets, imagines. In this sense, Hegel was on the right track in viewing culture as objective or social mind. Thus we may say that culture *supervenes* upon society like a mind supervenes upon a human organism, as long as we remember that culture cannot have the unity of a mind (since it is not an agent), that cultural "mind" is not immaterial (since it includes artifacts), and contra Hegelian idealism, culture is fundamentally, although not exclusively, a matter of practices.

This third point, famously associated with Pierre Bourdieu, must be clarified (Bourdieu 1990). The American pragmatists, beginning with Charles S. Peirce, put meaning, truth, and mind itself in the context of action. Concepts, words, and beliefs mean what their affirmation would imply for an agent's behavior. But a later contributor to this tradition, Justus Buchler, offered a further step. Buchler argued that while the pragmatists had sought to demonstrate the active nature of cognitive judgment, putting saying and knowing in the context of doing, the more radical point is to expand the notion of judgment *per se,* thereby to hold that "action *as such [is] judicative*" (Buchler 1955: 32). Rather than making all forms of human appropriation or discrimination matters of practice, Buchler severed, finally and completely, the presumed special relation of *verbal utterance* and *representation* to *rationality* and *wisdom.* Unlike many contemporary critics of the "logocentric" tradition who magnify linguistic primacy while criticizing it, Buchler allowed doing (practice) and making (construction) utter equality with saying (linguistic assertion) as the potential bearer of meaning, reason, knowledge, and validity, so that those normative terms apply indiscriminately to the three modes of judgment. This approach, crucial for conceptualizing culture, will be followed throughout.

Meaning Culture

All the things we call cultural must *mean.* The *how* of culture, what it does or the way it functions, has something to do with meaning. But it cannot be true that everything that means, or all meanings, are what we mean by "culture." If, to take a slightly narrower term, culture is like a language, it is not the case that everything I can say in my language is equally and in-differently part of my culture. There is a sense in which advanced mathe-matics, a system of sentential logic, and the instruction manual that came with my computer, while semiotic products of my society, are not cultural in the way that, for example, a Japanese tea ceremony or a Gothic cathe-dral or the figure of John Wayne are. If culture is semiosis, it must be rather *thick* semiosis.

What is meaning? In the broadest sense it is *implication*. If an object, event, or experience is capable of implying, referring to, or suggesting some-thing beyond itself in the mind of an intelligent agent, then it has meaning. In this sense, as Charles Peirce defined signs, what means must be some-thing that means something to someone (or, I would say, be *capable* of so doing) (Peirce 1955: 99). Meaning then has to do with connection among things, as opposed to their—to borrow another Peircean doctrine—sheer phenomenal quality (Peirce's "Firstness") or their brute facticity or physical resistance ("Secondness") (Peirce 1955: 75ff.). Qualia and difference impress, and are salient; but when they "mean," they must exhibit connection, rela-tion ("Thirdness"). Meaning comes to spread across the majority of the experienced world in the form of implication and is invoked and functions in experience in all sorts of ways (which need not imply that relation meta-physically outweighs particularity, disconnectedness, or irrelevance). While *everything* cannot mean, *anything* can, given the right circumstances. The first light of dawn means it is daytime, an open door can mean my apart-ment was broken into, and a particular array of photonic traces on a photo-graphic plate can mean that some physical theory is false. Even nothing, in the sense of absence, can mean. Coming home to an empty house after an argument with my wife on the telephone can have a lot of meaning. But not everything which means is a sign. Signs are humanly appropriated meaning-carriers that have a place in the process of thought or communi-cation. The first light of dawn is not manipulable, and so not a sign. If we wish, we can say that humanly created things alone can *be* signs, while other things can *function as* signs.

We turn now to a crucial point. Instrumentality has an ambiguous relation to culture. From Max Weber's diagnosis of modern *Zweckrationalität* (means-rationality) through Theodor Adorno's and Max Horkheimer's critique of "functional reason" and Heidegger's analysis of technology, to the more re-cent three-cornered debate among Jean-François Lyotard's postmodernism, Alasdair MacIntyre's premodernism, and Jürgen Habermas's "promodernism"—in all these analyses of modernity the critique of instrumentalism or cult of efficiency devoid of "value" has been a constant. This is all familiar. But what has gone unrecognized is that this has always been a debate about the relation of culture, understood as the domain of humanly constructed or posited ends, to instrumentality. There is something about the instrumental attitude—treating each thing as a fungible, exchangeable moment in a process—which removes the "cultural" valence of a cultural thing, like regarding a painting as nothing but an investment, or a religious service solely as the venue for a business deal. Not that there is anything immoral or unseemly here; there may be, but that is not the point. The point is that such an approach removes the meaning of the thing or event from the domain of culture. If a society regards a practice *as purely* instrumental, hence as exchangeable without normative loss for greater efficiency, then that practice ceases in some sense to be cultural.

The distinction of symbolic from everyday communication is relevant here. Knight makes the provocative claim that in ancient societies ritual, the first form of symbolic culture, cannot be reduced to signaling or messaging (Knight 1999). Despite the overlap—culture, of course, uses language—the modes and contexts of daily language use differ importantly from ritual and religious speech. Ritual is very "costly" in its expenditure of energy, repeating affectively loaded behaviors and sayings at high volume, over and over again, in a way quite different from the nonritual, everyday speech of preliterate peoples. His explanation is that ritual is not communication *per se,* but the collective creation and maintenance of a virtual world, an ontology of symbolic beings of various kinds: deities and ghosts (entities); chiefs and bridesmaids (roles); scepters and stop signs (material objects); sin and authority (concepts); baptizing and promising (acts). In the chronology of *Homo sapiens sapiens* these are late achievements of the Upper Paleolithic era, not "natural" expressions. Now, Knight and his colleagues presuppose something that for philosophers is an open question, a pragmatic world of fact on top of which a cultural deception has been added. But a slightly different formulation can still capture the point. There is something about culture which is in excess of, supererogatory to, the most basic or pragmatic dimensions of human existence. In culture a people adds something to their existence beyond the necessities of food, shelter, and reproduction, even if that addition is often inextricably bound up with those activities—as in a recipe, an architectural style, or the details of a marriage ceremony.

I suggest we regard cultural meaning, as opposed to any other employ-ment of signs, as meaning in relation to *ends*. An end, in the sense of goal or the Greek *telos*, is something experienced, known, and acted upon for its own sake. Ends draw attention, appreciation, thought, action. Ends arise ontogenetically as qualitatively compelling phenomena, chief among sali-ences, we may say. While an end emerges into experience as a compelling quality, if it remains an end over time it comes to serve as the "for-which" of a process that gives temporal organization to precedent events recon-structed as a dramatic structure of process-leading-to-an-end. Ends form the fabric that gives finality and shape, which is to say a certain kind of mean-ing, to human existence. Here John Dewey's account of means and ends is particularly useful (Dewey 1958). For Dewey means and ends are not two types of things but two respects in which the same event can be experi-enced, or what is the same thing, *two kinds of meaning* an event can have. Ends, or qualities, are moments of experience that constitute termini, expe-rienced as that-for-which and that-toward-which a process of experiencing was proceeding. They are *consummatory*, hence nonprocessural. They are the stuff of norms, categorized as moral, aesthetic, or alethic (cognitive), and both give meaning to and limit the processes they terminate, thereby restraining imagination, desire, and action.

There are ultimate and proximate ends. The former are the summary ends of human existence as understood by a social group, those values for the sake of which socialized persons live; the latter are the indefinitely many things which we experience and treat as consummatory. The ultimate ends are like the peaks of a hilly countryside; they culminate the view, com-plete the landscape, but the beauty of the surrounding fields and brush would not disappear without them. Ultimate ends are those whose value can be given no deeper account, whose finality is susceptible to explica-tion and interpretation but not explanation. Proximal ends, while consum-matory, do not leverage the value of existence itself; many people find politeness valuable in itself, but very few make politeness that for which they live. And certainly ends can do double-duty as means, which is to say, function simultaneously in two different orders of events with two distinct meanings. Romantic love is an end for those experiencing it, perhaps even an ultimate end, and simultaneously serves reproduction. But to understand romantic love as merely or primarily a means toward reproduction is to cease to be a romantic lover.

Some meanings cluster about ends, forming networks where the meanings in question each refer, however mediately, to ends that *root* the network. The interpretation of the end is the operation of relating the end to other things in such a way that the other things become the background for understanding the value of the end, and the background is endowed with value thereby. Culture entails social meaning-making and -interpreting, where "meaning" is teleological meaning, meaning connected, however mediately, to socially recognized ends. A set of meaningful things is cultural in so far as it is connected to, gains its meaning in reference to, socially posited ends. In terms of the relation of culture and society, whereas social action must always presuppose a grammar of intelligibility and propriety, that grammar, hence the social action in question, *is cultural to the extent that its rules of intelligibility and propriety are connected to, understood in terms of, socially shared ends.* In this way cultural things and processes intertwine with social things and processes to varying degrees, some social acts being more thickly and directly motivated and explained by ends, others less so. It is at the point where the experienced and understood meaning of the event, act, or object ceases to be consummatory, either proximally or ultimately, that it and the network of acts and things oriented around it ceases to be cultural.

Practices, Artifacts, and Narratives

Culture comprises three species of human appropriation of the world, namely, *practices, artifacts,* and *narratives.* These overlap; a representation may be an artifact and the focus of a practice. These categories are meant to capture Buchler's rendition of the old Aristotelian trilogy of practical, productive, and theoretical reason, or more modestly, doing, making, and saying (Buchler 1966). Such a categorization, if we were to pursue it to the "molecular" or micrological level, might well be unsustainable; we might find that human appropriation or judgment requires a more extensive list of categories. But left "molar" this categorization represents an advance on both the tendency to cognitivize culture into assertive beliefs and the tendency to pragmatize it solely into practices.

The whats of culture are artifacts. Artifacts, what is made, include fabrications of all kinds, high art, all manner of *technē, poiēsis,* all decoration, clothing, building, the construction and transmission of stories and speeches, the organization or configuration of elements, and so on. Not all made things are, however, artifacts. The tool whose structure and use is not endowed with meanings that are related to consummatory values is not an artifact. The screwdriver is not cultural until decorated, or experienced as itself the consummation of a process, or otherwise endowed with teleological meaning. In so far as culture is a set of meaningful items that characterize a people, in which they find and express significance, culture is artifacts.

Culture is also comprised by what a society believes, how it depicts the world and itself, whether this is expressed in plastic arts or verbal assertions, whether it aims to describe a given world or posit a better or ideal world. "Representations" may be the best term here. Representations tell about states of affairs, and they are supposed to be true. But not all representations are cultural phenomena, just as not all made things are artifacts. They become cultural when placed within social narrative. What does not fit into a narrative, hence dramatic, structure is not a narrative representation, hence not cultural.

Lastly, culture is practices. A practice is a discrete, repeatable, organized process of action. Following MacIntyre, practices have internal goods, dependent upon internal ends or purposes; that is, it makes no sense to claim to understand the practice and to engage in it while discounting the goods thereby entailed. They are the characteristic things cultural members do, in the way that they do them, carrying the meaning that they typically or normatively carry for members. Not all behaviors, even all behaviors common to or typical of a society, count as practices. The act of nose scratching I just engaged in is no cultural practice, nor is the slash-and-burn agriculture of the tribe for whom it is a pragmatic necessity at odds with their cultural self-understanding. The latter is social, of course, but not cultural. At least not yet.

To this horizontal categorization of cultural judgments and things we must add a vertical distinction. Practices, artifacts, and narratives can function on a *mundane* level characterizing more narrow, context-specific concerns as well as on a *symbolic* level as global, explicit ends-in-view, normative anchors of all other more contextually narrow appropriations. Practices, constructions, and narratives *become symbolic* as *ritual, icon,* and *metanarrative* or *myth*. While a particular way of decorating spoons (artifact) or of greeting strangers (practice) or a conception of who counts as a cousin (fitting into a narration of familial life) may be characteristic of a culture, and meaningful as such, we nevertheless may in our analysis pay more attention to religious rituals, metaphysics, and sacred icons. "Foundational" would be the wrong metaphor for the symbolic; symbols do not ground, but *complete* other cultural phenomena, retrospectively and anticipatorily serving as that-for-which they are accomplished and that-in-terms-of-which they are to be understood. The symbolic cultural items are *not* more cultural than the mundane; the mundane are just as fully implicated in a cultural network. Nor must it be the case that all the mundane cultural phenomena refer to or implicate the symbolic phenomena. Rather, the symbolic refers to the cultural phenomena that the *culture itself* regards as ends in themselves, as its "sacred" points, its grand stories of origin or destiny, its most treasured objects, which most nexuses or collections of related cultural phenomena at some point entail. The symbolic is the pinnacle of a continuous (which is not to say unified or harmonious) realm of cultural practices and meanings, just as, in an earlier figure, the hilltops remain continuous with the slopes and fields below. And as symbols they are inherently *vague*. They are reference points capable of diverse interpretations, as are canonical texts in MacIntyre's sense or myths in Baeten's sense. That a culture cannot "go beyond" them does not mean it cannot observe them or reflect on them.

Agency, Practice, and Ritual

Metaphysically, normatively, and logically, neither practices nor artifacts nor symbols are prior to the others. However, ontogenetically, psychologically, and pedagogically *doing comes first*. As Buchler suggests, each human being is born in a "state of natural debt, being antecedently committed to the execution or the furtherance of acts that will largely determine his individual existence" (Buchler 1966: 3). If sharing a culture means sharing a "way of life," then practices are the leading edge of what constitutes such a "way." I must learn to do what members of my society do, I must acquire its practices as the most basic dimension of my judgmental repertoire. And it is primarily through cultivation or training or acquisition of these practices that individuals are socialized, come to share the sensibilities of other members, and to divide up the world as the culture represents it. Pragmatism, which, like both Kant and Wittgenstein, accepts Goethe's figural response to the opening of the Gospel of John, that "*Im Anfang war die Tat,*" "In the beginning was the deed," need not be the metaphysical or epistemic truth, but it may well be the anthropological truth. If nothing else, our old and continuing theoretical tendency to focus on "beliefs," "worldviews," or representations makes it at least circumstantially beneficial to put practices, for once, first.

A practice is a series of acts, purposively organized into a unit such that the acts gain their intelligibility from that inclusion and their end from the *telos* of the practice. A practice is distinct from "technique" in that it is not purely instrumental. That is, society inculcates and vets the process, not just the product. Practices are modules, each a complex series of acts distinct from others, so a social actor knows when they begin or end. They are repetitive and social. The goods internal to practices must be valuable—that is, they must really be *goods*. In one of MacIntyre's favorite examples, knives *should* be sharp. Practices are, as for Pierre Bourdieu, manifestations of a practical intelligence that is not reducible to linguistic or cognitive intelligence (Bourdieu 1990). Expanding Dewey's early notion of the "sensori-motor circuit," we can say that a practice is a motor-affective-sensory-imaginative process of doing, a bodily and cultural engagement with the world, distinguished and delimited by social learning. As Michael Oakeshott insists, it cannot be adequately summarized by a verbal formula, hence captured by theoretical knowledge (Oakeshott 1991). Practices are the most basic web of meaning and value, self and society. They are fundamentally communicative, being always "gestural" in George Herbert Mead's sense (Mead 1974).

As noted, a society must have a set of largely implicit but occasionally explicit rules for how people are meaningfully to behave, which entail a grammar of intelligibility and propriety, of what acts, artifacts, and sayings mean, and what may and may not be done, made, or said. But there is an additional component of interaction: a shared *grammar of sensibility.* I mean a configuration of salience in perception and feeling, in what we sometimes call *taste,* which then is a constitutive part of the practical wisdom common among members. The culture must encourage in members a particular distribution of attention across the indefinitely complex array of experience and a corresponding distribution of emotional response, hence various sensibilities, dispositions to weigh certain experiences more than others, to feel some things more than others, to "natively" respond to experiences in certain ways. This is the affective substrate of the grammars of intelligibility and propriety that must hold in a person's relations to others. A fundamental part of what we call practical wisdom is exhibiting the right or proper sense of proportion, of what matters in personal and social life. This must be built into the structure of a person's experience, not merely into a reflective response to that experience. The individual who feels rage in inappropriate situations, but reflectively exercises self-control, not only fails to be a *phronēmos* or "wise" woman or man, but even a reliable or socially accepted woman or man. It is in this way that culture enters most intimately into the constitution of the process of experiencing characteristic of members.

The primacy of practice means that the self is primarily, although not exclusively, an *agent*. The agent is the dominant coagulation of or nexus in experience. I do not mean that the self is nothing other than what the person is taken, and takes herself, to be socially. Rather, of the totality of phenomena involved in the experiences characterizing a person, which are too overwhelmingly plural to be incorporated into any meaningful unity, those cohering about what can be socially expressed in agency must inevitably be dominant. The requirements of agency select saliences within the inner horizon of experience. Not that there is a perfect match; social requirements are not a purely procedural definition of the self. But components of personal experience that are in stark contrast to, or cannot be integrated with, a relatively coherent agency must be neglected under most circumstances.

At the symbolic level, practice becomes ritual, an end-in-itself that is known as such by the agent. This does not mean it is devoid of instrumental significance. But the culture comes to regard its practices as rituals at the point where they function as crucial normative components of social organization whose meanings *must* be internalized. The ritual both enacts an ultimate end of social existence, and in doing so, itself becomes such an ultimate end. Or, to preview a later point, ritual is practice become *dramatic*.

Construction, Artifact, and Icon

Constructions, artifacts, things people make, are certainly a major part of culture. Indeed, one might imagine that culture is pretty much all constructions. But this is not so. In the classical sense making or *poiēsis* is about the formation of materials into meaningful wholes. While much of what we call culture, and virtually all cultural *things,* are indeed the products of making, certainly making is not all of culture. Practices are done, not made. The notion that culture is all made is the result of the overuse and expansion of the metaphor of "construction" by contemporary theorists, who tend to label "constructed" anything showing the effects of human activity. Assertion and action then get subsumed under making. This tendency must be resisted. Making is one pole of a continuum that includes selecting, choosing, interacting, and affecting, unless we are going to claim that leaving footprints on K-2, or even *naming* it "K-2," are no different from having built the mountain itself from the ground up. It is true that people construct things. The things they construct are artifacts where they carry cultural meanings. The artifacts of a society have the special function of constituting a meaningful environment for members. It is the system of artifacts that has a right to the overused philosophical term "second-nature," a constructed world that supervenes upon nature.

And it is in this sense that construction does have a kind of primacy in the conception of culture. For while culture as a whole is equally a matter of doing, making, and saying, the entire *symbolic* dimension of culture, as opposed to the mundane, can from an external point of view rightly be considered something we *make.* By "external" I mean from the perspective of an observer, rather than a member, of a culture. For symbolic rituals, icons, and myths are arguably *added* to nature by human beings, and addition is more making than doing or saying. That is, while we engage the world by saying what it is, and by responding to or dealing with it, we also engage by supplementing it, clothing it in human terms, hence by arranging and forming natural materials into a new whole. But it remains the case, as we will see in Chapter 6, that this making is always the making of an *agent.*

Remarkably, the best recent account of this artifactual world comes from a work in social and political theory; but then, its author was a remarkable political theorist. In *The Human Condition* Hanna Arendt expands the concept of *Welt* and its dependence on practice from Heidegger's *Being and Time.* "World" for Heidegger was the horizon of all meaningful things, a horizon projected by *Dasein* or human being as the context for its experience. Whereas Heidegger's analysis of the physical projects that form, or form part of, this world stopped with tools (*zuhanden,* "ready to hand" things), Arendt makes human artifacts the structure of the world. Like a tent, Arendt's world is propped up and given structure by human *poiēsis,* making, or as she calls it, "work" (not to be confused with labor), including art, poetry, history, and crafts, all the manifold forms of human creation that leave behind durable meaningful objects. For even though political action is her focus, action is only commemorated and memorialized, hence capable of building something that outlasts the actor, if there is an artifact to capture it. The work-world of Arendt is clearly the world of culture.

As she notes, modern society privileges construction. Modernity makes man the maker *(homo faber).* In the premodern world two castes present alternate models of ideal humanity: the aristocratic model dictates that the sheer *being* of an individual marks its worth, granted by blood, while the scribal-religious class regards *contemplation* of the eternal as the essential task of humanity. Work was, in agroliterate civilization, a degraded category, embodied by peasants and merchants. In modern bourgeois society the measure of greatness is fabrication: here Kant's transcendental turn provides the epistemological twin to modernist art and Promethean capitalism. Certainly premodern people worked, but modernity shifts work to the center of its anthropology, thereby liberating work from the classical and medieval versions in which the fabricator is a copyist of ideal, tradition-bequeathed models. Modernity is the triumph of work, even if, as Arendt fears, in late modernity work threatens to degenerate into metabolic, meaningless labor.

The artifact or cultural construction that becomes a recognized end-in-view is an *icon,* a thing that is an end in itself for social members. Art-works are the most obvious examples, but so are many treasured objects. Iconic constructions provide to sensibility the aesthetically normative compulsions of a culture. They become centers of interpretation just as do the canonical texts of narrative tradition.

Representation, Narrative, and Myth

Representations are depictions and descriptions which claim to be true of what is described. It is here that the beliefs shared by cultural members have their place. I claim cultural representations are organized into meaningful patterns through narrative. That is the form in which representations come to be shared by social members as part of their culture. This is to argue that the primary form of the intelligibility of human existence, one which coheres with both practices and artifacts, is the narrative. It is in the historical depiction of events as they pass from beginning through middle to end via the activities of agents (human or nonhuman, that is to say, divine, supranatural) that culture provides this intelligibility. This might seem too restrictive. Certainly social members also share purely synchronic (non-temporal) representations or beliefs. But just as not all makings or actions are cultural, representations or beliefs that are not connected to shared narratives are not cultural.

Storytelling was presumably one of the first forms of culture, along with ritual practices and the artifacts of cave painting and bodily ornamentation. The canonical texts and folk wisdom of later agricultural civilizations are also primarily narrative. And in a postreligious age secular societies commonly substitute narratives of progress, national self-determination, and the achievement of liberty and individual authenticity as their dominant conceptions of the sense of life.

Narration is verbal representation normed, as noted, by truth. One might argue that our modern notion of truth-functional discourse has no place here, that ancient, segmentary narratives did not follow our modern notion of true representations as propositions whose correspondence to states of affairs can be evidenced or justified. One might imagine that the oral history heard by the fire functioned not to be the depiction of truth, but rather the reinforcement of a social bond, as Lyotard says (Lyotard 1984). He may be right, but that is beside the point. If the sociopolitical context of the story made clear that all present must then "believe" it without "evidence," must see the world in relation to it, must say the world *is* as the story says, then it was indeed offered as "true" *as well as* socially normative. The difference is not the absence of truth in the ancient context. Truth was there, just as aesthetic compulsion and moral-social normativity were there. But they were there *differently* than for us, in a predifferentiated state, as we shall see.

At the symbolic level the narrative structure of cultural representations becomes what Lyotard called metanarrative, or more simply, myth. Myths serve as the articulations of the ultimate ends of the culture and as such become *ultimate ends themselves.* Following Elizabeth Baeten's analysis, a culture's myths are the cognitive representations beyond which it cannot go, which provide explanation for other social activities but cannot be explained themselves, only explicated and interpreted (Baeten 1996).

Kingdoms of Ends

We can now offer a preliminary definition of culture. Culture is the *public repertoire of meaning-establishing and -interpreting processes and products, rooted in socially projected ends.* It is the teleologically *thickest* layer of a society's hermeneutic horizon. Culture is *not* a particular social sphere, not a rule-governed context of action. It is the indefinite repertoire in terms of which all such contexts gain their mediate significance, their "place." Just as a sovereign state cannot be part of a larger political unit (if it is, then it is not sovereign), a culture cannot function as a *part* of society or society's semiotics. It is rather a dimension of social experience which invokes social norms in narrative, practical, and artifactual meaning-structures. Differently put, culture is the net of interpretive products in so far as they are connected to socially normative ends. As to the question why I ought to commit some social act, rather than answering that I ought to do it because others expect it, it will feel good, will be practically beneficial—perfectly good social reasons—culture amplifies by answering: because it is right, or good, or sacred, or beautiful, or awesome, or true.

None of which implies that a culture *is* a system, or a substantive unity, but it can *function as* a unity. A culture's elements cannot be reduced to applications of a few central themes or ideals. An apt metaphor for its unity might be Giles Deleuze's "rhizomes," tubers that reproduce from any point rather than "arborially" in a "logical tree" (Deleuze and Guattari 1987). We may imagine a culture as a family of variously connected hypotheses spread out like clumps of kelp across a region of sea, swimming, as Peirce figured it, "in a continuum of uncertainty and indeterminacy" (Peirce 1931a: 70). Like an irregular construction of a child's tinker toys, every clump is connected to at least one other, but none connects to all or dominates the far-flung network.

The idea of a society of beings whose behavior is coordinated by ends-in-themselves may remind us of the attractive phrase coined by Kant for the imagined community of moral beings, "the kingdom of ends." Moral action requires that we act in conformity with that imagination, which is a necessary posit of practical, or moral, reason for Kant. For rational beings are and must be treated as ends in themselves. What is it about human beings that makes them ends for Kant? It is their moral autonomy, their capacity rationally to choose to obey moral law. For Kant the only ends in themselves are the beings with that capacity. Whatever the virtues of this approach, it denies that humans can reasonably regard something as *more important than themselves,* and this is an unnecessary truncation of how humans have in fact imagined the meanings of their lives. Human beings require more guidance in life than can be gotten from the notion that human individuals are the sole ultimate ends. For humans are the kind of ends *that must find other ends,* ends under which their autonomy, in so far as there is such a thing, gains its value. Kant should have called his system of moral beings the kingdom of *choosers of ends.* As for the kingdom of ends, *that is culture.* But unlike Kant's modern, cosmopolitan conception, the principalities of culture are many. Culture is more like a *feudal* kingdom of ends, locally dominant meaning-structures arranged in a decentralized patchwork of local authorities, in which no ruling end can be more than a *primus inter pares,* a first among equals.

3 WHO IS CULTURE?

First I am a Pathan because I have been so for thousands of years; then I am a Muslim, which I have

been for 1,300 years and, third, I am a Pakistani, which I have been only for the last 40 years or so.

—WALI KHAN (AHMED 1992: 133)

Culture comes in *cultures*, attached to particular societies. Cultures are not only *whats* and *hows*, but *whos*. This raises two thorny questions: what are the criteria for deciding what counts as a particular culture, and what constitutes cultural membership and identity? The latter connects to the question of what it means to be a "people," an "ethnic" group, or even a "race," briefly treated in Chapter 1. These connections are difficult to analyze, not only because of the sheer obscurity of the terms, but because such groupings trouble us modern liberal folk. If we open the door to the salience of cultural membership, will race and ethnicity and other "primordial" attachments sneak through, bringing intolerance with them? But open that door we must—it will not stay shut—and do some conceptual cleaning, even if sweeping initially kicks up enough dust to make the mess seem worse than ever.

We may try to set the bounds of *a* culture as a single *horizon* of shared practices, artifacts, and narratives, our judgment of "a horizon" being determined by the relative coherence of what is inside and its relative difference from what is outside. We may imagine extreme cases of discreteness, where one society bears a culture that is utterly unique and internally homogeneous. This is a perfectly decent procedure; starting with the easy cases usually makes sense. But easy cases are hard to find. It is dubious that we can identify cultures that share nothing (as we will see later, the very idea is senseless). Also, if as we have noted cultures need not be coextensive with polities or societies, then we cannot employ administrative or state boundaries. Further, we will always find internal disputes and differences in each society that are hard to distinguish from cultural differences. Even if, using Edward Shils's terminology, two cultural "centers" can be distinguished, they are likely to have indistinct "peripheries" where the percentage of persons in the locale embodying a trait goes continuously down, leaving us with the choice of labeling them deviant members of culture A or members of another culture B.

But things are not all that bleak. Unlike color spectra or other continua we might study, here the objects of our investigation help us out: *people identify themselves*. Self-acknowledgment of membership is a *prima facie* sufficient, if fallible, condition for cultural identification ("No, we are not Uzbeks. We are Tadjiks"). Beyond this we would expect, as noted in Chapter 1, those who identify with one culture to share a system of judgmental endogamy, the boundaries of a lifeworld of socially compelling expectations and norms. Above all we must remember that the kind of unity a culture exhibits may not be rigid. As MacIntyre claims of traditions, a culture is best characterized as an ongoing debate. Following Martha Nussbaum again we can expect societal cultures to be *thick but vague*. They deeply color the self, but are in most cases broad and pluralistic enough not to determine one narrow course of life. The point is, we do have some markers to look for, as long as we don't expect bright lines and red flags.

The level or zone of cultural phenomena matters here as well. At the "lowest" level, that is, most closely related to everyday social behavior, society and culture *must* merge. Interacting social members, even if they have different cultures, must share judgments of intelligibility and propriety. Sharing an understanding of what the social group takes to be the meaning of its practices, its rules of propriety, its natural language(s), is at the same time sharing a part of a culture. In a polycultural society, members of different cultures must, to the degree they are fellow social members, find each other intelligible and proper. Thus their cultures must overlap at the everyday level. At the less pragmatic and more symbolic level, however, culture includes rites, icons, and metanarratives for the constitution of meaning in a more global sense. Depending on the kind of social norms active, these can indeed diverge among social members. In the extreme case, modern liberal society, individuals or groups who bear distinct rites, icons, and metanarratives may yet function together under common norms of intelligibility and propriety on the everyday level in public and restrict the nonoverlapping portions of their cultures to privacy. Citizenship in such a society requires little sharing at the symbolic level.

More important for our purposes, however, is the meaning of the *verb* that stands between person and culture. A culture is not the kind of thing that can be "held" or "had" for external, instrumental reasons. While it makes sense to say that I learned Italian to do business in Italy, I cannot say that I *became* culturally Italian, that I *am* Italian, for such purposes. Parekh argues for example that being British is sharing not a body of values, or history, or civic institutions, but "a specific form of life...a specific way of talking about and conducting common affairs. Being British therefore means learning the grammar, vocabulary and syntax of the prevailing form of life and knowing how to participate in its ongoing dialogue... [it is] a matter of acquiring conceptual competence in handling the prevailing cultural language" (Parekh 1991: 203). This account would indeed capture much of what we mean by cultural *familiarity*. But it does *not* capture cultural *identity*. For what does it mean to have competence in "handling the prevailing cultural language"? This implies an instrumental attitude. There is nothing wrong with that; my point is conceptual, not moral. Is being able to "handle" British culture equivalent to *being* British? If it were, British-ness would be a kind of technique or competence. But cultural identity must be thicker than this; it must in some sense characterize my *ends*. As such, to treat a "culture" as something to be acquired for a prior purpose, and perhaps discarded later, is to admit that one has never really been a member.

Likewise we take culture to be something that cannot be gotten didactically. To acquire a culture requires the kind of long training that comes from living in or with the social group of which the culture is a possession. The usual way is through birth and maturation. This distinguishes "knowing" a culture from "belonging" to a culture, or cultural *facility* from cultural *identity*. I can be a scholar and lover of Egyptian culture and yet not identify myself as an Egyptian; indeed, I can adopt Egyptian values and still fail to be Egyptian, for as Kymlicka himself notes, shared ideals are not enough (Kymlicka 1995a: 188). I have a friend who immersed himself in things Japanese, including moving to Japan, learning a great deal of the Japanese language, studying Japanese philosophy, and finding a Japanese fiancée. This led to the bizarre situation in which he knew more about traditional Japan than most Japanese (including, awkwardly, his prospective in-laws). It may be that we can say at this point, or will be able to say, that he has "acquired" Japanese culture; certainly he is very familiar with it, knows an enormous lot about it, and so on. But is he a "member"? Has he "turned Japanese"?

No, for the Japanese do not accept him as Japanese. Knowing, and even agreeing, is not being.

This is precisely where, as we saw in Chapter 1, the linguistic analogy fails. Do I *have* a culture the way I *have* a language? The "having" of many languages is possible precisely because it does not make the demands on the self that cultural membership makes. A culture is not merely a competence, it is a social group. Having a culture is not like having a language; it is more like having a family, regarding which *having it* entails *being had by it*. Here having is belonging, and belonging constrains individuality while constituting it. We must now explore some of the human groupings through which the *who* of culture has been understood, forms of human association or identity from which the modern and especially liberal democratic mind often recoils. Today Western liberals often throw all of a list of suspected bases of community and conflict together, using the terms "nationalist," "tribal," "ethnic," and "racial" as synonyms. But each has a distinct meaning.

Race

If the reality of race has always been divisive in the United States, in contemporary theory the *concept* has become so. On the one hand, the continuation of integrationist and antiracist liberalism, which always denied the political importance not only of race but of biology, has led to a denial of the very sense of "race," no doubt with the best of intentions. On the other hand, a multicultural movement, trading on a Foucauldian view of discourse, actually promotes the notion of race against the attempts to erase it. If the racists used race to oppress, it argues, *we* must now use it to combat the results of oppression. Denying the importance of race is then a subterfuge that actually serves the *status quo.* During a dinner a couple of years ago among black and white intellectuals, I cringed as I heard a white liberal—not an academic, hence a well-meaning and decent human being, but out of touch with current theory—argue that, of course, the very concept of race is senseless. He was immediately taken to the rhetorical woodshed by a black Afro-American studies professor with whom he had thought he was expressing solidarity. Alas, he had fallen behind the theoretical times.

The most cogent case against race in philosophy comes from Anthony Appiah, who famously argues that nothing in the world corresponds to the

meaning the term has been given for the last century or so. For Appiah, simply, "The truth is that there are no races" (Appiah 1992). Races exist in the
same sense that witches do: there are none, but many people act as if there
were. The modern notion of race is the result of the nineteenth-century
"biologization" of the notion of culture, the view that culture is heritable.
The only real thing in the world the term "race" *per se* picks out is morphology, that is to say, skin color, hair texture, facial features, and the like.
Morphological distinctiveness is the result of sufficiently long ancient periods of genetic isolation. But genetic sameness across such groups is much
greater than the groups' differences from each other, just as differences
within each group are greater than differences between them. Racial deter-
minations of identity must then rely on two distinct judgments: a reference
back to a subcontinental genetic homeland of morphological homogeneity, then a series of rules in each generation as to what constitutes continuity
with the former (such as the American "one drop" rule according to which
having *any* black ancestors makes one black) (Appiah 1996). Such rules are
themselves changing sociocultural constructions. Thus if "race" means a
morphology that carries with it a culture, nobody has one.

Certainly the curve of human history is toward racial mixing; Theodore
von Laue's characterization of the modern world as the "Great Confluence"
holds for race as for economics and culture. Immigration and emigration
mean a society includes more people racially distinct from its long-term
genetic pool; thus the "racial we" is increasingly inadequate to the "social
we." The racial "we" gets further confounded by interracial mating. We may
also agree with David Hollinger that the contemporary American classifi-
cation of race is untenable (Hollinger 1995). As categorical schemes go, the
"ethno-racial pentagon" of colors—black (sub-Saharan African), red
(natives of the Americas), yellow ("Asians" and Pacific Islanders), brown
(Latin Americans), and white (European)—is a mess. The worst categories
are "Asian"—which ought to be "East Asian" so as not to include Israelis,
Siberian Russians, and Pakistanis, not to mention Polynesians—and Latino,
which is the best example of a cultural category masquerading as a race.
Many Latinos have mixed Native American and Spanish/Portuguese descent
and could be morphologically categorized as "brown," but commonly iden-
tify themselves and others through language and culture, regardless of color.
Perhaps most bizarre, the official pentagon leaves South Asians, North
Africans, Arabs, and Persians as "white," which, if it were true, would make

Caucasian racism against them logically impossible. This is not even to raise the problem that the pentagon's categories of racial morphology do not consistently correspond to color; by the criterion of skin tone alone, many native Australians and some South Asian peoples should be "black" (being as dark as many sub-Saharan Africans) and the majority of North Africans, Arabs, Persians, South Asians, and many others, by process of elimination, if nothing else, ought to join Latinos in the "brown" category.

We thus could say that for these reasons the discussion of culture has no special interest in race at all. Appiah's argument against race sensibly expresses his Ghanaian roots in a multiply morphological family where nobody could confuse color with culture or cultural identity. If the "Enlightened" West did indeed play the race card, constituting European modernity through invidious morphological contrasts, then that is a world well lost. But there is more to understand here than the history of an error. For if race merely means morphology, then Appiah's argument does *not* deny its reference. Racial differences are the real results of a bygone era of long-term genetic isolation. At some point in prehistory and early history, the ancestors of people who today bear distinctive racial morphologies must have lived and reproduced separately. To this day, some racial descendents continue to live both in genetic isolation and in the genetic "homeland." And where persons shared a homeland, they likely shared not only morphology, but other social and cultural traits as well. This is roughly Philip Kitcher's claim: "race" refers to the phenotypic commonalities in a group defined by sufficiently inbred lineages (Kitcher 1999). At this point the putatively scientific objection that intraracial differences quantitatively exceed interracial differences is heard. True, but so what? That is presumably true of *any* grouping of human beings we can imagine, including sexes. Indeed, the vast majority of my DNA is shared with mice, but nobody is arguing that membership in the human species is open for application from rodents.

Race is a set of morphological traits that are inherited, hence can serve as markers for ancestry, which societies *may* then pick out as salient whenever they think ancestry matters. There has been in some times and places, and still can be found, a contingent, *a posteriori* connection between morphology and culture. As such, race has functioned in many places and times as a sign for social, psychological, and cultural differences. Certainly, even in the best of correlations, morphology fails to be a sufficient marker, since there are many more cultures than races. Still, many people can plausibly

claim that in the local world they know, race is in fact *contingently* correlated with some sociocultural traits, that "we" are of one race and "others"
are of a different race. Such people can rightly regard themselves as descended from a people who had a particular social or cultural character to
go with its morphological distinctiveness. When a citizen of Kinshasa and
his country cousin see two youngish men in dark suits with briefcases walk-
ing a city boulevard together, one light-skinned with straight hair and thinner lips and one ebony-skinned with tight curls and fuller lips, the cousin
makes neither nonsense nor evil in saying, "The white man is a European."
His statement's only liability is its, admittedly, increased probability of empirical error in a changing world, a probability usually proportional to ignorance of local conditions. Thus the Kinshasan may respond, "Man, don't
you know that a community of whites has been living in this city for generations? That man is probably a son of Zaire like you." The liability to error
makes the cousin's inference no worse than many of our guesses. The evil
of such race-to-culture inductions lies not in the act of guessing but in
what is staked on the outcome.

Blood

Race is the ultimate, but not the only, "bad" source of cultural association
for modern liberals. Most of the "new culturalists" discussed in Chapter 1
regard connections of "blood and soil" to be only marginally less nasty.
Political references to blood are held to be reactionary, "essentialist," and
"biologistic." As noted, Kymlicka claims without argument that "descent-
based approaches to national membership have obvious racial overtones,
and are manifestly unjust" (Kymlicka 1995a: 23). Liberals fear the political
salience of the "natural," anything prereflectively given and unchosen. For
the post–World War II generation of political theorists and their students, the
intrusion of biology into politics can only mean eugenics and racism. Femi-
nists added their own repugnance, fearing that biology is only relevant for
patriarchal dictation of female "destiny." Even if race is Public Enemy Number One for progressives, blood remains high on the Most Wanted List.

But as suggested in Chapter 1, this is unfair. Blood is in one sense narrower and in another sense broader than race. For blood means *descent,* and
descent is a complex matter. It first of all refers to natality and parentage. It
is partly genetic. (Even in this respect it is complicated by gamete donation

and adoption. Is the singer American singer Shania Twain part Native American because her adoptive father is?) It is also partly social and legal, given that nonincestuous parents are not close blood relatives. My family includes lots of people from whom I did not descend: aunts and uncles, not to mention in-laws. Kinship is wider than descent. An interesting point about blood is that it can create ties among people who *do not share blood*. Descent generates non-descent ties. If it matters to one of my group memberships who my parents were, then blood matters, even if it is *not blood* that constitutes the tie among members. So if I am the child of police officers, but not myself a police officer, I am nevertheless tied in a way I may regard as important to the "community" of police officers. At any rate, the political manifestation of blood is not racial or ethnic politics, but *clan* politics. Blood-politics is rule by, as Gellner says, "cousins, not kings." It is Hatfields and McCoys, not Hutus and Tutsis. Under normal conditions even a small segmentary society cannot be constituted by a single clan, unless marriage partners are regularly imported from outside.

Nor is "tribalism" equivalent to racialism, ethnocentrism, or nationalism. The tribe is supralocal and subethnic, usually covering a set of clans living in a collection of villages over a region. It must be carried by some non-descent characteristics, like language or religion or a shared history. It is true that in a small society characterized by racial (morphological) homogeneity in which clans to some extent intermarry, so that kin crisscross society, it might be natural to conflate blood with ethnicity or tribe. But any influx of foreign marriage partners, or emigration of members who then isolate themselves from the homeland, drives at least the thin end of a wedge between blood and culture.

As Tamir notes, while liberal polities assert a civic, not a blood, tie among members, they nevertheless automatically extend citizenship to those who descend from citizen parents. For blood correlates to the *who* that teaches me a culture and to the *where* they taught me, in short, my *natal-maturational world*. Because children are inevitably part of their parent's surrounding community at the most form-giving age in the human life cycle, descent plays an enormous role in identity. Family is the most powerful and common way of acquiring a culture. Understood thus, blood is indeed crucial to many human ties and certainly to conceptions of ethnicity, nationality, and culture, in liberal as well as illiberal societies. Most families not subject to recent emigration inhabit a single polity, hence their familial loyalties may cathect the polity: to protect my family I may have to protect the state that houses them. Therefore, most polities that have popular legitimacy are endorsed by familial feeling even though not constituted by descent. If descent is somehow an unjust means of acquiring legitimate, obligation-inducing political identity, then *virtually all* extant polities are unjust.

Soil

The only competitor to biology as an object of liberal fear is soil. But of course it is more corollary than competitor, since descent is from a family, hence a community, *on some plot of soil*. Soil and place are feared by liberals as the justification for intolerance and ethnic cleansing. They are certainly right that the two are often linked; the most immediate goal of ethnic cleansing is the removal of the hated group from "*our soil*."

Liberal fears notwithstanding, we cannot avoid the fact that soil is commonly a significant correlate of culture. For soil is most simply *place*. My natal-maturational world is likely defined by the boundaries of a place. If we add local homogeneity, then the culture of the domicile and the locale are identical; their nonidentity is virtually the definition of minority status. If family and locale concur, failure to acquire their jointly carried culture is virtually impossible. Soil or territory, then, is essential to the historical reference that is cultural identification, because there must have been a geographically continuous population at the source of this reference. Wherever we find a societal culture, there had to have been *at some historical point* a plot of soil on which it developed as a possible object of identification.

Unfortunately, recent liberal political philosophy—and as Edward Casey has argued, recent Western philosophy in general—has shown at best a remarkable neglect of the significance of place in human experience, and at worst, an active hostility toward it (Casey 1995, 1999). For like blood, soil is typically pregiven, "natural," and unchosen. The liberal and intellectual antipathy to location has led to serious mangling of the significance of soil on the rare occasions when theory has turned to examine it. Jacob Levy nicely punctures the common anti-imperial story of European protocapitalist colonizers importing a foreign notion of *land as commodity* into their dealings with indigenous Americans and Australians (Levy 2000). That revisionist narrative was always too simplistic. The feudal and early modern West certainly did understand land as property, but precisely did *not* open it to commercial exchange as a commodity. Hence the principles of primogeniture (eldest male heir inherits all, hence land parcels are never split among offspring) and entail (prohibition of sale, or of sale outside the family) guaranteed the perennial aristocratic ownership of choice land. The reformers of the late eighteenth century (including Adam Smith, Thomas Jefferson, and even Edmund Burke) rejected these policies less because of a claimed "right" of the owner to dispose of private property as desired (which would have been a fully modern "liberal" position) than because of their desire to develop a talent- (rather than birth-) based aristocracy, spur commercial progress, and increase agricultural production. They deplored the "waste" of perpetually held but undeveloped and uncultivated land. The tradition they attacked—that is, their own—was thus not *so* different from that of indigenous peoples, like the American natives, who far from lacking a notion of property, typically regarded tribal land as *collective* property, in contrast to the preliberal European conception of land as *private* yet *noncommercial* (unexchangeable) property. In fact nineteenth- and twentieth-century Western nationalism fairly, albeit not precisely, mirrored that indigenous view, insisting on the coincidence of political sovereignty and ownership. The real incompatibility between natives and Europeans was that between hunter-gatherer and agricultural societies. For Euro-American settlers, the natives' claims to huge expanses of untilled land echoed the claims of their own homegrown elites to maintain game reserves at the expense of egalitarian farming opportunities. It was *fungibility* of land that was crucial to the development of modern liberal society; mere private ownership was not enough. In this sense, recent liberals wary of current nationalists' claims to their home "soil" ironically continue the capitalist tradition of commodifying land, a tradition responsible for the development of a liberal capitalist society ill-equipped to recognize indigenous land claims.

While all communities obtain in a place, only some cultures cathect particular plots of soil on a permanent basis, sing of its specific hills and valleys as their only rightful home. We may call this the *Jerusalem syndrome*. Tamir is entirely right that this identification is troublesome and often dangerous, simply on pragmatic terms. Given the history of conquest and migration, if we want our children to live in peace we cannot generally grant ethnic groups *unqualified* rights to particular plots of soil, just as ethnicities cannot generally be granted sovereign states of their own.

Nevertheless, even if we cannot grant a general right to soil, we cannot simply deny the moral weight of its claim either. For if ethnic cleansers demand the relocation of a minority, even to good land where the latter could enjoy sovereignty, would we not still object? Who would say today that loss of particular homelands for Native Americans was *not* a catastrophic violation of their rights? We admit as much whenever we grant financial or other compensations for forced relocation of natives. Recognizing the significance of the loss of a traditional territory need not mean that the right to homeland trumps all other rights, but it does acknowledge *some* kind of a right. For the power of the identification with place simply must be recognized.

As an example of the Jerusalem syndrome we might as well take Jerusalem itself. It is often forgotten that the Israeli government and military command before and during the Six-Day War of 1967 was dominated by hard-headed realists concerned with security, fearful of losing international support by expanding into Palestinian territory, rather than millenarian religionists longing for historical turf. On the second day of their defensive war against Egypt, Syria, and Jordan, with the military outcome very much in doubt, survival was their overriding concern. Nevertheless, upon taking the Temple Mount and the Western Wall in Jerusalem that day, a flood of primordial emotions overcame the leadership. Michael Oren recounts that at the Wall,

> [Military Chief of Staff Yitzhak] Rabin . . . watched with awe the scene of hundreds of soldiers, joined by Ultra-Orthodox Jews, dancing. "This was the peak of my life," he recalled. . . . "The sacrifices of our comrades have not been in vain. . . . The countless generations of Jews murdered, martyred and massacred for the sake of Jerusalem . . ." [Foreign Minister Abba] Eban, hearing about the victory in New York, wrote of "a flood of historic emotion [that] burst the dams of restraint and sent minds and hearts in movement far beyond the limits of our land." Among the most strenuous opponents of the war . . . [Religious Affairs Minister] Zorach Warhaftig recalled how "my heart was filled with gladness," as he rushed to kiss the Western Wall and embraced both [Defense Minister Moshe] Dayan and Rabin. (Oren 2002: 246–47)

The point is simply that place matters, sometimes very much, and however we negotiate such claims to soil we must at least recognize their human and political reality.

Ethnicity

In sum, all societies are based in descent and territory in some sense. Blood and soil matter everywhere, in nationalism and liberalism, civil societies and ethnic states. Modern civil societies of course allow nondescent membership, and de-ethnicize their membership criteria almost completely (with telling exceptions like the exclusion of naturalized citizens from the presidency).* Blood and soil are *not* equivalent to ethnicity. They are typically local. This was true in premodern societies, and is not contradicted in modernity, where rather than blood and place becoming supralocal, they simple decline in public significance altogether. In the ancient agrarian empires blood and place were not confused with either political membership or culture, which were typically far broader groupings. Language commonly obtained across a far-flung, distant network of clannish locales. Religion, at least in Christian and Muslim civilizations, ranged much further. Modern nationalism changed all that in the West by evolving a mass "nation-state" culture over a dominant linguistic region, transcending descent and local relations, beneath or within the larger circle of religion. Consequently, the question of cultural membership in the modern era is inextricably entangled with the meaning of nationality and its relative, ethnicity.

The term "ethnicity" as it is used in contemporary political theory is rarely burdened by clarity. Sometimes it is a synonym for nationality. Other times it serves as a kind of quasi-race, a kinder, gentler alternative to that feared term, allowing writers to mean descent and morphology without saying so. Sometimes it is condemned for that very reason, as an attempt to water down racial distinctions. But its historical meaning is plain. The English "ethnic" derives from the Greek *ethnikos,* which referred to a foreign people, normally in a somewhat disparaging way, like "heathen." This holds true also for the roots of "nation," which in Roman times meant non-Italianate peoples ruled by Rome. Although the connotations of the terms differ—*ethnikos* was linked both to *éthos,* character, and *ethos,* custom, while "nation" derives from *nasci,* to be born, hence refers to descent—their referent is the same: *a people,* understood either through their reproductive isolation or distinctive character. Unfortunately for us "nation" has been overwhelmed by the term national*ism,* hence sovereignty and states. Bowing

*As Phu Nguyen reminded me.

to aural custom, I will save "nationality" for the political mobilization of a people, usually in modern nationalism, and use "ethnicity," for the more fundamental condition of being *a people*. That is the root notion. The basic issue is, then, *what does it mean to be a people?* Or better...

Who Is a People?

Let us imagine the "ideal type" of a people in the sense of what the most complete form of the kind of homogeneity we mean by "ethnic" would be like. In such a condition differences among intrasocial groups could not be *cultural*. There would have to be one sociocultural horizon, one set of socioeconomic arrangements, one system of roles, one set of rules of intelligibility, propriety, and status, and one commonly held reservoir of meaning-endowing practices, artifacts, and narratives. This scheme does not imply equality; it could certainly include stark clan, caste, gender, and political differences. Let us further imagine that *no social outsiders share the local culture* (arguably a rare condition in the last several millennia). Such a society maximally fulfills the criteria for being considered "a people" by themselves and by outsiders. What would be true of such a condition?

First, in it we would find *the identity of society and culture*. Being a social member and being a cultural member would not be distinguished, because nobody would have one without the other. The conditions of membership in society and the conditions of membership in its culture would be identical. (In reality, the closest we would get to this condition would be small, isolated segmentary societies scattered across a region, where all such villages share the same language, religion, and so on, hence cultural membership would extend beyond local society. But still the crucial point would be that all social members belong to one culture.) Second, we would expect to find *the coincidence of spheres,* the disciplinary unity of the conditions of membership for that sociocultural group. That is, if a people calls itself the Ipo, then all social members must conduct their lives in an Ipo-way, speak the Ipo-tongue, worship the Ipo-gods, practice Ipo-sports, and so on. This people has not had to make distinctions among members who, while they share the Ipo way of economic life, do not share the Ipo gods or marriage rituals, or refuse the authority of Ipo chiefs, and so on. Third, the natal-maturational world, hence the primary kin-local sphere, would be *continuous* with the public social world. The culture may of course specify distinctive roles and norms in each, and there may well be interclan conflict. But as long as all social members regard themselves as one "people," their forms of family life will be continuous with the social order. No one, for example, will argue that kinship relations or religion should be "private" matters, irrelevant or inappropriate to public life, so as not to offend or coerce others. Last, the cultural life of this society will presumably be *thick*. By "thick" I mean that the shared culture is adequate to the determination of the sense and significance of human life. It fills the normative space for members. No further guidance is needed (except of course for deviant or idiosyncratic individuals).

We can then conceive of a variety of other, more pluralistic conditions as differing degrees of departure from this homogeneous condition. The first significant departure appears in conditions in which local societies subsist in a larger polity ruled by a *culturally distinct* center. This was characteristic of the great literate, agrarian empires that even today we count as our cultural forebears. By virtue of size they inevitably incorporated heterogeneous peoples, ruling regions and locales whose languages or religions were different from that of the imperial center. Here membership in the sovereign society or state is culturally different from membership in the locale or region. The greater the center's intrusion into the periphery—not only requiring taxes, denying local sovereignty, and providing protection from outsiders, but perhaps enforcing a religion, interfering with local jurisprudence, and so on—the more local members will have to distinguish spheres *within* their own lives and identities that cannot reflect or obey their local cultural norms. Furthermore, if legitimate political and religious authority are monopolized by the center, as in the Fertile Crescent empires and Egypt, for the first time distant peoples and events may surpass locale in normative or causal significance. There may in addition be polyethnic commercial trading and learning centers, but this complexity affects a small percentage of the population.

In a greater departure from homogeneity, a *civilization* may diffuse across half a continent, placing a layer of cultural unity across many linguistic groups and sovereignties, occasionally becoming the basis for more or less unified political action. In both the Western European and the Islamic cases, religion played this role. The result was a more complex notion of group identity, seen in the West in feudal society. In this orderly but decentralized system, life and political authority remained local while language and hence folk culture held over a region, and a symbolic cultural layer extended over much of a continent. Levels of identification thereby multiply, even if the local society remains primary, and can be mobilized under the right circumstances. The sovereign need share neither my local culture nor my language; my homogeneous locale, along with far-flung cultural-linguistic-religious cousins, may occupy a region ruled by a foreign monarch. Even the local lord, while culturally and linguistically similar to myself, is separated from me by a social hierarchy more salient than any cultural sharing. At the same time, a profoundly important layer of culture — religion — may enforce a far wider civilizational loyalty and identity. I bow to the distant authority of miter as well as crown, and may fight and die for either, my nonlocal identity playing the final trump to my local self. Of course, local contests continue to trump that unitary identity in daily social life. In reaction to transcendent, universalist religion, locale often exerts its home court advantage in creating folk religion, a "pagan" or animistic version of the script-based high culture managed by literate urban elites. At any rate, all of these movements away from simple homogeneity entail the *differentiation of the conditions of membership,* hence the de-fusion of spheres. Political, religious, linguistic, and social identity and membership can now differ, even if each remains quite stable.

Notice that up to this point local diversity has still not been mentioned. With the exception of the towns, where there may be commercial or administrative contacts with visitors and immigrants from culturally diverse provinces, the rural locales rarely deviate from the homogeneous condition. There is still no possibility of doffing the local identity; it can be trumped, but not discarded or rendered ineffective. In any case, it is only with country-wide or rural immigration, or population shifts to the diverse cities, that the sharing of the same local society by more than one "people" becomes widespread. At this point even local culture and local society begin to diverge; I may share social membership in the most diurnally relevant portion of my life with people whose culture, in some sense, I do not share, and thus my understanding of social membership must differentiate, distinguishing, for example, the forms of address due local fellow citizens as such from those citizens who are of "my people." Responses to immigration vary, of course. However locales or states respond — with intermixing, assimilation, tolerant mutual segregation, not-so-tolerant forced segregation, or violence — unless the others are stamped out, membership and the relation of society to culture have changed forever. Eventually we get, as Michael Walzer explains, a variety of regimes of toleration: the millet system (local religious-cultural autonomy under a dominant group's imperial taxation and military protection), consociations (shared rule between two or three communities with designated spheres of power), the liberal nation-state (a dominant yet tolerant cultural majority that guarantees civic rights for all), or the immigrant society (where no people is officially dominant) (Walzer 1997).

What then constitutes "a people"? We can now hazard that a people is formed by a *descent society* = *culture,* a group that subsists in the homogeneous condition, in which social and cultural membership are indistinct, and both acquired by descent or birth. But while this may be the ultimate reference, it is not the proximal or everyday meaning of the term today. For by those criteria, nobody I have ever met would have an ethnicity. So by extension we must say that in today's normal usage to claim "ethnicity" is to *claim descent from* a group that is *claimed to have at one time subsisted in the homogeneous condition of society* = *culture.* By today's lights, anyone fitting that criterion can rightly claim, "*That* is my people." Note that such claims can be false. No doubt all of us have ancestors who were members of such homogeneous groups, but often in the distant past about which we know virtually nothing. Those ancestors about whom we are likely to know anything may well have lived in relatively modern societies that were no longer homogeneous. It is this sense in which, as Benedict Anderson argues, nation or ethnicity is "imagined." But "imagined" here means selectively reconstructed, not invented. The claimed homogeneous society = culture—for example, the Scottish of my Scottish-American-ness—is likely an inaccurately simple portrayal of a diverse network of Scottish ancestors who, in a premodern and prenationalistic age, may have regarded each other as competing clans and tribes with little in common. My ethnic reference does indeed organize that past through a retrospective simplification and selection. But simplification is not falsification, for if it were, virtually all our "knowledge" would be false.

Ethnicity can coincide with morphology, hence race or subracial characteristics. Italian Americans and Irish Americans, like Korean Americans and Japanese Americans, often look different, have distinctive ideals of beauty, and so on. This is a contingent and historical matter. Peoples vary in their degree of morphological distinctiveness and in their valuation of such, and members may ignore such differences, or may distinguish among their fellows those whose appearance calls to mind less-mixed ancestors, giving their morphology a special status, for good or ill. For example, among many Latin American families it is not unusual to find people of very different skin tones. Still, Mexican-American writer Richard Rodriguez's mother warned him to avoid the sun, since he was already the brownest member of the family, and she feared he looked too "Indian," which for her was a marker of lower class (Rodriguez 1982). The point is that ethnicity is both cultural *and* bodily, the result of shared culture *and* shared society, hence endogamy. That is what it means to be tied *by* descent *to* a culture.

Last, if referring one's identity to an ethnicity is to have contemporary significance for behavior, two conditions must hold. First, the claimed people must *continue to exist* in some form, although not necessarily in the homogeneous condition. Ethnicity matters in the present if and only if there is a community in some place that shares the ethnicity. Second, there must be some kind of problematic social circumstances in which my ethnic membership is *relevant*. Ethnicity sinks in importance if the major social issues of my life call out only my other, nonethnic identities and associations in response.

The Function of Primordialism

What is it about ethnicity that seems to make it so seemingly powerful, primitive, and troublesome to the modern consciousness? How is it that it appears in the world as an evil temptation, a siren song from the depths, as bloody romance? What is it about understanding myself passionately as, say, a Serb, rather than a Croat, that seems more threatening than passionately understanding myself as a member of the Cahoone family, or the educated middle class, or the American Philosophical Association? What is the unique quality, hence the potential *intensity*, of that attachment?

Edward Shils gave it a name. As we know, the attempt to distinguish modern society from traditional forms of social organization was a preoccupation of the early giants of sociology. Each of the great thinkers took his own dualistic terminological stab at the question: capitalism versus feudalism for Karl Marx; *Gemeinschaft* (community) versus *Gesellschaft* (society) for Ferdinand Tönnies; mechanical versus organic solidarity for Émile Durkheim; status versus contract for Henry Sumner Maine; charismatic or traditional versus legal and routinized forms of authority for Max Weber. Shils makes the interesting claim that all these analyses of traditional society conflate three distinct forms of connection: *personal* connection based in individual interaction and hence the relational characteristics and roles of the persons involved (father, sister, coworker, friend, superior officer); *sacred* connection that subsumes relations under central teleological symbols; and last, *primordial* connection among persons through "objective" links of blood and territory (Shils 1957). For Shils, ethnic or national bonds are primordial, hence qualitatively and structurally distinct, not only from rational-legal or civic ties, but also from sacred and personal ties. His controversial claim is that they are unavoidable in *any* society, even modern civil society: the human mind must find ultimacy "not only in the spiritual transcendental sphere but in the primordial transcendental sphere as well." The horrors of fascism were not due to primordialism *per se,* but the *sacralization* of primordial ties under spiritual symbols.

Now, to call such primordial ties or qualities objective, natural, or absolute has for the contemporary scholar of culture an anachronistic ring. But these appellations are at least half-right. Natality, parentage, and locale are indeed objective facts. That is, given a set of concepts, for example, the definition of "sister" as female child of the same parents, one is or is not somebody's sister by public criteria. But only in some societies at some times have those objective markers of descent and locale been the primary means of group assignment, mobilized as important sources of social coherence. Kin and locale were far more important in premodern societies. As Robert Nisbet and Anthony Giddens separately argued, modernity is predicated on the reduction of the significance of local/kin or "communal" relations. Descent and soil can be objective yet at the same time socially indecisive.

This aside, Shils's account is insightful. It is reflected in mythology; since the rise of urban, agrarian-literate civilization many cultures have traditionally accessed not one but *two* distinct sets of ultimate referents or narratives, one from above and one from below. The former is the Divine, the otherworldly, the transcendent, the pure, the heavenly, the Ruler of the Cosmic cycle, often living in the sky or on the mountaintop. The other is chthonic, physical, dark, deep, reproductive, the Source, the earth itself or what is beneath and behind the earth. Presumably this opposition emerged once animism was largely replaced by transcendental notions of divinity, notions that, in the great agrarian civilizations, came to hold over far-flung peoples, leaving a gap in the legitimation of local and descent ties. Suffice to say that the Highest and the Beneath, the Towards-Which and the Out-of–Which are qualitatively distinct forms of ultimacy. Primordiality is the feeling of the latter, transcendence the feeling of the former. What then are the definitive features of the primordial form of ultimacy?

First and foremost, primordial bonds and identities concern personal and social *origins*. They tie us together through the past. They link me to a history. My people may understand themselves in terms of a coming golden age, the return of the Messiah, or the eventual attainment of secular utopia, but the primordial bond is my descent from, origination from, the tradition that projects such a future. The future can never be primordial. Hence primordial ties are *necessitous;* the past is that mode of time that cannot be the subject of action. Although I can selectively reinterpret it, I cannot change it. The future is unknowable, the present is yet to be comprehended. The primordial repeats the only temporality we can understand, the past.

Second, primordiality characterizes my *being,* not primarily my *doing* or *making.* Thus its acquisition and maintenance are effortless. Now, I do not mean that the primordial is somehow "natural" and that other connections are "constructed." Heavy duties and efforts may attend any form of identity or membership, the culture of an ethnic group being no exception. But those duties are *consequences* of identity; they do not *make* the identity. I can fail at them; indeed, I can even be outcast and disowned. I cannot *achieve* the identity or membership by the performance of the duties; rather, I fulfill them as obligations attaching to me *a priori.* Primordial attachments are unearned.

Third, what flows from the first two characteristics is, as Shils argued, that a primordial bond is *unelective* and *ascriptive,* and is experienced as such. It is not chosen. It makes demands and claims that cannot be ignored while the identity it roots remains relevant. It holds for a person in virtue of the person's "nature," what the person is regarded, by self and others, unchangeably as being. It is experienced as fixed. As noted, even in a modern liberal society where I may cease to regard my ethnicity as significant or select one of several descent ties for identification, I cannot choose to make a new ethnicity where descent ties do not exist.

Fourth, primordial attachments are *bodily,* hence *erotic,* in the broad sense of that term, connoting not sex *per se* but *bodily love.* As noted, my ethnicity may well be "written" into my bodily appearance by my parents' genes, then read and interpreted by culture. As such it can then double back and play a role in my own sexual life, hence also for my progeny. It is not without psychic significance that the only venues in life where most people experience intimate bodily care, experience another human being cherishing their body, are in infancy and during sex. We cannot avoid noticing that *primordiality works through sex,* through both sexual reproduction and through the intimate familial world of bodily care, mediated by the marital relation. It is hard to deny that primordial ties are the stuff of psychoanalysis. The natal-maturational world attaches our deepest feelings to immediate family, clan, the community in which the family lives, and the place these reside. As noted, human personality is notoriously *front-loaded;* the events and conditions of the first three or five or ten years are more salient and influential than any other period of three or five or ten years later in the life cycle. Thus kin-local relations are the warp and woof of the primordial. Primordial connections are thus eroticized just as the body, its appearance, family relations, and other maturational circumstances are eroticized.

The unique function or significance of the primordial can now be seen. *Primordiality alone renders intelligible, and normatively vets, the contingencies of my particular bodily existence.* In religions with a transcendent Divinity, although God has a plan, nothing about my religious life hangs on my having been the child of *these* parents, in *this* place, at *this* time, with this color of skin, with *these* genetic abilities and deficits, married to *this* spouse, with *these* children. The monotheistic personal God knows and cares about all this, to be sure. But the nature of the religious task in monotheism is to transcend these particulars. In transcending them, in demoting their importance, I recognize all other believers as my brothers and sisters, equal in the sight of God. I leave my origin, clan, locale, and body behind. Christ brought not only a new love, but a sword that might separate father and son, mother and daughter. Islam, the acme of monotheism, found its primary enemy in the clan-tribal network of Arabian society. Primordialism in contrast tells me that I *had to have been born* to *those* parents, in *that* place, with *this* body, within *that* community, speaking *that* language, because these *constitute my true nature.* From this perspective the true me is the primordial me of origin. What is the distinctive quality of self-recognition and satisfaction that contemporary people derive from researching family genealogy? The genealogical satisfaction comes from making intelligible and normatively "right" my bodily, genetic, historical origin and location, all those aspects of self that are not the product of choice or achievement, whose salience is recognized by all (with the possible exception of doctrinaire liberals). Returning to old models, ethnic or religious connections, the gender roles of our grandparents, the foods and clothing and manners of the family, all grant that feeling of "rightness." This is not to say, of course, that such a return *is* right. Even if philosophers today recognize many exceptions to G. E. Moore's attack on the "naturalistic fallacy" of deriving ought from is, modern citizens in the forum of public discourse are perfectly well habituated to deny that what *is,* what is "natural," or what is bequeathed by the past is *ipso facto* good or right. *But primordiality lives on the naturalistic fallacy.* It grants the normative status of the given.

"What Is She?"

None of the foregoing is a lament. I do not mean to urge the superiority of the primordial, or of "thick" cultures, to thinned, modernized, and rational-voluntary social forms. The point is simply that cultural thickness and primordiality remain facts, even if attenuated in the most developed societies, and that these facts are *not intrinsically* immoral, ignorant, and threatening. For as we shall later see, it is not at all clear that the Western way of modernization, whose dominant post–World War II form did indeed seek to overcome the primordial, will be the form in which modernization is best achieved by the developing world, or even by the postmodern West.

Nevertheless, clearly modern and postmodern society tend to efface the conditions necessary for primordialism. In those areas and dimensions of social life where it is correct to say that modernity is a world of "contract," not status, of individual initiative, liberty, and self-creation, not inheritance or acceptance, of making and doing, not being, primordialism is blocked or demoted. Likewise, ethnicity has a very tentative and convoluted meaning in societies like the United States. On the one hand, just as modernity inevitably reduces the identity- and affiliation-constituting power of clan and local community, the rise of civic-nationalism as well as educational, class, and career association tend to trump the meaning of ethno-linguistic community. On the other hand, the lack of a thick national culture leaves much room for ethno-racial identities magnified through intramural jockeying for a political and economic place in the sun. Some Americans identify with no other cultural grouping than "American," others are "hyphenated" by an old country-American combination, still others identify themselves with a thick ethnicity while maintaining a permissibly thin civic commitment, as we saw in Chapter 1.

But the situation is even more complex, and, as usual in the American case, it is the racial end of the spectrum of identity that leads the way. David

Hollinger has criticized our recent American habit of "racializing" ethnicity, of regarding racial morphology as the key to group difference. He laments the Irish-African-American writer Ishmael Reed's inability to march in St. Patrick's Day parades without drawing quizzical stares (Hollinger 1995: 21). However, that inability is not the result of ethno-racial identity *per se* but of one very particular historical artifact of a single interracial relationship, the American "one drop rule"—equally beloved of white racists and black nationalists—according to which one drop of African blood makes a person black. Retired basketball star Charles Barkley admits to pressuring the multiethnic champion golfer Tiger Woods to identify himself primarily as black, which Woods will not do, presumably out of respect for his mother's (hence his own) Thai heritage. "Ethnicity" sounds wimpy to racial nationalists—hence their opposition to viewing Afro-Americans as a *mere* ethnic group—only because the fading importance of ethnic distinctions among white or Euro-Americans has been drowned out by the history of white racism. Unfortunately, the historical animosity of the United States's two oldest non-native peoples, Afro- and Euro-Americans, joined at the hip like Siamese twins in a seemingly endless dance in which they cannot see past each other, tends to warp any discussion of race and ethnicity in America. As Appiah warned, this conflict may be social—race being historically taken as a marker of social groups in conflict—but it is hard to argue that it is *cultural,* the "cultural" differences between white and black Americans being, on a world-historical scale, very limited (Appiah 1997). Peoples come in greater variety than black and white.

Which is not to gainsay the musing of Glenn Loury, who remarked to himself after a speech to a racially and politically divided (and divisive) college audience, "Man, this race thing is deep" (Loury 1995). To take a simple, and not unpleasant example, a very good student of mine, an African-American woman of Haitian descent, upon glimpsing a rather artsy photo of my wife on my desk—black and white, with her sporting dark lipstick and dark glasses—asked me enthusiastically, "Is that your wife? What is she?" We both knew what she meant. She was excited by the possibility that one of her white professors might have a nonwhite wife. For this cosmopolitan, multicultural, sophisticated young woman, the morphology of descent was the first criterion and marker of social identity. No doubt, once having identified my wife racially, other identities would have become more salient for her. Nevertheless, race was the first question on her mind, even if only because of its function as a marker for ethnicity or origin. Thus, for good as well as ill, I agree with Cornell West that "race matters" (West 1994). So does ethnicity. But they matter *only where and when they matter,* being objective facts whose salience is the result of sociocultural selection and whose meaning is a matter of constant negotiation. By the way, my wife is about as white as white comes, being Dutch-American, an affiliation which might seem fairly devoid of sociocultural importance in today's United States. Unless of course you happen to be speaking to a Belgian-American in my wife's native northeastern Wisconsin, where you would confuse those two designations at your great peril.

4 MODERNITY: CULTURE OF REASON OR REASON AGAINST CULTURE?

As I have argued elsewhere, modernity is in some important sense *anticultural* (Cahoone 1988). This may sound absurd. The Enlightenment was certainly a cultural movement, initiating an explosion of literature, philosophy, and scientific activity. The sheer volume of production of modern cultural items—books, art, political discussion, and so on—dwarfs earlier cultural production. My suggestion may also sound ideological, either a conservative plea for the reinvigoration of a Greco-Roman or Christian-Medieval culture of unity, hierarchy, and transcendence, or a condescending implication that what modern Euro-Americans produce is *objective* truth while the rest of the world is mired in mere cultural particularity, that *our* knowers are culture-transcending scientists but *their* knowers are culture-relative witch doctors. I am implying nothing of the kind; modernity is as inescapable as it is beneficial, and while modern Western science does achieve a unique cognitive status, it remains a cultural product. My point is rather that the development of modernity alters the nature and social role of culture *per se*. The modern West, believing it had discovered a new, suprasocial, universal cognitive method, went on to discover unprecedented knowledge, amass unheard-of power, and create a novel way of life built on the constant transgression of tradition for the sake of progress. We may say it constructed a new kind of culture, and that is perfectly true. But its new kind of culture undermined the role that culture had played since prehistory. I will try to explain and justify this observation in the present chapter and the next.

We must note that such an investigation loads a new definitional problem onto our shoulders. For no account of modernity can be adequate to the phenomena. The novel civilization that became fully apparent in the West in, let us say, the eighteenth and nineteenth centuries, and which, in various forms and accompanied by various social cataclysms, has spread around the world, is complex beyond description. The difficulty is not the inaccessibility of the relevant historical phenomena but the variety of these phenomena and a surfeit of ways to interpret them. J.G.A. Pocock remarked of the eighteenth century that there is no one Enlightenment, but many Enlightenments discoverable in that most fecund of centuries, so while each of us can legitimately plump for our favorite version, we must accept it as one among many. My own favorite recipe for describing modernity would begin with the boiling away of community in favor of the dyadic confrontation of individual and state sovereignty (as in Giddens 1990 and Nisbet 1990), grate in the concept of spontaneous or emergent order (from Adam Smith to Charles Darwin), and mix with a pot full of social and intellectual differentiation, sometimes called rationalization, all cooked into a more or less (Max) Weberian stew. Nevertheless, while this would be my best dish, it is hardly the only item on the menu. Using an old mammalian metaphor, if I believe the elephant's most distinctive, forward-looking feature is her trunk, I must nevertheless acknowledge the tail, side, foot, ear, and tusk to which my fellow blind men and women persistently call attention. The reason for the indeterminacy is the complexity and size of the animal, not to mention that it's still growing. But even if a complete taxonomy of the beast is impossible, a fuller naming of its parts is nothing to sneeze at.

Where Did Modernity Come From?

We cannot avoid the philosophy of history; our modern self-consciousness makes it inevitable. The modern world *knows* that it is unique in human history and cannot refrain from comparing itself to its the past in order to gauge its own uniqueness. That knowledge is part of what makes it unique. This does not mean, of course, that we can accept a teleological or necessitarian view of historical change. History is a contingent affair, and no one knows where it could have gone, or where it is going now. But we do know something about where it happens to have been.

Leaping to the biggest of big pictures, Ernest Gellner argued in his sweeping *Sword, Plough, and Book: The Structure of Human History* that the human sojourn can be divided into three great periods: the segmentary, the agro-literate or stratified, and the modern industrial (Gellner 1988). These categories are by no means novel, although Gellner gives them a new twist. The first era is characterized by small, preliterate, relatively egalitarian, hunting-gathering groups, societies of, if you will, spears and eventually swords. The creator of spoken language and oral history, music, and often striking visual art and ornamentation, this form of life accounts for the great majority of the human sojourn, although we know least about it. The second refers to large, hierarchical societies with a marked division of labor that evolved from the invention of agriculture and writing sometime after 10,000 B.C.E., hence the societies of the plough and the book. The most extensive and longest lasting of these constitute what we call civilizations. In these two forms the majority of humans lived until very recently. Our current era, at most a three-century-old infant, if brazen beyond its years, is characterized by industrial production, centralized bureaucratic-legal organization, scientific knowledge, and technological innovation. In it progress is institutionalized through the constant outstripping of sociocultural integration—the inherited or traditional modes of social organization—by the "spontaneous" order of interlocking, functionally organized contexts of enterprise, that is, the coordination of human activities through jobs based on outcome efficiency and profit.

To accept this three-fold philosophy of history is to assert that there have been two momentous shifts in the human form of life once it was achieved, from segmentary to agroliterate and from the latter to industrialism. The recent shift has been, and still is, happening before our eyes, making it easy to examine, if inconclusively. The earlier shift is virtually lost to prehistory, with the exception of remaining segmentary populations, whose study is hampered by the methodological quandaries they provoke among anthropologists. Nevertheless, this is not to imply that the "surpassed" phases wholly cease to exist, either in their complete form in backwaters, or as undigested premodern elements in advanced societies. The addition of a new form of life usually spells the reorganization and reinterpretation of an older form, not its elimination. As Freudians argue of the mind, in human society as well the past lives on.

I take this account to be barely arguable. Certainly other economic and social forms have existed among island and coastal peoples dependent on the sea, cosmopolitan trading centers, themselves coexisting with and often parasitic on Agraria, and pastoral peoples, many nomadic. The latter became the dominant forces in a number of civilizations, most remarkably in central and south Asia. But as Gellner shows in his *Muslim Society,* pastoral society in some respects resembles segmentary society, and in most other cases where one can speak of a nomadic civilization, we find a segmentary herding people who, in conquering a sedentary agrarian population, settle down to create a kind of hybrid with Agraria, as Ibn Khaldun famously recounted in his *Muqquhadima*. Additionally, other questions can be raised about the division and the precise delineation of the basic characteristics of each form. But the deeper analysis is not, I think, a threat to the basic hypothesis. So let us back up and follow developments more slowly.

Segmentary societies are primarily small and local, even if they involve migration in pursuit of herds. Their religions are typically polytheistic and animistic, and not soteriological. That is, segmentary individuals do not need "saving," for they can hardly fail to have their lives legitimated by the social membership with which religious meaning is by definition intertwined. Gellner's essay into the murky, ever-revisited concept of the "primitive mentality" offers the helpful notion of "multistranded" thought and activity. Segmentary culture is characterized by the nondifferentiation of norms; each act is beholden to a multiplicity of value-constraints that the actors do not differentiate. For example, a social utterance may simultaneously serve as a report, a reaffirmation of a personal tie, and the ritual re-enactment of a social norm. Indeed, it is characteristic of early social life that it is differentiation, not multistrandedness, that needs to be explained. For Gellner this means that in segmentary societies the points of the cognitive-ritual system that allow unaltered inputs from the "natural" or "factual" world are highly limited. Some forms of disconfirmation could get through, of course; otherwise you and I wouldn't exist. But few do, or need to; social cohesiveness is more important. While this issue will require a more complete epistemological response in later chapters, basically Gellner is right. As he remarks of the vast majority of human existence, "Language is not merely rooted in ritual; it is a ritual. Grammar is the set of rules of a ritual performance. . . . Most uses of speech are closer in principle to the raising of one's hat in greeting than to the mailing of an informative report" (Gellner 1988: 51).

For us moderns, in contrast, the objective truth of an utterance is entirely differentiated from its social role; we can value truth independently of social fealty. The rationalization that Max Weber described as essential to modernity depends on dividing up the social functions of an act or utterance, so that only one kind of consideration is relevant to its validity at a time. Only thereby can progress become continuous. Rationality thus requires *commensurability* of acts or utterances, requires that those to be compared serve the same goal or norm (such as truth as correspondence to objects). To do this it must accept the incommensurability of distinctive types of utterance or act. Differentiation *between* types permits commensurability *within* type. Hence the normative, custom-conforming function, which exhibits the agent's or speaker's fealty, cannot be compared to truth-functional speech acts. Again, we who make such distinctions think of them as having been implicit in segmentary utterance, waiting for us to discover them, but for the segmentary mind our distinction is an invention of dubious justification. As Gellner puts it, *logical* cohesion and *social* cohesion are incompatible—the former requires differentiation, the latter multistrandedness. For multistrandedness is *the primacy of the social.* The price of (our) logical cohesion is the separation of the referential function of acts and utterances from their social function, which for a ritual society would rend social cohesion.

The domestication of plants and animals ushered in a new period, but only after thousands of years of experimentation and social evolution. It seems likely that from their southwest Asian epicenter, the grain agriculturalists—later to be matched by maize growers in the Meso- and Andean-America, and rice growers in the warm and wet areas from India around through southern and coastal China—continually exhausted their soils, becoming slow-moving agrarian nomads. Eventually the rich river valleys of the Nile, Tigris-Euphrates, and Indus provided yearly silting that enriched soil and permitted permanent settlement, stimulating the development of cities around 5,000 to 3,000 B.C.E.

Urban agroliterate societies brought something new into the world: *storage.* What we call civilization is the result of two great leaps in human storage capacity, bringing liberation from the here and now and a vast expansion of human constructive capacity, hence the creation of an increasingly artificial environment. For the first time people are able to store *cereals* and *culture,* dry grain for times of scarcity and information in writing. Each entails a hierarchical society, for grain must be defended by a military elite and codes must be interpreted by a literate elite. The restriction of swordplay to the few (farmers having famously beaten their swords into ploughshares, unlike those original citizen-soldiers, segmentary hunters) encouraged the political division into a vast farming population ruled by warrior-aristocrats (maintaining a sort of continuity with the segmentary war party and its, now called, martial values), themselves flanked by the other elite, the literate authority of scribes, keepers of written records and sacred texts. In some cases, as Marshall Hodgson put it, *court* and *temple* kept each other in check, in others they merged (Hodgson 1974). We can also say that civilization is based in cities, and, like Hodgson, speak of civilizations as "citied" cultures (as long as we do not make the mistake of saying that culture and progress are intrinsically urban, since it is more efficient rural food production that allows the cities to develop in the first place). And certainly with cities comes a third player, beyond court and temple: the market. There are no cities without markets.

To this new age we can add a conception which Gellner, and sociologist S. N. Eisenstadt, take from the German existentialist philosopher Karl Jaspers. Jaspers coined the term "Axial Period" for the remarkable global explosion of philosophical-religious genius that occurred during the first millennium B.C.E. (Jaspers 1953). Isaiah, Jeremiah, Zoroaster, the authors of the Upanishads, the Buddha, Confucius, Lao-Tzu, and the Hellenic Greek philosophers all lived within three centuries of the millennium's "axis" of 500 B.C.E. In southwest Asia, this brought the flowering of monotheism, whose most successful forms, Christianity and Islam, would later announce their revivals of the prophetic message, thereby eventually conquering between them most of the agrarian world outside the South-to-East Asian crescent of India-Indochina-China-Japan. In the Axial Age the implicit possibilities of a transcendental conception of God—which already existed in Judaism— were fully exploited. Something new enters the religious world: the need for salvation. Agrarian religion evolved the novel method of calling the individual conscience to confess its fealty to the Ideal. The soteriological nature of agroliterate religion presumes the possibility of being a social member yet having one's religious *bona fides* in question. In the religions of older animistic hunter-gatherer groups one could hardly be a social member and *not* be a faithful religious participant. Once the religious task has changed from performance of ritual to belief in doctrine and obedience to authority, religion becomes something to which social members can be recalled by the prophets and periodic revivals.

Agraria thus encourages a Platonic model of social reasoning, in which the validation of particulars entails their participation in, or conformity to, ideal norms or patterns. Social structure is divinely sanctioned, and divinity is *omnivalent,* that is, logically prior to any distinction between the true, the good, and the beautiful. God is an inherently multistranded concept, hence too is God's society. Here truth is indeed distinguished from political rightness, but then rationally *reintegrated* in the Divine. Literate metanarratives become essential to hierarchic, stratified societies. They make society binding on all human activities by inscribing it on the cosmos, forming what

Gaston Bachelard described as the anthropocosmic order (Bachelard 1964). Note that stratified society is not *more* integrated or unified than segmentary society. It is differently integrated, or as one might say, it is integrated, whereas segmentary society is predifferentiated. God, the Cosmos, and the hierarchical society replaces the yet undifferentiated whole of segmentary society with a *differentiated whole.*

To this account we can add our concern for the changing relation of social and cultural spheres. Among segmentary times and groups, society *is* culture and culture *is* society. We cannot distinguish social and cultural phenomena, or religious and political phenomena. The reason is not merely the great likelihood of local homogeneity. Social life is *the way,* the one and only way, the universe of activities and icons, which are not yet differentiated into the economic, social, or religious zones. The sacred/profane distinction, so important for Mircea Eliade, cuts across all activities and artifacts; it does not contrast what we would call religion from secular life, but rather the most impressive, symbolically rich, cognitively laden, and affectively complex zones of a unified social-religious life from their more mundane dimensions (Eliade 1954). So it would be perfectly apt to say that in segmentary life *culture is everything,* for in such a time society is everything, and culture is society. It is only in agroliterate or stratified societies, made inevitably more complex by their size, incorporation of distinct peoples, administrative complexity, and later their cosmopolitan trading and governing centers, that culture begins to be differentiated from society. *High* culture based in writing, and reproduced by a literate elite, becomes for the first time distinct from illiterate *folk* culture. High culture is led, of course, by religion, as the site of metaphysical representation, the ultimate seat of social norms, and the repository of education (that is, reading). The sociopolitical and religious statuses of the individual are now dis-identified, even if the symbolic code and political authority reintegrate them. Likewise, bringing diverse cultures under one imperial state-roof means that state or social membership can no longer be identified with cultural membership. It is against this backdrop that modernity evolved. The new world of commerce, science, republican politics, a growing wedge of secular culture, and the manifold traits of the modern industrial society did not obliterate, but overlaid and submerged, in some places only very thinly, the agrarian.

One last point, important as it is simple, needs to be kept in mind about this "Western" civilization that was the first to modernize. It is seriously misleading to refer to Ancient Greece and Rome, the Hebrew tradition, the history of Christianity, and the modernity that began with the Renaissance and culminated in the capitalist-scientific supremacy of north-central and especially Anglo-Saxon Europe all as the story of a triumphant "West." Ancient Greece, Rome, and early Judaism are *not* parts of Western civilization. The first two belong to *classical* civilization, a series of eastern Mediterranean empires and cultures that ended with the fall of Rome, itself issuing in three different civilizations: Western, Orthodox, and Islamic. For its part the Hebrew tradition lived a complex life amongst the peoples of the Levant for the two millennia preceding Christ. Nothing is surprising in this. As Carroll Quigley argues, what we call Western civilization is a product of *feudal* times, historically centered in North Central and Northwest Europe, and defined by Western or Roman Christendom (Quigley 1979). It follows the destruction of Greco-Roman civilization by *three centuries,* dating from Charlemagne's centralization of authority in the eighth century C.E., flourishes in the High Middle Ages, then undergoes a series of remarkable changes that create modernity. Even within this narrative we cannot speak of any kind of progressive Western civilization, any scientific or technical superiority, until the Renaissance, the Reformation, and the scientific revolution of the sixteenth and seventeenth centuries. That we can indeed trace characteristics of this modern civilization back to Rome, Athens, and Jerusalem does not make them all one civilization. Civilizations rise, fall, mix, borrow, and otherwise influence each other. That China and Japan have been heavily influenced by an Indian-born Buddhism does not mean that they are part of Hindu civilization, or that Hindu civilization is in any way East Asian. The point is that we ought to stop using that convenient four-letter word, "West," to weave a fantastic continuum, a triumphant four-millennium march from Abraham to Aristotle to Aquinas to Adorno. There is not and never has been such a civilization.

What Gets Colonized?

The most systematic of recent philosophical accounts of modernity and the contemporary world remains Jürgen Habermas's monumental *Theory of Communicative Action,* published in German in 1981. This work has been often criticized but never matched; no one else has provided a comparably interdisciplinary, social and philosophical vision of the dynamics of the modern world, along with a diagnosis of the problems, and promise, of our current condition. After two decades, while the debate over modernity and postmodernity has generated much heat and some light, his account remains the classic of its genre. It can serve to focus our discussion, while we highlight one of its largely neglected themes.

Habermas's account of contemporary society was rooted in three key notions: the distinction of strategic or instrumental versus "communicative" action, the corresponding distinction of system and lifeworld, and the colonization of the latter by the former. The system is the "systematically stabilized actions of a socially integrated group" coordinated by action consequences or, in the modern world, the interlocking network of money-and-power, capitalism and government bureaucracy. The lifeworld is the realm of interaction among social actors coordinated by inherently normative communication among the actors themselves, institutionally embodied in liberal democracy. For Habermas, modernity hangs on the release of the system and the lifeworld from traditional cultures, each freed to pursue its own "logic." Modernity is rightly characterized by Habermas, in a Weberian vein, as a differentiation of law, economics, and politics from tradition and from each other.

This allows him to reinterpret the functionalization thesis of Theodor Adorno and Max Horkheimer, who had argued that modern instrumental rationalization undermined the possibility of reasoning about ends or values. Habermas agrees that in late modernity the system of market and state expands its power to the point of taking over social spheres that had been in earlier phases of modernity coordinated by the lifeworld of communicative action. "When stripped of their ideological veils," he writes, "the imperatives of autonomous subsystems make their way into the lifeworld from the outside—like colonial masters coming into a tribal society—and force a process of assimilation upon it" (Habermas 1987: 355). But, he argues against Adorno and Horkheimer, modern rationality is not *all* functional. There is as well the communicative rationality of the lifeworld, the reason-giving of agents who must implicitly respect the freedom and equality of each in discourse aimed at achieving agreement on any given issue. This is the source both of the scientific method and of liberal democracy. There is in communicative action a "moment of unconditionality," of normatively governed freedom, uncorrupted by strategic purposes (Habermas 1987: 399). In his later work Habermas derived an ethics from such discourse (Habermas 1990).

The political project, then, is to reverse the oppressive "colonization" of face-to-face, communicatively rational human dialogue by the functional system of money-and-power.

Along with this goes a related development, which Habermas had explored in an earlier book: the rise and fall of the modern public sphere (Habermas 1989). In the Middle Ages there was no public sphere of political discussion to which citizens *per se* were invited, all land being owned by the aristocracy and king. Habermas recounts the early modern development of free towns, the movement of population to cities, increasing commercialization, and above all the spread of literacy and the rise of newspapers. But the colonization of the lifeworld in late modernity is at the same time a colonization of the public sphere. Commentators have periodically charted a decline of the public sphere in America for decades: Hanna Arendt in the 1950s, Richard Sennett in the early 1970s, Christopher Lasch in the late 1970s and 1980s, and Robert Putnam in the 1990s (Arendt 1958; Sennett 1974; Lasch 1979; Putnam 1995). They have lamented the decline of civility among strangers, participation in public organizations, the condition of public spaces, and increasing cynicism regarding politics itself. At the same time, our public spaces seem to be flooded with what Lasch called narcissism, and Jean Bethke Elshtain has recently labeled the politics of displacement, the displacing of private energies onto the public realm, the emotional catharsis of Jerry Springer and the reported sex lives of public figures (Lasch 1979; Elshtain 1995). In the language of Herbert Marcuse's *One-Dimensional Man,* this is a "repressive desublimation," a release of passion and intimacy that serves political repression, or in Habermas's sense, the continued undermining of critical public discourse. Paradox remains, however, in that on the one hand we seem overwhelmed by distant bureaucratic and corporate power that continually invades the private sphere, and on the other our public discourse and media culture seems saturated with personal, even intimate, coloration. We will return to this conundrum.

As others have noted, Habermas's concept is not entirely original (Cohen and Arato 1997). In *The Great Transformation: The Political and Economic Origins of Our Time* (1944) Karl Polanyi had sketched the fitful birth of the market economy. The heyday of laissez-faire capitalism from 1832 to the early 1930s required that all the factors of economic life be managed by a self-regulating market, hence the fiction of a "market society," the triumph of economics over sociology. But even its champions eventually became disabused of this fiction, recognizing that certain key "materials"—labor, land, and currency—could *not* be entirely subject to market forces, hence that capitalism had to limit itself to save itself. Unfortunately, it was fascism and bolshevism that in the 1930s attempted to return economics to its traditional position of subservience to society (as Peter Drucker argued in his 1939 *The Fall of Economic Man,* one of the first analyses of totalitarianism). To avoid those catastrophic systems, Polanyi argued, what liberal society requires is a return to the primacy of society, albeit one that holds onto the core of liberty and efficiency the market economy provides. Polanyi described the social strains created by the market as "shifting" among various "institutional zones," accumulating in one "comparatively independent" sphere or another. He analogized the condition of workers with that of colonized peoples (Polanyi 1957: 158). But unlike Habermas he claimed it is *culture* that bears the brunt of the distress. "A social calamity," Polanyi wrote, "is primarily a cultural, not an economic phenomenon.... Not economic exploitation, as often assumed, but the disintegration of the cultural environment of the victim is then the cause of the degradation" (Polanyi 1957: 157). The uncontrolled market created a "cultural vacuum."

How does Habermas treat culture? Ambivalently, we must say. For while he accepts culture in principle as a mainstay of free society, as long as it is a culture of open communication and not oppressive tradition, the structure of his theory betrays a common liberal fear of culture as a conservative force.

We can see this in his classic text on modernity. Habermas claims that modernity entails a "linguistification of the sacred," a transformation of norms that in premodern society received their power from divinity and ancestral authority into articulable, discursive social rules. From the distinction of the modes of utterance—truth-governed assertions, performatives normed by "rightness," and exhibitions normed by sincerity or authenticity—Habermas derives three functions of utterances in communicative action: reaching understanding, coordinating action, and socializing actors. These yield in turn the three related processes of cultural reproduction, social integration, and socialization, respectively, all to be coordinated by communication oriented to achieving mutual understanding. Thus culture is one of three zones in which communicative action operates, the one specifically tied to truth-governed assertion, hence reaching understanding, as in the "transmission of culturally stored knowledge" (Habermas 1987:

63). At the same time he describes the lifeworld as the "stock of knowledge," the repertoire of cultural-linguistic interpretive patterns which serves as the logically prior background for the subjective, objective, and social worlds. In a diagram depicting the special status of the lifeworld with respect to these three worlds, culture is made, with language, the medium of the lifeworld, and thus "constitutive for mutual understanding as such" (Habermas 1987: 126). In short, Habermas virtually identifies culture with the lifeworld; rather than one sphere within the lifeworld, culture is the realm of meaning from which participants supply themselves for the sake of all understanding. He even admits, sounding a bit like his philosophical rival, the hermeneutic thinker Hans-Georg Gadamer, that speakers and hearers cannot "distance" themselves from this cultural stock. So roughly speaking, culture is the cognitive reservoir that funds society's regulation of behavior. In this vein Habermas does indeed recognize an "impoverishment of culture" in late modernity (Habermas 1987: 327).

But having made culture the very basis of the lifeworld and communicative rationality, Habermas proceeds to restrict its role. He criticizes what he calls the "culturalistic" concept of the lifeworld, which he associates with American sociologist Peter Berger, for ignoring the solidaristic function of discourse. Culture's validity is dependent on, and rightfully criticized by, rationality and knowledge; its reproduction must be "evaluated according to standards of the rationality of knowledge" (Habermas 1987: 141). Apparently contradicting his own denial of our ability to distance ourselves from culture, he insists that in the modern era of communicative action "culture no longer remains at the backs of communicative actors; it sheds the mode of background certainty and assumes the shape of knowledge that is in principle criticizable" (Habermas 1987: 220). But where is this knowledge to come from that could criticize the storehouse of knowledge (that is to say, culture)? How do we acquire the ability to distance ourselves from, what he earlier identified with *the lifeworld itself*?

The point is that there are two conflicting concepts of culture in Habermas's theory. Where he thinks of culture as the stock of interpretive patterns that social actors carry into interaction, he in effect merges culture with the lifeworld, according it a correspondingly central place. Here all critique must operate *within and through* culture's resources. But where Habermas recognizes that such resources are predominantly inherited, his progressive-liberal instincts lead to him to fear culture as an obstacle to freedom. He then shrinks culture to an object of or component of the life-world so that knowledge and political discourse can act independently of it and criticize it. This vacillation on culture is symptomatic of a problem that plagues his entire theory.

Habermas's thesis that modernity released various social spheres to pursue their own "logics" is, I think, quite right. But, as others have criticized, the lifeworld-system distinction is problematic. First, it is too rigid. In his hands it simply recapitulates the old Kantian dualism of freedom and nature (Cahoone 1989). Certainly the lifeworld is interwoven with practical consequences, and the system includes moments of communicative action. While it is true, as I have argued, that culture concerns ends and cannot be fully instrumentalized without ceasing to be culture, we cannot separate out social zones, regions of social life, according to whether they are instrumental or not. The distinction is more subtle and complex, as we shall see. Second, it is too simple. Whereas Habermas calls attention to the two media of money and power, it would make more sense to refer to *four* media: money, power, *law,* and *signs.* Government as administration is part of the system. Law and power—meaning political power—are each bivalent: there is systematized law and unsystematized (or "lifeworlded") law, systematized political power and unsystematized power. For law and political power exist within civil society, below the level of the system, as well as within the system. Some of the inputs from civil politics arise to affect the system. This is something Habermas notes but fails to emphasize. In the contemporary system, law and the signs manipulated by what we can call the mass *mediaculture* are as much a medium of functionalization as money and power.

One way of putting this is that there are several distinct forms of internal "colonialism" that need to be differentiated. I will mention three: the colonization of local economic life, the replacement of local culture and civic life by mass mediaculture, and the sheer obsolescence of culture.

Regional, "national," and global corporations buy up and supplant local business. If this is a form of "colonization" in Habermas's sense—and I think we must say that it is—then independent local businesses must *not* be part of "the system" that is doing the colonizing. The system, then, is that realm of activities, properties, and their effects that are tightly bound up in the "logic" of the highly centralized, national, and increasingly, international market. What Habermas calls the "system" cannot simply mean business and government; it must mean big, distant, bureaucratic, powerful business and government (and as I have added, big law and big media). What remains unsystematized are largely *local* regions of economy, social relations, and culture, into which the tendrils of the system have as yet limited reach. IBM and CBS are part of the system, but the local *bodega* and repair shop, where neighbors swap stories while engaging in low-yield instrumental activity, are not. The greater the money, power, or audience at stake, the more systematic, the more integrated into the system, any social phenomenon must be.

This distinction can help to address the seeming paradox, presented above, of a simultaneous decline in the public sphere through a flight to privacy *and* a decline in privacy caused by public encroachment. It is true that in contemporary American life we witness the triumph of the public over the private. But what triumphs is not public life in general, it is a particular public, the *distant public,* primarily the electronically mediatized public sphere, while local publics are devalued. In the last century the local public realm has for many Americans been replaced by a public of strangers. The operative public realm today is that realm contiguous with the state and the major electronic media and entertainment outlets. This nonlocal public soaks up more and more of social, cultural, and psychological life; distantly regulated or initiated market and state activities penetrate and replace local, family, and interpersonal life to an unprecedented degree, making some of the most important of life's skills the management of relations to those bureaucracies, while the mediaculture increasingly values distant public life and achievement, hence fame, as the primary form of social recognition. But even the triumphant nonlocal public paradoxically loses part of its distinctiveness from privacy. For in its ubiquity, now without a mediating local public sphere, the distant or national public is flooded by energies earlier restricted to privacy or to the local, familiar public. Of course, for many Americans the local public remains crucial. But we are speaking here of tendencies, of the direction of change. For more and more, the local means less and less. And since it is inevitable that for the majority of Americans, and for an increasing number as we go down the economic scale, their primary "empowerment zone" of interest, expertise, and likely political action is in fact local, this shift has a profound antipopulist effect: the ceding of more political clout to the upper classes and to the professional politicians—not only electoral candidates, but bureaucratic officials, nongovernmental experts, and the journalists that manage their interaction.

But it is the effect on culture that is our main concern. Here we face a basic distinction. On the one hand, the systemic "mediatization" of culture *is* the mediaculture. This is in effect the creation of a new market, which Adorno and Horkheimer called "the culture industry," a collaboration of capitalism and culture that follows its own rules as a market subsystem. On the other hand, what remains of culture outside the media, shared across the locales that constitute America, is not colonized or shrinking; rather, it is increasingly rendered *obsolescent.* In late modern or postmodern America we witness the progressive displacement of non-media-culture from an influential role in social life. This is to say that experience, the social regulation of behavior, and the sense and significance of human life cease to be guided by a teleologically thick layer of society's hermeneutic horizon, an inherited, shared public repertoire of interpretive processes rooted in socially projected ends, and especially any symbolic reference to icons, rituals, and metanarratives. To some extent these decay, but to a greater extent they simply become irrelevant, in Wittgenstein's figure, a wheel that plays no role in the mechanism. We will trace the forms of this obsolescence in the next chapter.

The obsolescence of culture can indeed impact political discourse. Cultural obsolescence deprives political discourse of a teleologically laden medium, a set of culturally shared figures, standards, or narratives for social decision making. Even the "default" values of life, health, physical beauty, and sensual pleasure, which are always compelling regardless of the lack of more symbolic cultural agreement, must be deliberated and adjudicated according to some shared notion of equality, fairness, rights, justice, and so on. As Michael Walzer has argued, every scheme of distributive justice must presuppose shared notions of the meaning and value of the things that are to be distributed (Walzer 1983). How are such issues to be discussed, weighed, or measured, how are their patterns of distribution to be considered, how are they to be connected to fairness, survival, community, happiness, and tracked across different spheres of life without the employment of shared, moderately thick patterns of interpretation? As MacIntyre argued, such discussion becomes a sheer tallying of preferences in which discourse among opposing-preference groups has no convincing power (MacIntyre 1981). Without a shared, substantive cultural vocabulary, political actors may be free to speak, but have less to say and even less to agree on. This need not—indeed, in a free and pluralistic society it *cannot*—imply a short list of ultimate values to which all members must sign on. It implies rather that there must be an overlapping, thick-but-vague cultural consensus, as described in Chapter 1, implicating at least some substantive, more-than-default values shared by most social members.

Thus, among its other roles, I am suggesting that culture is *the stage-setting for political discourse*. Without it, we are condemned to communicate without the ability to presuppose end-signifying motifs, concepts, and values in common. Political discussants without overlapping cultural inheritances are reduced to only the most rudimentary considerations, like default values, and even regarding them citizens will be unable to resolve conflicts except by the most rudimentary means. Certainly with Habermas I hope for a reinvigorated discursive citizenship, but without a shared culture those public-spirited citizens will not have anything to say to one another. Even if we accept the whole machinery of Habermas's discourse ethics, with the later emendations of his epigones, can respect for the other be maintained, even conceived, without respect for what the other *values or stands for?* Habermas continues the error of egalitarian liberals who regard the democratic association of citizens in the present, the political forum and its presumed instrument, the state, as an adequate answer to the problems of a market-driven society. But I believe a third thing is required, beyond the market *and* the forum, namely culture, the inheritance of meaning-patterns that *inform the forum*. It is the colonization of culture, not the forum, that undermines the meaningful discourse among citizens. For solidarity presupposes culture.

Modernizing Culture

Among the various distinctions modernity enjoys, and suffers, is that it is the first civilization to *make culture a problem*. In perhaps its most famous strain, the eighteenth-century Enlightenment involved a self-conscious break with the past on the part of educated, political, and commercial elites, in which a putatively universal, impartial mode of validating human judgments in terms of Reason, Experience, and Nature (REN for short) replaced the prior standards that, from the perspective of the new mode, appeared dependent on Culture, Authority, and Society (or CAS). Reason is to operate on the data of Experience in order to ascertain the truth of Nature, or the natures of things. All three of these norms for cognition and practice are suprasocial and supracultural. REN aims to supplant what it now finds to be the merely traditional trappings of an unself-conscious society. While "cultural" in the sense of being a cultural development expressed in artifacts and historical metanarrative, it is nevertheless largely *anticultural*. For whatever else we may say about culture, it certainly has something to do with generationally transmitted interpretive networks, hence traditions (the Latin *traditum* meaning simply what is handed down), which operate with the force of authority to bind society together through compulsory norms from the past. Culture is, among other things, the storehouse where all the impediments to progress, all the customs and superstitions to be undercut by Reason, all the hoary forms of authority to be replaced by democracy, all the collective beliefs to be weighed in the scales held by liberated individual experience, are kept. The new, modern culture is a culture of *individualism,* where persons are both granted a degree of liberty from inherited custom and encouraged to "question authority" and create novelty, and *progressivism,* where for the first time in human history the past is officially denied its normativity and the future is supposed to diverge from it. Modern culture then presents us with an *antitraditional tradition,* a generationally transmitted message not to conform to generationally transmitted messages, an authoritative command to question authority, a collective commitment to the individual's right to violate collective commitments, a call from the (recent) past to ignore the past.

Let us explore this a bit more carefully. REN is asserted to be the new method and norm of judgment. Universal Reason, understood as a capacity that, while inculcated by particular cultures, rejects their authority; Experience, understood as a field of evidence that was always before our eyes but heretofore unseen because we saw as through a cultural glass, prejudicially; and Nature, the great object of our experience and reason, whose lawfulness provides the order we seek to know—these are understood to be independent of religion, society, and authority, even if they now will provide the validity of the latter. God may well stand behind them all, but the only public access to Him is through REN. REN must dislodge social, cultural, traditional forms of authority and belief. It is not an ideal on a par with the monotheistic God of Agraria, because REN is first of all a method, not a content, understood as progressive and fully differentiated from social, salvific, practical, and aesthetic norms. Skirmishes over Darwinism in American public schools aside, our commitment to REN is unshaken by conflicts with religion and authority.

But at the same time, in another of its strains, the Enlightenment invented the notion that each "people," understood as a homogeneous, territorial, endogamous group, characterized by some fundamental weltanschauung or virtue or capacity, ought to be equally free to express its portion of the divinely created Whole. Originally voiced by Herder and eventually motivating Romanticism, this notion became dominant in, of all places, our politics, creating nationalism. If the Enlightenment was the first century to claim to have transcended culture, it is also the first age to *define* culture. Romanticism and nationalism then became the carriers of a countertradition which is inevitably the obverse of orthodoxy. In its pure form nationalism claims that for each culture there must be a state, and for each state, a culture. This promoted egalitarianism and democracy, as I claimed earlier. Nationalism entails the *three-way convergence of state sovereignty, social order, and high culture*. As Gellner argues, modern industrial society evolved within states that declared the official status of one language, literature, history, or culture, thereby providing a "context-free" communications sphere across which freed labor, capital, and cognition could move.

But along with this, culture is made not only political but *philosophical*. The idea that deep presuppositions, worldviews, and cognitive habits, shared regardless of class by peoples, the notion that thought is social, historical, and particular is a modern view which in effect *semiotizes* or *cognitivizes* ethnicity, construes what it means to be "a people" through a socialized cognition. The more well-known Enlightenment of Reason may have intellectualized morality, made human reason the judge of norms, but it also, in this second strain, achieved a *becoming-philosophical* of social membership. To this day contemporary relativists and social constructivists regard culture as that-to-which knowledge is relative. This is a high compliment that the ancients and medievals would never have granted folk or popular culture. It remains relativism's strongest suit. Even epistemic realists, denying that culture goes "all the way down," nevertheless grant that culture is that deep structure of human belief whose determinative meaning must be undercut. In each case social membership is intellectualized.

At the same time, as Habermas argued, particular spheres of social life were granted charters to independence from culture, hence tradition. But surely this release of spheres cannot have been a simple jailbreak. Culture had to *vet* those incipient spheres as at least partially fulfilling its own norms. *Culture must have agreed to its own dismemberment*, granting at least limited permission for growth to science, markets, politics, law, and eventually art and mass culture, to pursue their logics. The spheres were *ambivalently*, never utterly, freed. But with their limited charters they nevertheless reconstructed each other and the cultural background from which they ever more confidently distinguished themselves. The payoff came readily: modern society achieved unheard-of levels of prosperity and power. Culture was not merely circumvented; it did not remain an authoritarian traditionalism somehow attached to exploding functional spheres. It cycled between accommodation-incorporation of the progressive spheres and an ostrich-like refusal to recognize reality, alternately cutting deals and digging in heels. But by the time everyone realized that what they thought was their culture was no longer, the benefits had become too great to give up. And they remain so.

The point is that culture was destined by Western modernity for a permanently ambiguous status. The rationality and differentiation that the released spheres of activity achieved became a part of culture generally, although never absolutely. A dialectical relation of mutual support and opposition was set up between each emerging, quasi-independent sphere and the background culture which is now a culture-that-permits-and-vets quasi-independent spheres. The spheres then do the driving. Culture doesn't drive. It never learned to drive because it never had to *go anywhere before*. In its history, it has mostly sat still, sometimes walked, in a crisis rode a horse or camel, but the speed of rail, liner, and the individualized transport of the horseless carriage was beyond its powers of adaptation.

Once ambiguously released, however, the scientific or cognitive, economic or productive, political-civil spheres, by expanding and rationalizing themselves, push society and culture forward. This reinforces both the sense in which they are, and are not, a part of culture; are not because they repeatedly violate cultural norms, yet are because they constitute so much of our way of life. Later, in postmodern society, culture becomes paradoxical in a new way. For, as should be evident, in so far as culture provides the context of teleological intelligibility in which social spheres are demarcated it can never become *a* sphere, a particular social context among others. That would violate *its* logic. But as we shall see, in the twentieth century to the extent that mass mediaculture becomes most of what members imbibe *as their culture,* culture then does become a sphere, indeed a commercial sphere, *within* social life, thus a part of the whole it is supposed to condition.

5 POSTMODERNITY: TOO MUCH CULTURE OR NOT ENOUGH?

Let us hope that the passage of time has shown that the controversial term "postmodern" means neither everything nor nothing, that it has settled down to the normal, imprecise, contested linguistic life of meaning *something*. That contemporary society is postmodern is arguably true, but only if we accept that the postmodern is merely the advanced course in modernity, not its end. The break or discontinuity it claims obtains *within* the modern, sociologically and cognitively defined. For it is implausible to claim that the recent ("late" or "post" modern) world represents a break from the nineteenth through mid-twentieth centuries comparable to the break between, say, the eighteenth century and the Middle Ages. Recent decades have not overturned the most novel features of the modernity that was born in the Enlightenment, became a strapping youth in the second half of the nineteenth century, and whose adult personality, if not future antics, were clearly discernible by the early twentieth. Whatever one's favorite account of the modern period, no one can deny that it introduced the science, technology, capitalism, industrialism, social egalitarianism, and cultural pluralism that remain daily lessons. Nothing more recent can match that break with earlier social history, not the eclipse of metanarrative, Newtonian physics, or European imperialism, not the rise of electronic media culture, quantum mechanics, or the knowledge-and-service based economy. Once we accept its location within modernity, "postmodern" can nicely indicate the recent deinstitutionalization or decontextualization of key elements of modernity, whereby more traditional features of early modern society, themselves holdovers from the agrarian world, which had balanced or harmonized the modern elements, have been undermined. It is then a plausibly decent name for the recent acceptance of the increasingly complex and troublesome nature of the modern, for a permanently problematic modernity, a postutopian worry that we all now imbibe as if with our postmodern mothers' milk. So "postmodern" will do, at least until something better, or just newer, comes along. Our current job, at any rate, is to identify some of the characteristics of this postmodern world and its relation to culture.

The Not-so-New Class

We have mostly been concerned with the structural changes of modernity. But if the postmodern brings a novel form of life, there is still a class which, if not the creator or producer of cultural change, is nevertheless its most important carrier. Just as the bourgeoisie and its attendant classes arguably brought us the modern world, the postmodern is carried by the New Class. It is admittedly not so new. Woodrow Wilson warned against handing the country over to "experts," James Burnham's 1941 book *The Managerial Revolution* recognized the increasing prominence of the layer of managers, lawyers, and information professionals, and Milovan Djilas's *The New Class* argued that Stalinist-era socialism had spawned a new bureaucratic management with its own class interests. Then came the "postindustrial" knowledge-economy diagnosed independently by Alain Touraine and Daniel Bell, and adopted into postmodern theory by Jean François Lyotard. If anything, the New Class has grown in importance in the last decade, swelled by the computer and telecommunications revolutions. Two recent discussions are the late Christopher Lasch's *Revolt of the Elites* and David Brooks's delightful *Bobos in Paradise: The New Upper Class and How They Got There*.

A particularly useful investigation is Alvin Gouldner's largely neglected *The Future of Intellectuals and the Rise of the New Class*. Gouldner identified the Western version of the New Class as the highly educated possessors of "cultural capital," including college faculty, engineers, managers, accountants, government officials, attorneys, media personnel, and human service and medical professionals. He divides them into humanist intellectuals and technical intelligentsia. Together they form the "cultural bourgeoisie." They are most importantly marked by a linguistic practice, the Culture of Critical Discourse (CCD). This "grammar of discourse" is characterized by a concern to justify assertions in terms of truth or rightness in order to obtain the "voluntary consent" of addressees without invocation of authority. The New Class's ideology is an ideology *about* discourse, about how beliefs and language are to be treated and handled, accompanied by the conviction that social action is *rightly* steered by such discourse. CCD conceives "pure" speech to be status- and situation-independent, reflexive and self-monitoring, hence devoid of the contaminants of inequality, status, authority, force, and tradition.

Gouldner's point first of all is that the New Class *is a class,* hence primarily interested in its self-promotion vis-à-vis competing classes. The cultural bourgeoisie is a *guild.* But "unlike the old working classes it is basically committed to controlling the content of its work and its work environment, rather than surrendering these in favor of getting the best wage bargain it can negotiate" (Gouldner 1979: 20). Its members must professionalize as they bid to claim superiority to the "old class," the capitalist bourgeoisie. Their medium is not money (like the old bourgeoisie) or land (like the yet older aristocracy), but *speech.* The new class is committed to autonomy, inner-directedness, the "chosen rather than the imposed," the self-moving rather than the "externally driven." Rationality is then conceived as autonomy: arguments must "stand on their own legs," one must "consider the speech not the speaker," undetermined by the external forces of authority and tradition, or impulse and nature. The New Class accepts, unacknowledged, the bourgeois inheritance which holds that doing and producing are the supreme human functions and proper legitimation of social status, the banner under which the bourgeoisie had fought the aristocratic conviction that status lies in sheer being or birth. But the New Class's version of doing and producing is *semiotic.* Doing things with words, or other signs, is their business, and the *creative* use of signs their goal. We may say, stealing from Habermas, that the New Class is the *linguistification of the bourgeoisie.*

Gouldner does not fail to notice the virtues of the New Class. It is probably a better master than most elite classes, especially given its liberal commitments to procedural equality. But its members are prone to resentment over their "blocked ascendance," namely, that at the end of the day they have less money, status, and power than the business class. And their power is limited. They are generally a managing, not an owning, hence ruling, class (although there is nothing "petty" about a bourgeois class that includes the richest man in the world, Bill Gates). But despite the lack of ultimate proprietorship, their level of control is profound. Gouldner tellingly remarks, "CCD treats the relationship between those who speak it, and others about whom they speak, as a relationship between judges and judged. It implies that the established social hierarchy is only a semblance and that the deeper, more important distinction is between those who speak and understand truly and those who do not. . . . To participate in the culture of critical discourse, then, is a political act" (Gouldner 1979: 59).

The New Class thus tends to merge two ideal models of cognitive and political responsibility: *judge* and *scientist,* importing a scientific model of knowing into a juridical model of decision making and conflict resolution, emphasizing rule-governed presentation of evidence and impartiality. For the New Class, Gouldner writes, "Speech becomes impersonal. Speakers hide behind their speech. Speech seems to be disembodied, de-contextualized and self-grounded" (Gouldner 1979: 29). Their universalization of their method, CCD, is the universalization of their own power. "This inflexibility and insensitivity to the force of differing contexts," he tells us, "this inclination to impose one set of rules on different cases also goes by the ancient name of 'dogmatism'" (Gouldner 1979: 84). This may sound odd; as lovers of discourse, the New Class is committed to the open-ended nature of dialogue. But in this very "openness" Gouldner finds a set of abstract rules that ignore or prohibit important modes of identity and tradition from appearing in their "open" forum at all. We shall return to this.

Let us amplify three key components of Comprehensive Critical Discourse. First, the *denial of incommensurability.* All that is meaningful and cognitively valid is believed to be translatable into a single neutral idiom of culturally, historically, and geographically decontextualized, impersonal utterance, or what Gellner calls context-free communication. Meaning and validity are delinked from status and social role, so that content of statements can be judged independent from context of utterance and the social standing of the speaker. Second, the *ubiquity of justification.* All belief that seeks public expression or enforcement must be legitimated by inquiry and evidence, subject to highly stringent justificatory demands rather than vetted by authority, faith, or tradition. Last, *value-relativism and value-skepticism.* Value-questions are undecidable by the rules just described, hence are *surds* asserted by individuals. They are to be treated equally as data. This very fact guarantees liberty and toleration. As factual claims that persons do value certain things they can be registered by preference-counting (democracy) or negotiated by discussants (liberal capitalism).

Expanding on Gouldner, the New Class's unique concern with status over money likens them to another class familiar in Western history. If, as Gellner has argued, modern society involves the *universalization of the clerisy,* the education of all citizens into literate high culture to establish the necessary universe of communication for a mobile work force, the New Class of CCD constitutes its *high priesthood.* Like the feudal clergy, the New Class discovers that given the proper bureaucratic conditions, power and influence can accrue to learning itself. Members of the New Class are the finest products of contemporary education, the best students in class, who most thoroughly master the context-free cultural semiotics delinked from place, peoples, and past that is our ruling discourse. They are the vanguard of the universalized culture of semiotic homogeneity.

It may come as no surprise that the New Class tends to have political views that befit its status. The New Class is progressive, cosmopolitan, and potentially internationalist. It tends to neutralist, rationalist liberalism, whether libertarian and antigovernment or egalitarian and committed to redistribution and government control, and in the past two decades has absorbed a strong commitment to cultural diversity under the neutralist umbrella. It is no coincidence that neutralist liberalism and the New Class matured together in the 1970s and 1980s. The egalitarian or welfare-state sector of the New Class accepts its role as the defender of the victims of the bourgeoisie, that class whose thunder it has always hoped to steal. Politics is primarily a matter of setting up Good-neutral rules of right which can be justified by a culture-neutral inquiry. Christopher Lasch contrasted its values with those of the petty bourgeoisie, skilled workers and small business owners, who prize the virtues of loyalty, responsibility, and above all, a sense of limits and hence the fragility of life and achievement. He remarked of New Class members, "They find it hard to understand why their hygienic conception of life fails to command universal enthusiasm. They have mounted a crusade to sanitize American society: to create a 'smoke-free environment,' to censor everything from pornography to 'hate speech,' and at the same time, incongruously, to extend the range of personal choice in matters where most people feel the need of solid moral guidelines" (Lasch 1995: 28). As Galston argues, those petty bourgeois commitments, which formed the historic basis of self-respect for the traditional clients of the Democratic Party, were devalued in the 1970s by neutralist egalitarians in their overweening concern for the least advantaged (the underclass) and marginalized social groups (such as homosexuals), shifting the petty bourgeoisie to the Republican Party in the 1980s, most notably as "Reagan Democrats" (Galston 1991: 162). The standoff has remained ever since. The "culture wars" of the 1990s were then largely battles between New Class and the spokespersons of petty bourgeois values.

The New Class adopts a series of positions that are self-undermining or at least self-threatening. Perhaps this is inevitable for a class that claims to transcend class. Given its role as vanguard of the postmodern era, these paradoxes tend to be suffused throughout our society.

First, the commensurability of communication and justification requires compartmentalization. Understanding utterances outside context in effect places them in one communicative mode, as constative utterances or truth-functional claims that can be justified by evidence or argument. But whatever cannot fit under that rubric must then be excluded. Incommensurability then returns between the truth-functional claims and all other utterances, particularly those expressing value-orientations. For CCD these cannot be adjudicated. In other words, to paraphrase a Weberian point, *rationalization entails the refusal to treat ultimate questions, question comparing contexts, rationally.*

Second, cultural self-determination is justified by equality and freedom. No one, no people, is to be ruled by another; the only legitimate rule is self-rule. So liberal rationalism justifies both individual rights and national or tribal self-determination. Units should be autonomous, be they individuals or societies. But the autonomy of individuals and the autonomy of groups threaten each other, as we saw in Chapter 1. So, autonomy is in conflict with itself. That is, *the autonomy of individuals and the autonomy of collectivities are both mutually necessary and antithetical.*

Third, while authority is rejected as a legitimation of truth, it returns in the form of *expertise* in the methods just described. Liberal society is managed by authority in the form of rationalist expertise. The New Class says: "In a free and equal society, *I* will rule." This is a kind of meritocratic egalitarianism. Lasch called it the new paternalism of allegedly neutral experts and bureaucrats, which replaces the patriarchs of old (Lasch 1979). For the *anti-authoritarian society has to be authoritatively managed.*

Fourth, in a culture of criticism everything is questioned. But as Adorno and Horkheimer argued, if everything is subject to open-ended criticism, so is any critical ideal. The objection to the status quo turns out to be as indefensible as the status quo, which leaves the status quo standing as that to which we are no longer, to be sure, naively committed but *ironically resigned* (Horkheimer and Adorno 1972). Equidistant between carrots, the critical donkey stays where it is. So, *the critical devaluation of everything leaves us with a postcritical acceptance of the given.*

Fifth, since it claims to be neutrally all-inclusive, CCD insists that it is commensurable with any culture. Liberal rationalism is a culture of universal tolerance which claims it can incorporate all other cultures. Now there are lots of cultures on earth that are not liberal, reject CCD (at least on ultimate matters), hence enforce thick cultural values and practices. CCD is committed both to granting these validity—thereby tolerating them—and to asserting its own superiority and universality—thereby being intolerant of them. *It must, and it cannot, tolerate the intolerant.*

Sixth, CCD claims to be an idiom, mastery of which can resolve all resolvable issues because it is impartial regarding whatever claimants come before it. The proper response to conflict is to rise above it. Issues unresolvable in that impartial idiom have no claim on rational human attention. But if rationality is impartial, all partiality is irrational. That is, *CCD is partial to impartiality, hence partially condemns all partiality.*

Last, as we said, the New Class is by virtue of its mandarin status the educated or *semiotic bourgeoisie,* a cultural clerisy. But at the same time it insists that its methods, and the world it imagines as "the True and Only Heaven," is a world devoid of cultures in the sense of distinctive peoples with substantive, intransigent commitments. Its anthem, featured as the soundtrack of corporate commercials, is John Lennon's *Imagine:* "Imagine there's no heaven. . . . Imagine there's no countries. . . . Nothing to kill or die for. . . . No religion too. . . . Imagine no possessions"—the call for an egalitarian utopia whose only remaining social inequality, one suspects, would be that between the highly educated and creative cosmopolitans who most identify with that message and the unenlightened. The New Class accepts the liberal notion that the more one learns the less one embodies, that education makes one less committed to the superiority of any form of life, that "acculturation" and "cultivation" are antonyms. Thus, *the height of human culture is to have no culture.*

Members of the New Class thus tend to be emancipatory dogmatists, elitist egalitarians, self-styled princes and princesses of the anti-authoritarian society. In a conflict with their opponents they sincerely offer themselves as neutral judges to adjudicate the matter. Now, if you must fight with someone, it is true that you are probably better off fighting with someone sincerely devoted to truth and justice, as members of the New Class are. They may fight fair, and may even compromise, or admit your victory once the competitive process has produced its results. But if you become their intractable opponent, watch out. For they must regard your opposition not merely as a conflict of interests—since they believe they have no interests—but as your opposition to truth, justice, and reason *per se.* You must then be "irrational" or "uneducated" or "politically incorrect," which is to say, *immoral*. As Carl Schmitt put it, those who claim to represent humanity as a whole must regard their opponents as *inhuman* (Schmitt 1996: 54).

Leibnizian Postmodernism

One structural disagreement between the analyses of our time proffered by postmodernists (such as Lyotard or Luhmann) and promodernists (such as Habermas) is a social version of the old philosophical problem of the One and the Many: do we witness today the deconstruction of society into a (postmodern) multiplicity of social "language-games" or rather the coalescing hegemony of a unitary (modernist) "system" or "empire" of money, power, and mass culture? Putting it this starkly makes each side sound rather simplistic; certainly there are aspects of unity *and* difference in our world. Nevertheless, a real argument exists between those who see in the present a tyrannical unitary technical-economic system that they hope to oppose with a renewed social solidarity, and those postmodernists who see instead disintegration and pluralism, for good or ill. I suggest that we can produce a model that harmonizes these two claims, with the not inconsiderable additional benefit of being true.

As we saw in the previous chapter, Habermas argued that in late modernity the lifeworld of human communication is progressively replaced and colonized by the "system" of money and power. As implied there, we can now say that this metaphor rightly captures a *static* picture of local communities facing the network of nonlocal capital and nonlocal administration, mediaculture, and law. What Habermas called the system is actually *the process* of interaction among vast markets, fields of activity, and the collective agencies acting in them, each composed of competing/cooperating individuals in functional roles, engaged in rational improvements in the context of overlapping and mutually impacting "games," or rule-governed contexts of mostly agonistic social activity and discourse. The total interaction among these social contexts is fluid, although at any one moment there is a constellation of games and their agencies with which all lesser games, agencies, and players must contend. What we call *the* market is nothing but the interlocking interactions among a huge number of subprocesses, each attempting to survive by the rules of its own particular game in the market-administrative-legal-mass cultural environment. The postmodern society of autonomous contexts *is* this environment; it is what the globalized process looks like at the level of individuals, agencies, and roles. This claim simply expands the Weberian differentiation thesis, the breaking apart of social spheres from tradition and into internally commensurable, rationalizable spheres. Each context—science, economics, politics, and even art—freed to pursue its own logic, reorganizes itself by internal rules. This is what made progress possible. The meta- or supracontext is the environment formed by the collection of all social contexts. Each faces the environment constituted by all.

The key to this view is that social agencies and contexts are simultaneously autonomous *and* interdependent. Autonomous in that they develop according to internal rules, expressed in the theory of *autopoiesis* or self-making systems (Luhmann 2003; Maturana and Varela 1980). But at the same time all generate externally relevant effects, hence constrain one another, to varying degrees of salience. None is independent of the outside constituted by the other agencies and contexts; each represents those effects in its autonomous internal rules and problems. Continuing the metaphysical metaphor, this is a roughly Leibnizian picture of monadic social contexts, each with its own inner principle of growth and each reflecting changes in all relevant others. The element of Leibniz's metaphysics that is missing here, of course, is his notion of a prearranged harmony created and sustained by God. The combination of autonomy and interdependence implies that more and more games become internally rationalized and progressive *and* there are fewer and fewer boundaries to the effects games have on one another. Every game and agency expands, rationalizes, in relation to its internal goals and rules, but every game tends to take on technologies of the environment that is the sum of all. All are transparent, nothing is hidden.

What must be added to this roughly postmodern view is the fact that the most dominant economic games, along with the progressive research games of technology-creation, and the administrative games with their legal rules, are the progressive driving forces of the process. Rather than describe this as system hegemony we ought to recognize that this "multiheaded" progressive force pluralizes all social activity into autonomous language games or contexts. The metaphors of sovereignty (from politics), mechanical regulation (as in systems theory), and difference (from semiotics) do not hold here. What we see is a burgeoning set of internally normed, interlocked, practical-linguistic games, which, in their explosive progress, force pluralization and contextualization on the rest of social life. These driving contexts do not establish unity or empire or system or hegemony; on the contrary, *they continuously break down any substantive metacontext of social activity,* the cognitive representation of which Lyotard called metanarratives. The network of driving forces is not a *thing;* it is a process that *erodes all things.* The total complex of these complexes indeed forms a "reality" or "environment" for all other social contexts and individuals at any moment. Like the physical universe, the social universe is expanding from every point (with exceptions to be noted below). I am suggesting that the postmodern condition is merely the advanced course in Weberian modernization. We are still working out the implications of a society of "spontaneous order" in which units are free to rationalize themselves, first initiated and conceived in the eighteenth century.

The relevant categories of social contexts are then three. First are those that constitute the progressive economic, technological, administrative-legal games, and some components of mass culture. This is the *driving sector,* the core of the process. It is driving, not determining; its members push against, rather than rule, other contexts, creating continual pressure for change. Second are the non-driving contexts that are nonetheless progressive and rationalizing, like art, intellectual culture, other parts of mass culture, and a host of voluntary and political associations which seek rational improvement or advantage according to their own norms and hence create novelty. This is the *riding sector.* Third are the social contexts that are outside the dominant network most of the time, and are in themselves nonprogressive, like the normative institutions of family, friendship, certain voluntary and interest associations, and local economic, politics, and culture (indeed, I have argued, civil society itself). They constitute the *by-standing sector.* They may or may not be, to use Peter Berger's terms, "de-" or "counter-modernizing" but they are at least nonmodernizing, not internally normed by progress or rationalization, and thus are usually under threat from the first two sectors.

We may profit from Charles Jencks's claim that postmodern architecture, rather than abandoning nostalgia or metanarrative, incorporates traditional gestures into an otherwise modernist frame through "double-coding," the combination of signs from two opposed languages. The agencies of the progressive sectors of postmodern society do not forsake unity or metanarrative. On the contrary, as Leibnizian monads, each represents or projects a vision or goal of expansive unity, or metanarrative. One might say that each context facing out into the environment understands other contexts through an at least projected unity, employing George Herbert Mead's figure, a "generalized other." The postmodern condition is not one in which we abandon metanarrative but in which metanarrative and rationalizing instrumentality, unity and difference, the language of tradition and the language of progress, are mixed together and the inconsistency fails to be problematic. Everybody is free to project what metanarratives they like, and free to notice that shared metanarrative does not matter. *The process works regardless.* We follow the contextual rules of particular functional linguistic-practical contexts while simultaneously spouting grand narratives belied by our performance. Weber argued that the differentiation of spheres and values made us no longer agroliterate monotheists, but "polytheists." In the postmodern condition we are simultaneously polytheists and monotheists *without the worry*.

For there certainly are metanarratives in postmodern society, most notably in the United States. But they subsist in a distinct fashion. First, there are the official and public metanarratives of society that everyone takes seriously: progressivism or the commitment to social progress as the meaning of existence, and individualism or the view that human individuals are the centers of value and the ultimate court of true judgment in the world. They are powerful, broadcasted by mass culture, flown on banners, and sworn to as oaths. But they are thin and procedural; their narrative structure underdetermines questions of the meaning of human existence and any hierarchy of values. What gets invested with effective loyalty is a *how*, not a *whither* or *why*, a common pragmatic attitude, ability to adapt to novel contexts, context-free problem solving, as well as a remarkably open cognitive system. Genuinely thick metanarratives, on the other hand, are still held by perhaps most citizens, and metaphors and references to these litter our public life. But they generally have practical consequences only in private life or in voluntary associations. When citizens announce thick metanarratives in public, everyone recognizes them as socially unnecessary, to be taken with a grain of salt, that is, tolerance. Thus, what the "loss" of or "incredulity" toward metanarratives means in fact is not their absence but their ambiguity or social impotence when substantive. If thick and determinative, metanarratives are merely private or contextual; if public or universal, they must be thin. Social actors themselves recognize that coordinated social action does not require thick belief. Thus, most Americans may endorse conservative rhetoric, but it is precisely at the point that conservative political groups seek to establish nativist or Christian policies that they back away.

Now, the Leibnizian picture presented above may seem too fragmented. The modernist is right to say that we cannot conceive of ongoing social action that is not rule-governed or meaningfully contextualized. So it would seem the differences can only obtain against a background unity. But the postmodernist retort (or, what the postmodernist *ought* to retort) is correct: while every interaction must be rule-governed or backgrounded, there does not have to be *a* context of contexts, a rule of all rules. Agencies bootstrap themselves into temporarily and contextually rule-governed interactions with one another. A set of rules Q, projected by individuals or agencies R and S in certain of their context-dependent roles, provides the background against which R and S have a meaningful interaction. But when S turns to interact with an individual or agency Y, another background Z will be invoked, and so on. There is in each case a "third thing" but not *one* third thing for all cases. My point is not the metaphysical claim that there are no supracontextual norms, only that contemporary society has no need of that hypothesis. No doubt many people accept as given that there is a common generalized other or, more subtly, that the metanarratives projected by the various contexts of society are converging or will converge. But we do not see evidence of that in contemporary society. The demands of the driving sector are cognitively and culturally minimal and, if you will, falsificationist: they rule out thick metanarratives, but don't mandate any. The open-ended issue, which each generation will have to recalibrate for itself, is how to make sense, or coherence, of the differentiation of the progressive, single-stranded, rationalized sectors and the nonprogressive, multistranded, nonrationalizing sectors of human life.

Is Culture Obsolescent?

During the Soviet era Czech émigré novelist Milan Kundera argued that in contemporary Europe culture had "bowed out" (Kundera 1984a). After a friend's manuscript was confiscated by authorities in communist Prague, he and Kundera wandered the city discussing which great cultural figure in the West they could contact to take a public stand. Despairingly, they could think of no one who was not compromised by sectarian politics. Europeans had ceased to believe in the moral autonomy of cultural creation, Kundera lamented, in the intrinsic values constructed by learning and writing. For in

Soviet-dominated Europe there was no independent culture, while in the West nobody—including the intellectual-cultural elite itself—valued culture except as something to be consumed. The great modern "age of culture," which had, for Kundera, replaced religion as the repository of European ideals in the eighteenth century, was retreating like a melting glacier. That we occupy a vastly different geopolitical environment today does not gainsay Kundera's question: do we now live in a postcultural era, a time beyond culture?

Some may respond that this question is absurd; surely today we are not devoid of culture, we are inundated with it! The sheer volume of cultural artifacts and cultural producers, the enormous industries devoted to producing and selling culture in the broad sense—film, television, radio, books, news and entertainment weeklies and monthlies, all manner of toys and print reproductions, fashion, sports, the ubiquity of journalistically transmitted political discourse, and so on—is unprecedented in human history. Likewise, in our pop version of poststructuralism we seem more concerned than ever with cultural signs, with images of reality rather than reality itself. But the point is not the absence of cultural activity or artifacts; it is whether our *attitude toward* them renders them incapable of doing what cultural activities and artifacts have traditionally done. Indeed, a changed function of culture may be the requisite precondition for massive cultural output. Still, if not absurd, talk of the end of culture is at least politically suspicious. Presumably it is an elitist Eurocentric conceit, a lament over the decline of a high culture that was the property of mid-twentieth-century upper-class whites in the towns and suburbs of London, Berlin, Paris, and New York in the face of an upsurge of ethnic, linguistic, and cultural pluralism from below. But the issue here is not the replacement of one culture by another, or the lack of unity in culture. It is whether the meaning and experience of *culture per se* has undergone a structural change. Here there is good (or at least plausibly good) news, and bad (or at least sobering) news.

The bad news first. There are indeed a series of contemporary effects, more complex than the "colonization" Habermas suggested, that arguably undermine or encroach upon cultural practices, artifacts, and narratives *per se* in a variety of ways. First, there is *decontextualization,* the splitting-up of shared cultural contexts that roughly backgrounded all social action, leaving, so to speak, bits and pieces of culture stuck to particular social contexts and practices to operate without any shared, cross-contextual background, as Alasdair MacIntyre has argued (MacIntyre 1981). In moral life it leads individuals to turn to purely vocational, bureaucratic, or role-specific moral rules, having no other reliable and shared basis for moral judgments. Second, there is *de-culturation,* the simple elimination of cultural elements as unnecessary or incompatible with gains in efficiency or cost, as when pushing buttons on a bank machine replaces small talk with a teller. Where cultural elements are not actually eliminated, they tend to be reinterpreted in a way that costs them their cultural function, which can happen in two ways. They can be *functionalized,* regarded as publicly valuable only in an instrumental sense, or *privatized,* regarded as meaningful or valuable in a purely private sense that has no legitimacy in public. What then remains of publicly shared culture often approximates a *default culture* focused on those values which remain when other public values are undermined, in particular the *biovalues* of life, longevity, health, pleasure, and physical beauty.

The social reproduction of culture has changed dramatically. For the first time in history people get *acculturated at a distance,* not primarily by kin and locale. Throughout history family and neighbors were the sole means of inculcating the majority. The sources of high culture were nonlocal, extending from cultural elites in cosmopolitan centers, but the agents of acculturation were always local. To be sure, today kin and locale continue to work their socializing magic. But now, even if the familial and local culture are idiosyncratic, or largely fail, the media, plus the schools, plus big business and government, will train the child in the wider culture. While this may have its benefits, it must give us pause, not only because it means the continued erosion of locale, as noted earlier, and a running battle between parents and the New Class culture-makers, but because it presumably must alter the acculturation process itself, the way the young come to be cultural members and what their "culture" means to them.

Last, contemporary culture exhibits as a prominent component an *anti-culture,* in which culture depicts itself as anachronistic, trivial, merely private or merely functional (Cahoone 1988). For among the things represented and interpreted by the cultural medium is *the cultural medium itself.* Both at the level of intellectual culture and the popular mediaculture one can encounter the message that all cultural practices serve economic or political purposes, the evaluation of cultural products solely by financial criteria, and campy cynicism regarding the ultimate meaninglessness of narrative representation. Again, the point is not a turn from high to lowbrow or popular culture; it is not that today our children prefer the sitcom to Shakespeare. It is rather that part of their acculturation, their medicultural training, is learning that *culture does not matter,* that inherited literatures and the wisdom of the past serve no purpose. It is true that Shakespeare will suffer from this trend more than the sitcom, since Shakespeare demands more effort and education. Nevertheless, people do not avoid Shakespeare merely because it is hard, but because it is hard *and* because we feel Shakespeare has nothing important to teach us, just as the sitcom has nothing important to teach us. We don't take Shakespeare seriously, *and we don't take the sitcom seriously either.* Shakespeare is a joke, like the sitcom is a joke; but the latter is an easier joke. In fact, the sitcom is happy *to consider itself* a joke, to wink at us in ironic self-comment and acknowledge its merely economic function. The media-constituted public realm thus becomes saturated with nonmeaning, open lies, and frank calculation. We train ourselves to regard what are on their face cultural forms—dramatic narrative, images, rhetoric, artifacts—*as nonmeaningful and nonvaluable.* We get used to discounting, ignoring, and trivializing cultural things.

Now, all that is on one side. Yet there is some good news about our postmodern culture that makes it impossible to say, with Kundera, that culture has "bowed out." Certainly mass electronic culture does not exhaust our culture; there remain minority ethnic, regional, and local cultural eddies and inlets. Perhaps most people live double cultural lives, moving between the local and communally inherited on the one hand and mass culture on the other. Nor is mass or mediaculture simply empty; the cultural obsolescence just described is a powerful component of its description, but it would be foolish to argue that it exhausts the whole. Certainly culture is bigger than ever. In our age of universal literacy, universal schooling, an ever rising number of college attendees, and the postindustrial swelling of the "semiotic" spheres of the economy—from knowledge to entertainment to news—we virtually swim in signs, spoken and written words and images and narratives. To this is now added globalization after 1989, which has tended to spread the mass culture of the countries with the largest economies, the United States above all, over the globe. So the critic ought to be cautious about any simplistic condemnation of the novelty and complexity of postmodern culture.

First and most obviously, postmodern mediaculture is the first culture in history that is *commercial* and *built to change.* These two traits go together. Certainly earlier cultural artifacts and practices had economic value. But only today is the constant creation of cultural artifacts, as Adorno and Horkheimer lamented, an *industry.* Marx's analysis that under capitalism "all that is solid melts into air," like Schumpeter's attribution to capitalism of the method of "creative destruction," fits mass culture more than any aspect of social life. The result is, as noted, a source of despair for many critics, but with its economic and fluid nature goes the malleability and diversity of our culture. Whatever postmodern capitalist culture is, it is not rigid. As they say of New England weather, if you don't like this culture or the role it bequeaths you, wait five minutes.

Second, our culture is arguably more *egalitarian* than at any time since the agroliterate revolution. The distinction between high and low culture has virtually disappeared. All cultural products live in the same semiotic dimension, self-consciously accessible to more or less all consumers. In retrospect it seems that the construction of national high cultures in the nineteenth century, with the drive toward universal literacy, set the stage for the twentieth's "revolt of the masses," meaning the repeal of class (and in the United States, racial) exclusions. The upwardly and outwardly expanding lower-middle and working classes had an appetite for culture. When the distinction of high and low culture was deconstructed, roughly at the same time as the post–World War II expansion of higher education, the result was a more and more homogeneous cultural environment in which all classes absorb the same media in all regions, their local and historical cultures taking a back seat.

Third, this equality extends beyond consumption to *production*. The making of culture is no longer in the hands of a tiny educated elite. Almost anyone can contribute to culture today. Of course regarding distant or mass culture there are vast concentrations of power in the giant media conglomerates; the elites of New York and Los Angeles, with some canny spinning by Washington, D.C., mostly decide the mass media topics of the week. But tally the number of writers of books, movie scripts, reviews, letters to newspaper editors, callers to talk radio, and posters of internet material. Then add to this all contributors to *local* culture across the country, from people who create programming for public access cable stations to the participants in town, county, and neighborhood ethnic festivals, the designers, gardeners, and home decorators that display their wares in local fairs, in public venues, or even on the public face of their property. I hazard the sum is a larger percentage of the populace than any time since the dawn of stratified society. Ours is an *open* culture, no longer controlled by authority.

But we must close with more sobering news about a structural phenomenon implicit in what has been said. As noted, in the twentieth-century culture, or a large part of it, became an *industry*. The critique of this development has mostly concerned the economic attitude to which this subjects culture. But there is another effect: for the first time in history *culture gets framed*. Part of what we mean by culture is the interpretive horizon of teleologically connected meanings in terms of which the frames or boundaries of social contexts are set and understood. As such it cannot be *one of* those contexts. But in so far as postmodern mass culture is a business, culture becomes one of the industrial spheres of rationalizing activity. Electronic mass culture is not all of our culture, but it is a very significant part and it certainly offers itself as the whole. We thus face the following ambiguous condition. We have, and inherit, a horizon of meanings which valorize the construction of differentiated social frames within some of which progress can occur. But as mediculture this background of social action becomes one sphere of the foreground. This denies us the employment of culture as background while permitting us to examine our own culture as an object, which paradoxically makes the *whole* of our social world into a *part* of our social world. This is characteristic of our postmodern predicament.

The Postmodern Cognitive Predicament

Modern Western society signified a break with all previous social orders. There is an "asymmetry" of human cultures. The failure to recognize this signals a self-reflexive inconsistency on the part of the theorist and obscures one of the largest facts and problems about the contemporary world. If symmetry or relativism were true, then no culture would contain cognitive assets that put it in a general position of advantage with respect to all other cultures. If that were so, then modernity would present us with *no* new fundamental issue that has not been faced by any other historical period. If you can't quite bring yourself to believe that, then relativism must be false on this point.

So let's face facts (yes, actually, there are a lot of them). A novel cognitive style has evolved over the last three centuries which yields unprecedented and undeniable results. The style is epitomized in science, but it spreads over other forms of practical endeavor. Let's call its yield *knowledge,* at least tentatively, absent a full epistemological justification. Certainly if pragmatic capacity is any evidence of knowledge—we don't have to agree that it is the sole or primary evidence—then this new cognitive style yields a tremendous amount of knowledge. It is also true that a productive-industrial mode of organization of material life linked to that cognitive style yields unprecedented and undeniable material gains, including weapons technologies, so that the societies possessing the noted cognitive style tend to become dominant world powers. We can philosophically question the validity and doubt the ethical, aesthetic, and spiritual benefit of these gains, but we are not at liberty to abandon them. As Marion Levy Jr. wrote, modern techniques are irreversible; they cannot be discarded without tremendous suffering (Levy 1972). The provision of perennial human needs is in our age dependent on modern bureaucracy, industrialism, technology, science, and advanced communications. Cultures that have not fully embraced these developments face an environment in which others have them. Nothing in the contemporary world, not its material life, its politics, its cultural conflicts, can be understood if we deny the *prima facie* advantages of science, technological innovation, and industrial production. Certainly the last century has exposed plenty of troubling implications of life on the new side of history's Big Ditch, from nuclear weapons and global warming to the evening commute.

Modernity thus implies a commitment to the scientific method, broadly construed, a search for publicly available evidence, the rejection of the influence of other sociocultural norms on cognition. This is a procedural commitment, not a substantive one. Modernity primarily entails a *way of seeking* truth, not the truth of a given world-picture, or the latter only secondarily. For the former inevitably upsets the latter. Gellner notes the remarkable fact about our society that we accept that our ontology is *flexible,* that it rightfully changes with the science of the day or decade. Indeed, the revolutions of twentieth-century physics seem to guarantee that our "official" ontology will never again be capable of social assimilation, as both Aristotelian and Newtonian physics were. The account of the universe based in relativity and quantum theory cannot be integrated into the worldview of even educated citizens, cannot be put together with commonsense experience. It is unthinkable that future scientific advances will do other than widen that gap. Just as our procedural commitment to emergent order based on autonomous rationalization of spheres in other areas of social life upsets any vision of the future, cognitive progress prevents the secure imagination of the whole.

As we saw in the preceding chapter, Enlightenment culture attempted to reorganize itself around, and judge itself against, Reason-Experience-Nature or REN, rather than Culture-Authority-Society or CAS. But when this cognitive form *observes itself*, it generates a host of philosophical or hermeneutic problems. First, it comes to recognize itself as one function among others each engaged in its own business, like politics, art, economic production, and so on. Second, the cognitive function cannot legitimate itself, because legitimation would require justification through reference to an outside, including a practical justification in terms of scientific cognition's social benefits. Third, this leads to constructivism, which is arguably the trend of post-Kantian philosophy, although its roots are in Hume. A cognitive examination of the cognition of nature progressively reveals the cognitively self-constructed nature of that cognition, reveals, to use older languages, the operation of "custom" or "transcendental" machinery or "*Geist*" or the theory-ladenness of observations or the "historical" or "linguistic" constitution of the alleged object. It discovers, as William James put it, that "the trail of the human serpent is over all." If the Enlightenment, in one of that brilliant century's modalities, had announced that REN, not CAS, would be the norm of and constraint upon cognition, then its later modern progeny discovered that Culture, Authority, and Society had *reappeared within* those norms. The post-Kantian claim—continued by idealism, phenomenology, pragmatism, Wittgenstein, philosophy of science from Kuhn to the social constructivists, and postmodernism from Derrida to Luhmann—that the world we encounter is our product, concurs with Promethean capitalism, modernism's conception of the task of art, and our Baconian conception of science's power. Not only on the factory floor and in the executive suite, but in the seminar room, the SoHo loft, and the Oval Office as well, the model of the human is *homo faber*.

I will argue later that constructivism, in anything like a literal form, is untenable. Nevertheless, it is the spirit of the age, and this is revealing. For my point is that the self-observation of REN returns us to CAS, as Richard Rorty has argued. From "objectivity" we turn to "solidarity" as the ground of our cognitive strategies. Rorty's opposition is telling, but its application is not. For solidarity is first and foremost the apt term, not for our "postmodern," postobjectivist condition, but for *premodern* epistemology. As we have argued, before modernity society was virtually everything for almost all human beings in history (and prehistory). Social convention and authority have been the virtually ubiquitous determinants of belief-acceptance and language-use, openness to nonsocialized or anomalous experience being strictly limited. The widespread acceptance of the rightful distinction of *true*

from *socially legitimate* is very recent. The aim of logical coherence inherently violates social coherence. Now, we might say that rational inquiry has
always had as its inherent possibility from the time of Buddha and Plato that
it progressively abstracts from culture. But it never fulfilled that possibility
until modern science, which is indeed virtually neutral with respect to cultures. It is not, of course, *strictly* neutral. Like every symbolic form, it has its
presuppositions. But it is precisely the development of a systematic procedure of cognition that is *maximally* independent of culture, including the
culture in which it arose. It is a cognitive institution which pursues truth and
technē by isolating them from all other cultural norms. Its development
required and enabled a movement from omnivalence to differentiation, the
separation of inquiry from the soteriological, aesthetic, practical, and social
concerns in which it was traditionally embedded.

In this respect Rorty is right that the postmodern involves, again not
inescapably, a resocialization or reculturation, a rediscovery of Culture,
Authority, and Society beneath the (at least self-reflectively available) layers
of Reason, Experience, and Nature. But the second time around, as Marx
said of the Eighteenth Brumaire of Louis Bonaparte, is different. Rorty,
Berlin, and others call this difference irony. I think this is too precious.
More broadly and straightforwardly, the return to the social is *procedural*.
The solidarity that Rorty claims as our cognitive commitment is a procedural solidarity, a commitment to liberal, bureaucratic, and scientific rationality, accepted as the critical mesh through which our continued reference
to the real must be strained. In postmodern cognition we return not to the
thick inherited cultural narratives of earlier social history, but to justificatory
procedures that are social but thin. We are self-reflexive and pragmatic,
rather than naive and theocratic. Nevertheless, such commitments are strictly
held: constructivists and postmodernists do not suggest a return to religion
or faith, even ironically. Cognitive closure may be impossible, but some roads
are closed off. We doubt our ability to justify the binding nature of our practices, but remain bound to them nonetheless. We bang out another critique
of the "myth" of scientific objectivity on laptops created by that "myth,"
and call engineers and not shamans when they break down. Arguably it is
our very realism, our science, our rejecting of omnivalence in favor of the
differentiation of logical or cognitive from social norms, which leads to
procedural commitments ever in search of an unavailable foundational content. For refusal to identify social convention with truth is the hallmark of

modern cognition. We reject the "primitive" segmentary identification of culture with nature, and the Agrarian cultural assertion of divine or transcendent norms, in favor of a purely noncultural constraint, whose precise determination escapes us. Differentiating logical from cultural validity takes away the possibility of completing our circle, of justifying our inquiry within a graspable whole. Hence our, apparently permanent, paradoxical position.

6 PLAYING REALITY

"Revolutionary" was certainly a term of praise for Karl Marx. So it may be surprising that in one of his most famous passages Marx notes capitalism's revolutionary role. While it was for him the most repressive economic system in history, as the apotheosis of unequal economies, the exit from history into communist utopia, Marx gave it its due. Unlike all earlier systems of domination capitalist modernity is honest, its evil is naked. It demythologizes itself, tearing off the premodern masks by which ruling classes had gilded their power with aristocratic crests and divine robes. In contrast the capitalist says, "You aren't going to do what I say because I am superior, descended from the founders, or constructed of gold to your bronze. You're going to do what I say because *I've got the money.*" Thus in a famous passage from the *Communist Manifesto* Marx writes:

> The bourgeoisie, historically, has played a most revolutionary part... wherever it has got the upper hand, has put an end to all feudal, patriarchal, idyllic relations... pitilessly torn asunder the motley feudal ties that bound man to his "natural superiors," and has left remaining no other nexus between man and man than naked self-interest. . . . The bourgeoisie has stripped of its halo every occupation hitherto honoured and looked up to with reverent awe... torn away from the family its sentimental veil. . . . All fixed, fast-frozen relations, with their train of ancient and venerable prejudices and opinions, are swept away, all new-formed ones become antiquated before they can ossify. All that is solid melts into air, all that is holy is profaned, and man is at last compelled to face with sober senses, his real conditions of life, and his relations with his kind. (Tucker 1978: 475–76)

It is ironic to note that half a century before, Edmund Burke, the archetypal English conservative, opponent of modern republicanism and equality,

had made a remarkably similar diagnosis. Burke attacked the French Revolution for its attempt to reform traditional political arrangements according to abstract Enlightened principles. In one of the most famous passages
in his *Reflections on the Revolution in France* he reacted to the events of October 6, 1789, when a Parisian mob marched to Versailles and took the king
and queen into custody.

> It is now sixteen or seventeen years since I saw the queen of
> France, then the dauphiness, at Versailles, and surely never lighted
> on this orb, which she hardly seemed to touch, a more delightful
> vision. . . . [L]ittle did I dream that I should have lived to see such
> disasters fallen upon her in a nation of gallant men, of men of
> honor and of cavaliers. I thought ten thousand swords must have
> leaped from their scabbards to avenge even a look that threatened
> her with insult. But the age of chivalry is gone. That of sophisters,
> economists, and calculators has succeeded; and the glory of Europe
> is extinguished forever. . . . All the pleasing illusions which made
> power gentle and obedience liberal, and which, by a bland assimi-
> lation, incorporated into politics the sentiments which beautify
> and soften private society are to be dissolved by this new conquer-
> ing empire of light and reason. All the decent drapery of life is to
> be rudely torn off. . . . On this scheme of things, a king is but a
> man, a queen is but a woman; a woman is but an animal, and an
> animal not of the highest order. (Burke 1987: 66–67)

Thus did Burke and Marx, the canonical conservative and the arch-
revolutionary, express a common discomfort with modern apparel, or rather
the lack thereof. Modernity tears off the traditional fabric of life to expose
the naked ape beneath. We can now say that fabric was nothing other than
culture, the costuming bequeathed by tradition. Note Burke's conflict, however. It is impossible not to believe that he truly regarded the French queen
as more than a *mere* woman. At the same time he refers to such notions as
"superadded" ideas and "pleasing illusions," implying that they are not true
but good, that we *ought* to believe them for social and moral, not cognitive,
reasons. Either way, modernity rips off the garments that make social life
bearable and virtuous. This leads to the most basic philosophical question
about culture and reason: is culture illusion? Must reason and truth reject
culture? Or is culture *necessary* illusion? Are human norms, and perhaps
even our sense of reality, dependent on artifice?

There is a particularly useful path of access to this question, one traveled by an eclectic historical line of thinkers who theorize culture as the development of a particular form of artifice, a human propensity that would seem to stand at the opposite pole from any sort of realistic or pragmatic dealing with the world. That dimension is *play.* The analogy of culture to play employs both sides of the ambiguity of the term, understanding culture as both free, creative, impractical activity and as the construction of drama. The point is implicit in Marx and Burke, for whom costuming, or in children's parlance, *dress-up,* is essential to premodern social life. Pursuing the question of play will lead to a deeper analysis of the function of culture in human experience and thought.

Schiller: Free Play

Play owes its modern philosophical elevation to German romanticism and in particular to Friedrich Schiller's *Letters on the Aesthetic Education of Man* (1795). He argued that the dual human impulses toward sensuous concreteness and eternal form achieve their union in the play impulse, which seeks "living shape" or beauty as in art. Work results from the sanction of need, hence is serious; superfluity and superabundance manifest as physical play. But physical turns to aesthetic play when "free form" is imposed. Play is *the* premier manifestation of freedom. Like other proponents of play, Schiller feels the need to answer the objection, is it not a cheapening of art to call it a "mere" game?

> But why call it a *mere* game, when we consider that in every condition of humanity it is precisely play, and play alone, that makes man compete and displays at once his twofold nature. . . . Man is only serious with the agreeable, the good, the perfect; but with Beauty he plays. . . . Man shall only play with Beauty, and he shall play *only with Beauty.* For, to declare it once and for all, Man plays only when he is in the full sense of the word a man, and *he is only wholly man when he is playing."* (Schiller 1977: 79–80)

This is a lot to claim for play. But Schiller's explanation is straightforward, given the general terms of German idealism. Because play is the opposite of work, is not serious, unproductive of needed goods, it is therefore free, like art. But like art, play is at the same time formal, an attempt to embody a structured whole. Play is not arbitrary or chaotic, it has rules that players must follow. Thus in its completed form play gives us a *free necessity,* an externality freely created by Spirit to which Spirit must then conform. This means that play alone expresses the whole or inner man, our freedom and our recognition of necessity, our inner instincts and outer, physical, social environs. Consequently, play arises at the meeting of the two halves of human nature, the impulse toward the concrete or particular and the impulse toward the abstract or universal. It is in this synthesis of particular and universal, sensuous and abstract, necessitous and free, that only play—and that adult play which is art—attains the highest fulfillment of human experience.

Mead: Just Gaming

The American philosopher George Herbert Mead presented perhaps the first fully naturalist and pragmatic account of human consciousness. He famously preceded the dominant philosophical perspectives of the mid- and late twentieth century by making social communication the womb from which meaning, mind, and self emerge. In his well-known *Mind, Self, and Society from the Standpoint of a Social Behaviorist,* Mead imagined creatures, higher animals and humans, engaged in a process of mutual adjustment of response. A does something in response to a situation, B responds to the new situation set up by A's act, then A responds to the new situation that includes what B has done, and so on. This is "gesture." Humans alone are capable of *significant* gesture, in which A responds not only to B's but to its *own* gesture. That is, A's gesture calls out the same response *in itself* that it calls out in B. This can only happen if A is able to calculate its gesture through its anticipation of B's perception of and response to it, hence capable of taking the standpoint of B.

Play and games complicate this gestural dialectic, hence make sophisticated communication and thought possible (Mead 1974). Play is the adoption of the character of the other in pretending, acting "as if," being another to oneself. Games are the epitome of this process. In games the participants must be capable of imaginatively occupying a whole series of other viewpoints more or less simultaneously. I can play baseball acceptably well only if I can imagine the likely response of nine other people to events or to my own acts. It is from games that we begin to imagine a "generalized other," a social viewpoint on our own actions, the source of both morality and objectivity. So this generalized otherness which grants objectivity develops from an "as if," the capacity to modify one's behavior in light of the *ir-real,* something not actual, namely, how I *would* see events from the perspective of someone I am *not.* As Peirce had argued earlier, reality, in a sense we shall explore later, only emerges subjunctively, in terms of a perspective on states of affairs "I could" or "I would" but do not now embody (Peirce 1955: 272–73). Thus playing games is the school not only of self, society, and morality, but of reality as well.

Huizinga: The Play's the Thing

In his *Homo Ludens* (1938) or "Man as Player," Dutch historian Johan Huizinga provided a systematic interpretation of culture as play. For Huizinga play situations are constructed, artificial, marked off from the rest of social life as "nonserious," not a continuation of the projects, interests, or functions of the rest of life (namely, work). Play is, as he says, borrowing the phrase of Romano Guardini, "zwecklos aber sinnvoll," empty of practical aims but full of meaning. Players are free but play is rule-governed, hence action is ordered. There is always something at stake in play, hence tension, something to be lost or won. Last, part of the significance of the play is that it is "making a show," an appearance for players or audience in which participants are in effect actors.

What is remarkable about Huizinga's account is less his analysis of play than the range of social and cultural activities he traces to play: including rites, sacred performances, contests, art, poetry, religious sacrifice, riddle-solving, social costuming, and fashion. He argues that even legal trials and war evolved as ritual contests mirroring an agonistic conception of truth and divine favor. The heroic virtues are play virtues: honor, bravery, glory. When one adds to this list the representations of such activities and virtues in art, music, oral narration, poetry, and history, then Huizinga's remarkable claim for the importance of play becomes plausible: "Culture arises in the form of play" (Huizinga 1980: 46). What he really wants to say is that culture *is* play, except it becomes apparent that culture and civilization are capable of losing their play-element, which for Huizinga means that they have lost their true nature and function. He writes that "as a civilization becomes more complex, more variegated and more overladen, and as the technique of production and social life itself become more finely organized, the old cultural soil is gradually smothered under a rank layer of ideas, systems of thought and knowledge . . . which have all lost touch with play" (Huizinga 1980: 75).

Huizinga argues that today we live in a decadent "age of seriousness," of work, of time devoted to production, social aspiration, education, and knowledge of "reality." The belief in progress is the antithesis of play. Starting with the French Revolution, "Culture ceased to be 'played.' Outward forms were no longer intended to give the appearance, the fiction, if you like, of a higher, ideal mode of life" (Huizinga 1980: 192). Leveling and democratization destroyed costume. Today the "systematization and regimentation" of contest has even invaded sport itself; we have a professionalization of sport, "sport among those for whom it is no longer play." Whereas, he insists, "Real civilization cannot exist in the absence of a certain play-element . . . [the] limitation and mastery of the self, the ability not to confuse its own tendencies with the ultimate and highest goal, but to understand that it is enclosed within certain bounds freely accepted" (Huizinga 1980: 211). Huizinga does not falter before the logical conclusion. Plato's *Laws,* the Book of Proverbs, Luther ("All creatures are God's masks and mummeries"), and the Hindu concept of divine *lila* (play) all describe the world as the play of God, "outside of morals, neither good or bad." It is the deepest wisdom to conclude that "all is play" (Huizinga 1980: 212).

Ortega y Gasset: Finding Game

There is a special meaning of "game," which in English goes back a thousand years, that deserves mention. In his fascinating essay "Meditations on Hunting" (1942), Jose Ortega y Gasset argues for hunting's unique place in human psychic history. The premier occupation of segmentary man, arguably the first occupation and skill, and perhaps the first subject of human art (as in the cave paintings of Lascaux), was elevated into sport by the privileged landowners of the agrarian period. Hunting became the premier peacetime demonstration of valor, strength, and endurance and came to be considered legitimate training for aristocratic and royal sons and one of the major leisure activities practiced by the wellborn (along with gambling, racing, physical contests, dancing, and conversation). It was envied by those below; one of the first acts that (successful) modern revolutionaries committed against the aristocracy was to tear down their fences to open game preserves.

For Ortega, "sport" hunting is for humans a reentry into the zoological order, a return to the natural regulation of species. It is thus "an imitation of the animal" (Ortega 1972: 124). This imitation rests on artificial conditions in which man freely renounces some of his technical superiority to try to "take possession" of an animal with whom man has a specific "venatic" relationship. Thus "the fisherman who poisons the mountain brook to annihilate . . . the trout swimming in it . . . ceases to be a hunter" (Ortega 1972: 45). The animal is allowed its "wiles," principally evasive ability. It is most definitely not appropriated, as by Agraria, in the form of "livestock," species under human control. It is the prey who stimulates the hunt: "The only adequate response to a being that lives obsessed with avoiding capture is to try to catch it" (Ortega 1972: 120). Each shot is then a "risk," since it is likely to reveal the hunter and spoil future chances. Ortega regards the hunting relationship as profound. It is an intimate, ritual handling of death, the construction of a situation in which life is at stake, in which humans re-experience their ambiguous location in the animal order. The ambivalence is reflected in the moment of the kill, where, he claims, "Every good hunter is uneasy in the depths of his conscience when faced with the death he is about to inflict on the enchanting animal" (Ortega 1972: 88). Hunting then poses a rather remarkable example of *an artificial return to the natural,* a re-positioning of the human player in a sort of contest with an animal, a relation that is reciprocal but not between equals, a return to predation through the player's acceptance of limits on the use of power.

Winnicott: Playing Reality

British psychiatrist D. W. Winnicott formed a powerful account of the role of cultural artifacts in human development and their relation to play. In the essay "Transitional Objects and Transitional Phenomena" (1951), he argues for the necessity of "transitional objects" in early childhood, typically the beloved blanket or cuddly toy (Winnicott 1999). This play-object is the first "not-me possession," but it represents far more—indeed, it is the first representation, the first symbol. It stands for a novel zone of experience, of which the child cannot rightly be asked whether it is created or discovered, subjective or objective, *just* a projection of its feelings or *just* a blanket. Its psychic role in allowing separation from the primary parent rests precisely on its being understood neither as an erotically charged adjunct to the primary parent's body, nor as an uncathected object of indifference; it must occupy an intermediate zone of experience. Put another way, what makes separation possible is that we never do separate, not fundamentally, for the emerging zone of separation must be immediately filled with something that is not-mother-but-not-indifferent-either. That filling does not disappear in maturation, but is "diffused" across the whole domain where meaningful living takes place. Winnicott argues that domain is *culture*. As he says in a 1967 essay, among adults it is culture that fills the role of transitional object as the dimension of life which is neither internal nor external, subjective nor objective (Winnicott 1999). This "intermediate zone" turns out to be for Winnicott the center of existence, "the place where we live." Without it the world becomes divided into an unstable subjectivity that projects desire and fantasy and a value-less material reality whose only valence would be as the constraint on, or negation of, desire and fantasy. It is telling that the exploration of this topic is so deep that it compels Winnicott to put himself and his profession into the analysis.

> You may cure your patient and not know what it is that makes him or her go on living. . . . Psychotic patients who are all the time hovering between living and not living force us to look at this problem, one that belongs . . . to all human beings. I am claiming that these same phenomena . . . appear in . . . cultural experiences. It is these cultural experiences that provide the continuity in the human race that transcends personal existence. (Winnicott 1999: 117–18)

Winnicott's notion of transitional objects is rooted in an earlier argument of his that the child's capacity to be alone emerges through the experience of "being alone in the presence of someone else," that is, the experience of being within sight and sound of, say, a parent, but without having to encounter, attend to, or deal with the present other (Winnicott 1965). The presence of the parent not only secures the area, preventing anxiety, but enables the child to learn the possibility of being with another without effort or the fulfillment of demands. It is this meaning that is carried by the transitional object. It becomes a "symbol of union" with the primary parent through the process of the parent going away long enough to provoke anxiety but returning before the anxiety becomes traumatic (that is to say, before it generates a felt break in personal continuity), thereby establishing a zone of supra-instinctual enjoyment.

Play and the play-object for Winnicott are then an area of concentration or interest, into which objects from external reality are drawn for inter-action under rules that are of the child's free creation or adoption, in which there is active and skilled manipulation of these objects in service of a con-structed theme or meaning made possible by trust or security provided by a parent or similar figure. This realm is precarious, threatened by erotogenic excitement, meaning that intense feelings can swamp the experimental "transitional" zone. Its unique position makes the division of other things into subjective and objective, inner and outer, possible, opening the way for noninstinctual valuation—that things may mean without directly serv-ing instinctual demands—and hence the very perception of undesired real-ity. Winnicott writes, "The transitional phenomena are allowable to the infant because of the parents' intuitive recognition of the strain inherent in objective perception," the strain of representing and interacting with what is recalcitrant to fantasy and desire (Winnicott 1999: 15–16). The transitional object is then a symbol standing for union-in-disunion, the possibility of a world neither frustrating nor orgiastic, neither dead nor effortlessly control-lable. It anchors a region where the self *makes things that matter.* It is, Win-nicott claims, the source of the *feeling of living,* "what life itself is about."

Bateson: "This Is Play"

In a 1955 essay Gregory Bateson made the remarkable claim that commu-nicative play presents an instructive logical paradox, itself the subject of much debate in early twentieth-century logic (Bateson 2000). Engaging in play with another requires a "metacommunication," itself internal to the play context, which must then be logically paradoxical. The joust, for example, must proceed in a situation guided by the metacommunication "This is play." To take a nonhuman example, the apparent bite one playing dog gives another must, in Bateson's terms, denote a real bite but in such a way that it does *not* denote *what a real bite denotes,* namely, hostility. This is a version of the ancient Paradox of the Liar, which arises whenever we try to interpret statements like "I am lying." If the statement is true, it means that the speaker is telling a falsehood, hence his statement must be false. If the statement is false, then what the speaker says is not a lie and must be true. Bertrand Russell's famous analysis of this problem considered the set of all sets that do not contain themselves. Such a set must but also must *not* contain itself. This problem caused Frege, the godfather of modern logic, to doubt the adequacy of his own logical system and led Russell to formulate his "theory of types" in an effort at solution (Kneale and Kneale 1962: 656).

Bateson is suggesting that the mundane phenomenon of play, as well as drama, ritual, and art, are real-world expressions of this logical problem. In order to play with others some prospective participant must signal that "the following act is not to be taken seriously." (In the case of art we may think of Michel Duchamps's famous painting of a pipe, titled "*Ce n'est pas un pipe*," "This is not a pipe.") Bateson concludes, not that these activities are devoid of sense, but that they presuppose a complex logic of communication. In a stream of behavior an agent indicates that the behavior now arising, or about to arise, is not to be taken in its "normal" way. This can only arise once the participants achieve the capacity to recognize their signals *as* signals and thus the ability to meta-communicate, to signal *that* one's signals ought to be understood in a certain way. For Bateson the logical paradox is irremediable and productive; it marks the development of a crucial human capacity. Human communication as we understand it is impossible without the ability to create such paradoxes.

Callois: Playing the Self

Having reviewed Huizinga's book, the French philosopher and anthropologist Roger Callois responded with his own account of play in *Les jeux et les hommes* (translated as *Man, Play and Games*). Callois distinguishes four types of games, separable into two pairs: *agon,* or contests, and *alea,* or games of chance; *mimesis,* or imitation, and *ilinx,* vertigo or ecstasy. *Agon* is a structured rivalry in which members desire to win on the basis of merit. *Alea* or games of chance involve no merit (except, we might say, the courage to risk). Such games are passive in the sense that one can only wait for fate to decide the outcome. *Mimesis* is the loss of self in another identity. *Ilinx,* as in carnival rides and amusement parks, is the creation of vertiginous, ecstatic states. *Mimesis* and *ilinx* are more primitive and predominate in segmentary

societies, whereas *agon* and *alea* remain prominent in what he calls civilization, presumably agroliterate, citified societies. Indeed, "the transition to
civilization as such implies the gradual elimination of the primacy of *ilinx*
and mimicry in combination, and the substitution and predominance of
the *agon-alea* pairing of competition and chance" (Callois 2001: 97). All four
vary in the degree to which they tend toward *paidia*, uncontrolled fantasy
or "tumult," on one hand, or *ludus*, skill-employing play in which problems
are created for the sake of solving them, on the other.

Callois implies that play and games form the root metaphors of a variety of modern social institutions. Capitalism is *agon*. Our "serious" social
life is competition. We imagine, or want to make the competition, like a
contest, hence purely fair and equal, purely meretricious. But this results in
a great avocational need for *alea*, for games of chance, where merit can be
overcome, where anyone can win at any moment. We also create "disguised"
games of chance, forms of competition in which luck is decisive but a
veneer of merit is added (as in many television game shows). Our notion
of justice is tied up with *agon* and *alea*. They likewise reinforce identity in
a context of the negotiation of social status. On the other hand, mimicry
and vertigo permit the abandonment of identity. Callois invokes the Nietz-
schean distinction between the Apollonian and the Dionysian, the order-
giving and order-breaking spirits of archaic Greek culture, relating them to
agon-alea and *ilinx-mimesis*, respectively. Like Nietzsche, who connected
the Apollonian and Dionysian to dreaming and intoxication, Callois argues
that neither of the play pairs is realistic; each avoids reality, one by the construction of the pleasing illusion of a self and the other by the disintegration, hence dedifferentiation, of self and other. Callois suggests that the
movement from segmentary to civilized life entails the movement from the
desired loss of self in intoxication, or the Dionysian element of *ilinx* and
mimesis, to the dreamlike Apollonian constructions of *agon* and *alea*.

Callois makes an important point of what he calls the absolute status of
games. The equality of the players is established despite their unequal positions outside the game. The rules are absolute because they are arbitrary,
that is, have no meaning outside the game. The response to the child or
newcomer who asks why there is such a rule is a frustrated "Because that's
the way we play!" The rules cannot be derived from outside. Play and game
thereby embody *fictive necessity*, made-up obligation. Rather than "nonserious," Callois calls them "nonproductive," meaning they do not produce what
is needed outside the play or game: in play "property is exchanged," he

writes, "but no goods are produced." Hence—and this is Callois's real improvement over a strain of thought about play from Schiller to Huizinga—rather than being nonserious, play and games are *nonhistorical*. The results of the preceding game are not retained, there is no progress between games. Each new game starts at zero. Play and game are nonefficacious reenactments of productive and serious activities, and thereby possess "the permanence of the insignificant" (Callois 2001: 81). For this reason Callois resists the direct connection of play and culture. While the "spirit" of play is essential to culture, "games and toys are historically the residues of culture," cultural activities whose "serious" meaning has been lost or truncated, as when war is mimicked in peacetime by the tournament. (This judgment, I would argue, is due to his inadequate definition of culture. War is clearly a social activity, but not particularly cultural, however much it has cultural ornamentation and stimulates cultural motifs, hence the tournament is not an inefficacious "playful" residue of war, but a cultural activity. Nevertheless, Callois is right that culture is not play *simpliciter,* as we shall see.)

Gadamer: The Art of Play

More than any other twentieth-century philosopher, with the possible exception of Ernst Cassirer, Hans Georg-Gadamer embedded human cognition in culture. In his *Wahrheit und Methode (Truth and Method),* all understanding is a matter of dialogue between interpreter and interpreted, hence the cultural traditions of each. This is not the place to exposit or evaluate Gadamer's hermeneutics; we shall focus only on his notion of play and what it signifies within his account.

Gadamer emphasizes the "primacy of the play over the consciousness of the player" (Gadamer 1994: 104). The play requires a bounded space, a playing "field," a "closed world." The game "masters" the players in the sense that roles taken on by players can be utterly false. Art begins in and culminates such play, for play presents the primary aesthetic process of "transformation into form" *(Gebilde).* The drama, for example, is the repetition of origin whereby the unfulfilled possibilities of real situations are actualized, revealing their truth in a "repetition that brings the essence forth."

All this is presented in a section of Gadamer's book titled "Play as the clue to ontological explanation [of the work of art]." It introduces the notion of "fusion" of present and past events, later to be articulated as Gadamer's central concept. The dramatic or historiographical repetition of a past event actualizes a fusion of the performance and the original, both in drama and ritual; the original, as a "temporal" entity, exists only by *repeating itself as different* (Gadamer 1994: 123). His notion of *Wirkungsgeschichte* or "effective history," historically effected/effecting consciousness, is that all historical research is already affected by the object which it investigates, by a "pre-understanding" that is partly the result of that very object as it has been understood through the tradition. Hence, knowledge of the object can never be "objective" or "complete." But how then do we know the past? It is Gadamer's achievement to suggest that our involvement with the past, our being affected by it, being part of it, hence lacking "distance" from it, far from being an obstacle to knowledge is *the necessary condition for understanding* the past. True understanding occurs when the "horizons" of the historian and the historical document "fuse" *(Horizonsverschmelzung),* when "we regain the concepts of a historical past in such a way that they also include our own comprehension of them" (Gadamer 1994: 374). We reconstruct the question to which the historical artifact or text or event is an answer by making it for ourselves a "real" question. Following Plato, all our knowledge of past cultural artifacts or texts is a dialogue with the artifacts, not an observation of them. We know them when we "make [them] our own."

From Play to Culture to Reality

All this may sound mildly interesting. Certainly many of the phenomena we have discussed as play are parts of culture, and perhaps play informs culture as a whole. But what can this tell us about any supposed role of culture in our understanding of *reality?* If a modern, might we say, "post-cultural" understanding of reality has cast a skeptical eye on culture as pleasing illusion, how much further removed from the real is play?

In drawing this connection we may start in what may seem an odd place, the feeling of *un*reality. One version of that feeling is nicely described in Evelyn Waugh's *Brideshead Revisited,* when the young Charles Ryder is leaving the scene of his youthful romantic adventures.

> But as I drove away and turned back in the car to take what promised to be my last view of the house, I felt that I was leaving part of myself behind, and that wherever I went afterwards I should feel

the lack of it, and search for it hopelessly, as ghosts are said to do, frequenting the spots where they buried material treasures without which they cannot pay their way to the nether world. . . . I had come to the surface, into the light of common day and the fresh sea-air, after long captivity in the sunless coral palaces and waving forests of the ocean bed. I had left behind my—what? Youth? Adolescence? Romance? . . . "I have left behind illusion," I said to myself. "Henceforth I live in a world of three dimensions—with the aid of my five senses." I have since learned that there is no such world. (Waugh 1964: 190–91)

There is a deep truth here in the final sentence's recognition that in a real experiential sense reality can evaporate. That is, among the issues of Charles Ryder's life, loves, and accomplishments, or lack thereof, there remains a crucial underdetermination of decision by fact, a feeling that the tangible, stable, and mundane could, on the breath of a whim, be turned upside down, something that Milan Kundera called the unbearable lightness of being (Kundera 1984b). This is one of the senses in which *reality can seem unreal.* For the "real" has several meanings, and each one of them can only be encountered given a certain condition of the experiencer. A functional sensorium is not enough. Nor is desire, will, or the urge to survive. Nor is even objectivity, by which I mean a socially understood system of lawfully interacting objects. Something more is required. Not that feelings of unreality are, so to speak, bad, something to be gotten rid of, defended against. They may be, as in the Waugh passage, highly important and illuminating experiences. But one imagines they can only be so if the subject's general experience is one of reality, if the unreal is a passing, and not a normative, phenomenon. At any rate, my point is that the *sense* of reality is complexly funded. Simply put, reality is an acquired taste.

Here Charles Peirce's phenomenological categories provide a useful template for describing how "real" and "reality" function in human experience. One aspect of experienced reality is its sheer phenomenal quality, the redness of the red dress, the bite of the wind, which Peirce called "Firstness" (Peirce 1955: 75ff.). In a second sense the real is difference, opposition, the resistance of physical bodies in space, the "Secondness" that Peirce nicely exemplified by the feeling of a shoulder against a door. Third, reality is intelligible and represent-able order, the primary sense of "objectivity" confirmed by social agreement and ultimately science, which Peirce called "Thirdness" (he does not imply that *all* is orderly). Peirce's categories are offered here not as metaphysically right or complete, although I do suspect the three are necessary, that experience lacking felt quality, spatial resistance, or ordered intelligibility would indeed feel "unreal." Expanding Peirce's description, whatever else we are, we each inhabit reality as an intentional consciousness with a functional sensorium revealing phenomena, as a physical object among other physical objects, as an animal driven by needs to respond to environmental stimulus patterns, and as an intelligent, fully socialized observer, and tester, of objective regularities. I suggest that another mode of encountering the world seems a necessary part of our experiential repertoire. We also inhabit reality as *agents* who act with *understanding* in a world containing *ends in themselves.* This means not that *all* reals are ends in themselves, but that *some* must be, and the world in general is experienced as structured by the significance rooted in these ends. The role of the human experiencer which encounters reals in this way is agency. My point will be that culture provides the conditions necessary for experiencing the world in this way. That is, culture provides conditions necessary for perceiving, negotiating, and understanding reality *as an agent does.* There are three such conditions provided by culture: a normative environment, framing, and drama.

The Normative Environment

There is an affective and normative dimension to our experience and perception of real things. "Real" is a normative and affective term as well as a descriptive one. Real means *not merely apparent,* not merely phenomenal. It means salient, resistant, intelligible, available for contemplation and/or manipulation and/or enjoyment and/or suffering. It is a term, if you will, of *respect,* of recognition. The recognition of the reality of a thing is a recognition of its importance, its being something that must be dealt with, not wished away. As noted, Dewey rightly argued against a reified stimulus-response model of human behavior that stimuli are constructed, or prepared, by motor activity, so that sensation–action is a circuit. Merleau–Ponty likewise saw the role of tactility and the "flesh," the bodily surface, as a "subject-object," a spatial thing that feels by acting (Merleau-Ponty 1968). I would add *affectivity* to this circuit. Sensation and action require as well affect, what Heidegger called state of mind *(Befindlichkeit)* or feeling. Reality is as much as an achievement of affectivity as of perception and motor activity.

We experience the affective and normative environment in our status as *agents*. In a broad sense, agency is the status of a human being as a comprehending actor in the world, a particular being in a process we call living, whose temporal sojourn is in some sense a unit, and whose surround is not only tolerably regular or intelligible, but structured by *significance*. Agents are personal, the peculiar owners of their experiences and history. They are selves. Agency is not *all* about acting or doing, but the other modes of the agent's appropriation of the world—its undergoing or experiencing, its physical subsistence, its arranging or constructing, and its cognition of the world—are within the perspective of agency processed *through* a history of and potentiality for action. It is as agent that I am, in Buchler's terms, "born in a state of natural debt, being antecedently committed to the execution or the furtherance of acts that will largely determine [my] existence" (Buchler 1955: 3). Likewise, the world for agency is a domain whose intelligibility, inertial force or resistance, and qualities are organized around meaningful and valuable beings, *beings that are ends,* valued in themselves and not merely as objects of, or means toward satisfying, desire or need. It not the case that all objects and events must be ends or that ends must be devoid of instrumental value or desired consequences, but some components of the world must be ends to provide its significant structure. This notion of the world as a structure of significance bears the echoes of Heidegger's concept of *Weltlichkeit* (world-hood), Arendt's world of artifacts, Johannes von Uexküll's *Umwelt,* or surrounding environment, and J. J. Gibson's conception of the "affordances" of things (Heidegger 1962; Arendt 1958; Gibson 1979; von Uexküll 1926).

If "subject" means consciousness, or more generally, *us,* and objectivity is what consciousness perceives outside itself as uncontrollable by thought, then there is something about culture which falls between, which *spans* the subjective and the objective. Pure phenomena can of course be salient and compelling; I do not presume they are a desultory, passing array of qualia. But clearly the infant brings something to experience besides sensory capacity. It brings *needs,* or if you will, *will.* As Hans Jonas argued in *The Phenomenon of Life,* wherever there is life, there is metabolism, and metabolism is the first arising of autonomy, the homeostatic process by which an entity maintains its existence as a particular identity throughout an exchange of materials with environment (Jonas 1966). As soon as there is metabolism, things start to matter in an experiential sense, to be relevant to the maintenance of the organism. This is the *beginning* of agency, freedom, identity, and affectivity; an entity does something, namely, modifies self and environment to remain in existence as itself, and so remaining is a crucial issue, hence whatever impacts that likelihood matters. It is also correlated with a more complex form of objectivity. Desire or will, as embodied in action, discovers obstacles that must be negotiated, troubles that have to be faced. One might say, life brings teleology into the world.

But as Winnicott argues, need-satisfaction does not grant the reality of the need-satisfying object. While it prepares the experience of objectivity by focusing attention, it undermines the independence of the object. For the infant, the fact that when it cries the "object" magically appears—"I want food and, poof, she's there"—indicates the ontological continuity of the object with its own needs and fantasies—"She is part of me." As long as the object obtains in a zone of experience flooded by desire, it is not real in the sense of an independent object. There must evolve a zone of mild, moderate or sublimated interest. Psychodynamic theory traditionally regarded frustration, and hence separation from the primary parent, as the mechanism of realistic disappointment. "Reality" would thus be the name for what *withholds*. Winnicott's alternative is that such withholding could not become the kind of reality with which mature agency could interact; given the psychic environment described, it would be a "dead" reality, hence in a very important sense *not* real. Play is the first working-out of the experience of things independent from yet affectively related to the agent. Nobody plays without emotion; if they do, they're not playing. Enjoyment, fascination, pleasure, delight, anger, fear, envy, and so forth, must be present in play. It is in play that we work through the fact that thoughts can lead to events, but only via the mediation of muscular movement, that reals can be *made* by us, hence that "reality" is a phase or modality of being into which our thoughts and feelings can enter and achieve form, that something can be outside the magical continuity with self and yet at the same time be affectively worthy, real in the sense of deserving the agent's respect. *Play is the delimited environment for experiments in emerging agency in relation to meaningful reals independent of the subject.*

It arises, I suggest, out of *repetition*. At first this repetition is probably introduced by others in the simplest forms of play, like moving an object, hiding and revealing a face, repeating a song. Later the child will manipulate the repetition and reappearance itself, and this will be the first self-produced meaning. Repetition creates the fundamental experiential form of intelligibility: the fulfillment of anticipation. Something in the world stimulates anticipation, and then the world matches this anticipation, giving the experience of satisfaction, as the return to the tonic chord in music will later, hence a primitive kind of control—the self is able to do something about the world, and the world confirms the validity of its doing, even though this will be interpreted initially as magical omnipotence. Eventually the experience of the outside as genuinely outside *yet* in tune with the inside, as matching the inchoate self's vitality, emerges as repetition ceases to be the magical continuation of the self, becoming instead a *dialogue* with the world. The imitation of series of actions comes to have the same satisfaction, the fulfillment of anticipation, only now in the register of the creation of meaning by the "agent," the child. *Mimesis,* imitation, hence what we call representation, has its root here. Things are real in so far as they are actually or potentially repetitive.

As the child matures, the role played by the received and selected objects of play come to be taken by objects that are made, transformed by imaginative handling and construction. The made objects, which become for Hanna Arendt the world of "work," provide the primary instance of objective ends, things that matter, and matter not merely in their function as satisfying needs, nor as means to such satisfaction, but as *ends in themselves.* This is particularly important, as Winnicott argued. For the spaciotemporal object that is in some significant sense made becomes the prime instance of value-things, or to use a tired terminology, a subject-object. It is that of which Winnicott says that we cannot ask whether it is subjective or objective, a fancy of the mind or a material object whose "meaning" is extrinsic to it, without undermining the special "transitional" role it plays in experience.

Now, my argument may seem to ignore an obvious alternative to play and culture as precondition for a fully viable sense of reality. As several branches of philosophy have learned in recent decades, knowledge or intelligibility of the world is based in some crucial sense in intersubjectivity. Simply put, objectivity is social: the individual's perception of things can only be understood as objective through the confirmation, testing, and disconfirmation that social communication brings. As Mead put it, to have an objective view of the world is to view it from the perspective of the "generalized other," the perspective of an open-ended community. Thus one might say against my current claim, "Look, we've known for most of a century that, yes, society, social communication, or social action is necessary to the experience and/or understanding of reality. Pragmatism, ordinary language philosophy, hermeneutics, etc., have long since held this. And you yourself have cited this work! So why make the extravagant claim that culture, not just society, is crucial to the sense of the real?"

I am arguing that beyond the admittedly social constitution of reality for us, culture, as it supervenes on society, *adds* something to our objective perception that social interaction devoid of culture cannot. It adds to the socialized perception and intelligibility of things the organization of those things around ends in themselves, that is, around things understood as valuable *not* merely because they serve organismic or social purpose. The successfully socialized human of course has the capacity to test its experience in terms of the perspective of others, and picks out of its environment objects and events that speak to its socialized needs. But it can also cherish objects, gaze at the beauty and profundity of natural things and events, revere and wonder at things. When things are valued not for their role as need-satisfiers, tools, or markers of social approbation, but as ends, culture is at work. Culture thus provides *normative objectivity over time;* what is and has been valid in itself. It is the school of real, objective value. It provides the ontological basis of social norms. Without a cultural ontology, a cultural description of existing things that are ends, there would be no "worldview," no understanding of a suprasocial world, that would justify social rules of propriety and intelligibility. In effect, without the cultural ascription of value to things, societies would have to accept the *truth of conventionalism,* that their norms are humanly constructed, unreflective of the world beyond human agreement.

Now, as suggested in the preceding chapter, postmodern society has eviscerated the role of cultural ontologies. It is true that our era, as noted, eschews most of the ontologies of gods and spirits, leaving for its "official" ontology science, whose shifting and unperceivable metaphysics is uniquely unsuited to a social role. That is indeed an important fact about our society. But this does not mean *all* culturally posited entities are socially anachronistic. We may take one crucial case: *persons.* Scientifically speaking there is no clear line separating what we call humans from nonhumans. Humanity is a matter of degree. We are made of roughly the same stuff as nonhuman creatures, sharing with them the vast majority of our DNA. Ethology continues to shave away previously unquestioned human uniqueness, such as language, whose use by gifted primates and dolphins under experimenters' tutelage keeps advancing. The modeling of human thought by digital and analogue devices shaves from the opposite side. Most of all, what we regard as persons today is one of a large number of hominid species that have populated the Earth in the past, at various levels of sophistication (that is to say, similarity to us). Would a thawed-out Neanderthal be allowed to vote in the next presidential election? What about *Homo erectus?* But despite the continuum of current humans and other species, virtually all our social and normative life depends on positing a discontinuity, a strict line between the human and the nonhuman which must appear arbitrary from a scientific perspective (a line even scientists must respect when deciding whom to admit to their universities). This line is, as Elizabeth Baeten puts it, mythical, meaning not a traditional belief known to be false by contemporary inquiry, but a normative belief unjustifiable by inquiry that nevertheless *must be presupposed by society, including by that inquiry itself* (Baeten 1996).

Adapting a Heideggerian figure, we may represent the context of experience as a place, a background, a *clearing,* in which everything meaningful, in the sense I have meant, "takes place." Hence we can hazard a further analysis of culture: *culture holds open the clearing.* That is, it holds open the place from which subjective and objective emerge as symbiotically related yet distinct phases of experience, of which, as Winnicott says of the child's experience, the question "Is it created or discovered?" must remain ambiguous. This makes a place for the teleological meaning of human existence, human society, and reality. Its absence is the death of meaning, which occurs either when fact ceases to mean and so ceases to be fact, or when meaning ceases to attach to being and so ceases to be. Culture maintains the context in which the *ends can be real,* and *reals can be ends,* hence the self's feelings are real and the real is felt by the self.

Framing

Culture does this in part by *framing.* Phenomena cannot be experienced or understood as real except through frames, which is to say, appropriated "under a description." In this sense Kant was right, and Cassirer's application of Kantianism to cultural or "symbolic" forms was prescient. The art object, the festival, the sporting event, the legal contest, not to mention perhaps the most crucial case, "plays" or staged dramas, have their frames, dates, boundary lines, courtrooms, and prosceniums. Frames distinguish inside and outside. What do they keep out? All other contexts, but in the present case, primarily work, economic necessity, acquisition and production, brute physical necessity, and history. Frames must cancel many of the cognitive and social rules operative outside; so in the play I am not my usual pauper self, but a king. Those who are social unequals in the outside world are equal under the rules of a sport. This already means the play frame must be constructed, artificial, partitioned. Play requires boundaries that hold off the activities of the world outside.

Of course, all social contexts require frames of some kind. But play frames are particularly opaque, since they must rule out so much. As Callois claimed, "serious" activities progress in the sense of accumulating both products and changes in technique or experience, so are historical. The unique status of play is that in play we can *see the framing,* we are aware of the institution of boundedness. Most of all, play situations are bounded as *ends in themselves.* Play is perfectly circular; it is the epitome of the cyclical notion of time familiar from Mircea Eliade's analysis of segmentary societies (Eliade 1954). If instrumentality in its normal form is ruled out, the rules and vicissitudes must be played for their own sake. Play is thus not only *sui generis:* it is *the sui generis itself.*

This character is inherited by cultural frames. Thus what Huizinga lamented in a modern or postmodern context is an undermining of frames in which the bounded-ness of any social frame is regarded as mere appearance, its "reality" being its place in a universal process of cause-effect, instrumental manipulation, and progress. As Arendt claimed about the modern subordination of all social and political life to economics, modernity promotes a dynamic, processural view of the world in which each item and event is a point of receding intrinsic significance. Something about modern instrumental rationality or functionalization breaks down the cultural frames of social life, spilling out their contents as fungible means toward practical ends. Culture is then the *unframed framing of social contexts with teleological meaning,* meaning irreducible to practical accumulation.

For culture is all about the reality of socially drawn distinctions. G. Spencer Brown begins his provocative logic of distinctions with the stipulation, "Draw a distinction" (Spencer Brown 1994). Well, culture does that. The installation of distinctions, arranged in a system of orders, is the logic of culture. Sneakers are proper in one context, leather shoes in another; what can be said to my wife cannot be said to my neighbor; a religious belief cannot be utilized by a liberal state; during the ceremony before the hunt the buffalo's horns make me a beast, but if I don them tomorrow during supper, my children will laugh at me. Distinctions hold only within contexts, and culture maintains the most important value-laden frames for social contexts. Without framing, no normative distinction can hold up. A world in which all is one cannot have culture in it. In Bateson's language, culture frames. What undermines culture is either the reduction of distinctions to unity, or the reduction of all unities to what Jacques Derrida called *différance* or sheer difference (Derrida 1973). Culture presents the meaningful reality of the distinctions societies draw. Its teleological connections argue for the necessity, validity, and reality of the key frames. If those are illusions, then culture is an illusion.

And we know this because we also have the impulse to destroy all frames and distinctions. That is the Dionysian impulse, which Nietzsche describes in *The Birth of Tragedy,* to destroy the *principium individuationis,* the ego or principle of individuation (Nietzsche 1956). It is not only the self and its distinction from the world that are thereby eliminated, but all distinctions, anything holding apart from anything else, all the frames that make it possible to preserve contextual integrities. The Dionysian impulse says, "No, that's the end! No more subtle rules and distinctions that force reflection and refraction, that diminish by slowing energy. Enough foppery and decoration. Enough of 'each thing is what it is and not another thing,' of 'this is not the time for that.' We shall roar through all portals and windows, all limitations." But Dionysus is outmatched. Unity loses to difference. For the living make, and must make to keep living. Thus does Dionysus become a *moment in* the dialectical development of culture, the destruction of meaning and form takes its place in the history of meaning and form. Philosophical skepticism and nihilism, explosively antistructural forms of art, even violence itself, become part of the narration of contexts whose boundaries they deny. Hume and Nietzsche are studied in courses in modern philosophy, Jackson Pollock hangs in the museum with Rembrandt, De Sade becomes an historical precursor of Genet for students of comparative literature. Culture is thus the *socially shared framing of social contexts,* the making of contextual distinctions that allows the differentiation of value-spheres. In culture these frames are literally made, since they are marked by activities and artifacts. The cultural products "hold up" the frames. Human beings cannot stop understanding by making. That making is our medium, and its name is culture.

Drama

In lamenting the failure to suspend disbelief that he found in contemporary cultural experience, the American historian and social critic Christopher Lasch wrote, "The illusion of reality dissolves, not in a heightened sense of reality as we might expect, but in a remarkable indifference to reality. Our sense of reality appears to rest, curiously enough, on our willingness to be taken in by the staged illusion of reality. . . . [T]he very idea of reality [is] dependent at every point on the distinction between nature and artifice, reality and illusion" (Lasch 1979: 160). I think this is true. More particularly, in our existence as agents our sense of the real is derivative of *narrative*. With Alasdair MacIntyre, Samuel Fleischacker, Michael Oakeshott, Kenneth Burke, and Bernard Lonergan I am suggesting that the characteristic form of intelligibility under which events are understood by cultural beings is narrative. The cultural construction which provides the framed teleological meanings available to human understanding is fundamentally *dramatic*. This drama is the construction of human agents, metaphorically "clothing" reality in an idiom that answers to the needs of those agents. We can live, act, and know in a fully human way only in a world structured by our own making. This construction is not a barrier to or shield from reality. To put it simply, *making is the way we know.*

Narrative is the organization of events into a historical process that proceeds, as Aristotle formulated it, from a beginning, through a middle, to an end, and in which the passage of events occurs at least partly through the acts of agents. It is inherently teleological in that the narrative is drawn so as to depict events in their meaning for the transition to a purposive end (even if the end is tragic). It must both tie events together and set them off from all other events. Narrative is the domain from which a series of fundamental human notions are drawn, like action, agent, role, character, motivation, performance, and history, notions that in turn largely make freedom and agency intelligible, and even serve as models of the possibility of causal explanation. The very distinction of "doing" from "undergoing" seems to require a teleological or dramatic element, just as apparently nondramatic accounts of "events," happenings, or "news" entail the division of processes into bounded episodes characterized by the classical trinity of beginning, middle, and end. As Mark Freeman suggests, "Narratives . . . rather than being the mere fictions they are sometimes assumed to be, might instead be in the service of attaining exactly those forms of truth that are unavailable in the flux of the immediate" (Freeman 1993: 224). Without this, reality becomes phenomena without salience. The *feeling of reality* is gone. Absence of connection to goals undoes the sense by which will is connected to reality. As such, cultural things in the form of narration are *the* model of intelligibility for humans, the form of reality for us being primarily dramatic.

It has been argued that *consciousness itself* is narrative. John Dewey incorporated a narrative theory of consciousness into his naturalistic account of experience.

> Thus the purport of past affairs is present in the momentary cross-sectional idea in a way which is more intimate, direct and pervasive than the way of recall. It is positively and integrally carried in and by the incidents now happening: these incidents are, in the degree of genuine dramatic quality, fulfillment of the meanings constituted by past events. . . . Every case of consciousness is dramatic; drama is an enhancement of the conditions of consciousness. (Dewey 1958: 306)

Remarkably, this conception has been echoed by contemporary cognitive science. Antonio Damasio has argued that the structure of perception is narrative. What he calls "core consciousness," the "pulselike" rudimentary and fleeting stimulations of feeling, is a constant constructive process of "non-verbal story telling," a prelinguistic narrative of "images" or patterns, which is how the organism represents its own changing state to itself (Damasio 1999). This consciousness orders and appropriates the bodily responses to physical influences as events "owned" by a self. Consciousness thus constructs a particular way of interacting with the world, one that enhances perception of those objects whose presence induces feelings by patterning them as being available from a character's perspective.

It is useful to distinguish the narrative structure of experience as the first-person intelligibility of experience from the second-and-third-person telling of a story. The telling becomes the archetypal cultural event of rendering life, experience, and world meaningful and intelligible. It is the experience of meaning/intelligibility made into *art,* whose illocutionary function—what type of act the utterance performs, e.g., a reporting—is cognitive or representative, even if its perlocutionary function—what consequence is accomplished by the utterance, e.g., socialization—is practical. As David Carr points out, the story "gathers" the otherwise lost moments of experience into a meaningful, memorable whole (Carr 1986). Unlike the character of the story, the narrator knows the end, hence the point, of the action of the characters. Events and actions are selected that carry the intimation of the dramatic end in themselves. As Carr explains, this is an ideal of human intelligibility to which real-life agents aspire but can never fulfill. I can carry into my experience the imagined perspective of a future narrator, a temporalized version of Mead's generalized other, through what we could call, leavening Heidegger with Carr, *anticipatory retrospection.* Such is a possible mode of my present experience. We seek this attitude of the storyteller on our own lives because it alone renders life intelligible, that is, understandable as the life, not of an organism or point in a social system or an unconscious dynamism—all of which are legitimate and important truths about me—but the life of an actor, agent, or character.

This does not mean everything cultural has a direct connection to, or itself embodies, dramatic narrative. It means most of the cultural phenomena of a particular society can be understood as grouping about such narratives, like data points around a mathematical line or curve. Neither does it means there is only *one story going on.* Many stories, as MacIntyre suggested, collect about key experiences, icons, and rituals. Arguably we are all like those medieval commentators whose subplots were written into the margins of their inherited scriptural stories. As Peirce said of signs, stories multiply. The story of the founder, like a coral reef, accretes the tales of the others who retell it, and the stories of subsequent leaders, as well as new interpretations of all of these.

Consider a postmodern American poem.

> "There must be some way out of here,"
> said the joker to the thief,
> "There's too much confusion,
> I can't get no relief.
> Businessmen, they drink my wine,
> Plowmen dig my earth.
> None of them along the line know what any of it is worth."

"No reason to get excited,"
the thief, he kindly spoke,
"There are many here among us
who think that life is but a joke.
But you and I, we've been through that,
and this is not our fate.
So let us not talk falsely now, the hour is getting late."

All along the watchtower,
princes kept the view.
While all the women came and went,
barefoot servants too.
Outside in the distance
a wildcat did growl.
Two riders were approaching, the wind began to howl.

(Bob Dylan, *All Along the Watchtower*)

A rather unjovial joker despairs over the lack of appreciation of worth endemic to his instrumental social world, not unlike Job's perception of vanity or MacBeth's lament of life as a tale told by an idiot. But Dylan's thief takes a different view. Offering no justification, he ascribes to fate his own escape from nihilism. Yet he intimates that the joker is not speaking truthfully. And his warning compels: there isn't much time. There are things to be done. What are they? Here, in a remarkably conceptual move, Dylan conjures something so compelling yet generic that it is less a story than the sheer *idea* of story, a story about story-ness, a figure for *narrativity itself*. Something unknown but crucial is about to take place, as if we have been *thrown,* as Heidegger would say, into a Gothic tale at its climax, knowing neither what led us here nor what will happen, a present nestled between suspense in two directions. It brings a shift in our perspective whereby a mystery unfolds, a drama in time, perhaps a wildcat growling in the dark night as, unbeknownst to the castle's inhabitants, riders approach. The oscillation of experience between meaningfulness and absence of meaning, which is at the same time the oscillation between reality and unreality, hangs on the susceptibility of the world to narrative explanation. Only in narrative is the world meaningful for human agents. Our first question, upon discovering ourselves in any new and confusing context, is in sense if not in so many words, "What's the story?"

Now, there are obviously other ways of making the world intelligible. Science is all about intelligibility, but not narrative intelligibility. Even if it must insert beginnings-middles-and-endings into the physical register— for example, the recounting of the origin of things in Steven Weinberg's *The First Three Minutes*—its "stories" hardly compare to the kind of narrative we find in myth, history, or dramatic art. As noted, human beings function and experience in plural registers, for example, as material objects in a physical environment, and not only as dramatic agents. The world can be understood a variety of nondramatic ways, for example, as a single pantheistic substance (in the works of philosophers from Parmenides to Spinoza), as a collection of subatomic particles (in the works of philosophers from Democritus to Bohr), or as a realm of illusion (in the Hindu philosophy of Advaita Vedanta). But one of the modes of human being is agency, the status of a unitary potential actor with sensibility, will, and cognition, who affects and is affected by the world over a limited life span. The world for agency is a field of interaction open to human experience and manipulation, success and failure, where something is always at stake, of which William James wrote, "It *feels* like a fight." It is in our status as agents that culture provides an intelligible world. If culture is illusion, so is agency. Even those metaphysical schemes that appear to deny drama, when employed in life as orientation for conduct and imagination, typically embrace drama; the Buddhist narrative of the heroic Gautama coming to understand that the world of agency is ultimately unreal is itself a drama of the first order.

Conclusion

Culture is the mature, socially generalized domain of the telic organization of reality, populated by practices, narratives, and artifacts that are cathected as ends in themselves, but nevertheless as social, external, objective. It offers repetition or re-presentation of the ends in terms of which the world and society attain intelligible and meaningful order. Culture presents the world as organized about those processes and things which speak to agency, hence affectivity and intelligibility, and the agent as a thing in that world which exists in continuity with that world's nexus of value. Culture is the place of a society's public drama. As such, *culture is the school of meaningful agency,* hence of the real world as it is intelligible to agents. For what we must come to accept is the self as a source and proprietor of a cathected world, a world construed as valuable and meaningful, who is nevertheless a thing within that world. The world is ours, or more precisely, appears only in and through our projection, *and* we are in that world, part of an objective cosmos independent of us. Managing that paradoxical status is the business of culture.

7
WHY THERE IS NO PROBLEM OF CULTURAL RELATIVISM

Relativism is nothing new. Throughout the history of Western philosophy, when we find skepticism, we often find relativism. The most extreme skepticism of the ancient Greek world, created by Pyrrho but best described for us by Sextus Empiricus, was explicitly based in the relativity of perception to the perceiver. Like them, skeptics have often counseled obedience to local social convention, having eschewed any higher or more universal principles. But *cultural* relativism is peculiarly modern. It is only since the eighteenth century that we find thinkers espousing, or fighting, the claim that the validity of acts and utterances is relative to cultures *per se*. Cultural relativism would not exist as a concept but for the intellectual and sociopolitical revolutions of the Enlightenment. The reason is not that the new age brought international exchange and interaction among cultures; there had always been such interaction. Nor is it a novel deflationary Western self-consciousness as merely one among many civilizations; arguably the modern West has never had such a consciousness, or only in very recent bouts of ambiguous revisionism. Rather, it is due to a uniquely modern collision of politics and philosophy and society whereby, for the first time, all seemed inexorably to condition each other.

As we have seen, it is during the simultaneous demise of Western imperialism and philosophical foundationalism in the second half of the twentieth century that Western thought took a further cultural turn. Dewey, the later Wittgenstein, J. L. Austin, Quine, Gadamer, Habermas, and Derrida all made meaning public rather than transcendental or private, hence historically variable, thereby opening the door to relativism. Today few philosophers endorse relativism but many court it. In reaction to this reaction some think that "cultural relativism" is a bogeyman only anachronistic foundationalists could fear. If we give up outmoded hopes of justifying knowledge from the ground up, they say, then relativism loses its power to threaten. Clifford Geertz's "Anti Anti-Relativism" makes just this point (Geertz 1989).

In supporting his "frank ethnocentrism" (Rorty 1991a: 168), which endorses universal rights and rational critique as the culture of the modern West rather than as valid in themselves, Richard Rorty has suggested that Hilary Putnam and other philosophers should cease to conjure up the "relativist menace" (Rorty 1998). For Geertz and Rorty the demise of objectivity is unproblematic. They affect what we could call the Alfred E. Neumann response to relativism: "What, me worry?"

It will turn out that, oddly enough, Geertz and Rorty are right but for the wrong reasons. The point is not to stop worrying and love relativity. Relativism is arguably incoherent, and its abandonment of realism, the belief that the validity or truth of our utterances is determined by their fealty to reality, would indeed have serious social consequences (Cahoone 2002b). The point is rather that a properly conceived realism remains unthreatened by a limited cultural relativity that, while undeniable, is not the last word on human cognition.

Relativity and Rationality

The recent background of the relativism debate arose from a remarkable convergence of four distinct strains of thought between 1958 and 1962. The first, explicitly anthropological, was inspired by the 1958 publication of Peter Winch's *The Idea of a Social Science,* in which he applied the work of the later Wittgenstein to anthropological interpretation. He was quickly criticized by Alasdair MacIntyre and Ernest Gellner, initiating what came to be called the rationality debate. Next, in "Translation and Meaning," a chapter in his *Word and Object* (1960), W.V.O. Quine argued for the "indeterminacy" of translation between natural languages that shared no expressions. Donald Davidson would later make a major contribution to that line of thought, arguing that "conceptual scheme relativism," and with it global skepticism, is nonsensical. Third, also in 1960, the hermeneutics of Hans Georg-Gadamer's *Truth and Method* argued, as we saw, that we must accept the historically embedded nature of cognition as the source of, rather than an obstacle to, truth. Last, in 1962 Thomas Kuhn's *The Structure of Scientific Revolutions* claimed that scientific revolutions involve "paradigm" shifts so deep and far-reaching that the meanings of terms from one paradigm to the next may be "incommensurable," making rational, noncircular evaluation of the paradigms impossible. These formed the background for the philosophical debate over relativism in the late twentieth century. More recently MacIntyre, Samuel Fleischacker, and Lorenzo Simpson have proposed nuanced accounts of the logic of intercultural communication and evaluation that open the way for a realist rejoinder to relativism.

While Winch's 1958 book initiated the debate, his response to its critics is most relevant for us. In the essay "Understanding a Primitive Society" (1964) he criticized anthropologist Evans-Pritchard's study of an East African people, the Azande. Winch argued that while having improved on the Eurocentric approach of Levy-Bruhl, Evans-Pritchard still assumed the irrationality of those Zande beliefs that contradicted modern Western science (Wilson 1970). Winch's critique is straight out of Wittgenstein's *Philosophical Investigations:* norms of rationality have meaning only *within* a practical-social situation of language use. The Azande *are* realistic, consistent, and rational, but according to *their own* distinctive criteria. For "rationality is not just a concept in a language like any other. . . . It is a concept necessary to the existence of any language: to say of a society that it has a language is also to say that it has a concept of rationality" (Wilson 1970: 99). It is also striking to recall Winch's motivation, made clear in his political conclusion: "What Marx called the 'alienation' characteristic of man in industrial society. . . . Our blindness to the point of primitive modes of life is a corollary of the pointlessness of much of our own life" (Wilson 1970: 106).

As we noted in the preceding chapter, the most prominent twentieth-century attempt to promote an account of what could be called cultural knowing, comes from Gadamer's *Truth and Method*. The first task of Gadamer's work was to establish that there exists a tradition, or rather a family of traditions, in Western thought which acknowledges forms of understanding that lie outside "method" or more precisely "scientific method," including *phronēsis* or practical wisdom, the theory of "judgment," taste in aesthetics, and rhetoric in politics. Focusing on aesthetic and historical understanding, Gadamer argued that reason operates *through* history, tradition, and culture, not *outside* them. Rather than make objective knowledge impossible, reason's immanence is our sole means of access to truth. True understanding, for example of a historical artifact, occurs not by doffing one's historical prejudices but by mobilizing them into a dialogue with the other. But this means there is no rational understanding outside or independent of cultural tradition. Consequently, "truth" in interpretation requires, for Gadamer, that dialogue achieve a fusion of the interpretive horizons of interpreter and interpreted.

Quine denied the very possibility of such a fusion. As he famously argued in *Word and Object,* when the native points at a rabbit hopping by and shouts "gavagai!" an observant anthropologist may take *gavagai* to mean "rabbit." But the meaning of *gavagai* is in principle *under*determined by the observable stimulus conditions of the speaker and any ostensive act (pointing). No behavioral situation would allow the anthropologist to distinguishing the native's foreign ontology, whether she meant by *gavagai* "An individuated physical object we call rabbit!" or "The unfolding of a process of rabbit-ing!" or "An instantiation of the ideal form of Rabbit-hood!" Indeed, as a behaviorist who denies that meanings are mental entities, Quine claims that there is no uniquely right translation, since *there is no fact of the matter* that could decide which is right, no hidden object in the native's mind for the anthropologist to be right or wrong about. Quine extends the case to a general conclusion: "To the same degree that the radical translation of sentences is under-determined by the totality of dispositions to verbal behavior, our own theories and beliefs in general are underdetermined by the totality of possible sensory evidence time without end" (Quine 1960: 78). He thus endorses what he elsewhere calls ontological relativity, the underdetermination of our own ontological schemes by observations between which evidence can never decide (Quine 1969).

The most important attack on the very problem of relativism in post–World War II Western philosophy arrived as an extension of Quine's view in Donald Davidson's "On the Very Idea of a Conceptual Scheme" (Davidson 1984). In a criticism of the global relativism of the linguist Benjamin Whorf, Davidson denied that relativism of a robust sort can make any sense at all. He rests his argument on the recognition that a relativism of *meaning,* which would be inevitable for a global cognitive relativism, would undermine the relativism of *validity.* If the meanings of statements were culturally relative in a strong sense, then we could not discover that two cultures made contrary statements, since one culture's translation of another culture's claims would be "deprived of things to go wrong about." We can never find enough evidence to assert a deep relativism of meaning; the translation of another culture's claims *must* employ the principle of "charity," by which the translator assumes a sizable background agreement of beliefs in order to translate any claim in question. Without the assumption of commonality we cannot even begin to interpret their statements. Elsewhere Davidson presses this argument further. Just as we can never find evidence necessary to justify statements like, "That culture over there shares none of our beliefs," we can make no sense of the claimed possibility that the preponderance of our system of beliefs could be false, that we might be wrong about everything. Thus "most of our beliefs must be true" (Davidson 1986: 314).

Relativism and Culture

With the historical resources now developed we can now turn to our systematic task. Relativism, if it is to mean something philosophical and troubling, hence worth discussing, must claim that the judgments we take to be valid or true are so because of their relation to traits of judges or judgments, rather than traits of what is judged. Of course, even realists admit that the traits of judgments, theories, and languages matter, but deny that they are decisive. As such, relativism is a form of epistemological antirealism, denying that what is judged, as something independent of the judgment, determines the validity of the judgment. Note that in what follows I will be solely concerned with epistemic relativism, relativism about the validity of knowledge-claims. In particular, nothing said here implies that moral norms must all be universal; there may well be such thing as "moral relativity" (Wong 1984). Also, I will not treat "objective relativism," the metaphysical claim that real things are constituted by their manifold roles in diverse contexts. Last, nothing herein specifically rebuts more technical forms of relativism, like Joseph Margolis's relativistic attack on bivalence — although I would reject such approaches for other reasons (Margolis 2000; Cahoone 2002c).

What then does "cultural" add to "relativism"? Presumably it makes cultures the things to which the validity of judgment is relative. So if culture is a society's network of practices, artifacts, and representations, and the interpretive patterns embedded in them, cultural relativism must imply that cognition of reality is social, mediated through and dependent on semiotic structures like language, gesture, and art, *and* that those social-semiotic structures are particular and historical, different systems being inherited by different human societies.

Now there are some versions of cultural relativism we can disqualify with dispatch. First are any global hence self-undermining relativisms, such as Davidson analyzed, relativisms which say, "There are cultures so different from ours that we don't agree on anything," "Cultures are incommensurable," and so on. As David Wong has pointed out more recently, such claims actually undercut the relativist's ability to problematize Western judgments of cultural superiority, for that ability requires the critic to *understand* the subordinated culture and sympathize with its validity. The interesting forms of relativism presume a significant degree of cross-cultural understanding (Wong 1989). Second, and related, is what Bernard Williams calls vulgar relativism (Williams 1981: 142). This is a moral position with which we are all familiar. It holds that any culture's attempt to judge another, or to demand another culture's conformity with its own judgments, is cognitively unsupportable and/or morally wrong. Upon reflection we can see that this position in fact *violates* relativism. It asserts a universal morality of noninterference or toleration. In fact, it is just a universal "democratic" or "liberal" or "rights-based" morality, albeit one whose sole injunction is against interference in the self-determination of each cultural unit. A truly relativistic notion of freedom, absent any constraining universal rules, would have to say that whether a culture is morally justified in imposing its rules on others is *itself* relative to that culture. If one culture thinks cultural imperialism is fine, then it *is* fine, *for* that culture. Vulgar relativism is a universalist morality that mistakes itself as relativism. Last, there is a lesson for cognitive relativism in the most common argument against *moral* relativism. That argument is a combination punch, a *reductio ad absurdum* argument followed by a charge of inconsistency, namely, that those who assert relativism will eventually find themselves condemning evil (such as the Holocaust) nonrelativistically. In effect this is to argue that there are no relativists in foxholes. But the smart relativist will soon discover that the best tactical response to this *reductio* is to adopt the passive voice, not to *say* " 'True' means 'true-in-a-perspective' " but merely to undermine any nonrelativist assertion. It is when following this tactic that relativists like Richard Rorty are most successful. I have argued that they are not in fact successful, but their reticence certainly restricts their liability to charges of self-reflexive inconsistency (Cahoone 2002b). We cannot assume a silent relativist herein, but the principle holds that the less the relativist says, the better.

Thus, a genuine, consistent, and plausible relativism must be a third-person view of the limits, and true meaning, of judgmental validity. By itself it has no unmediated moral implications. For the intercultural communicator can always respond, "Yes, our principles, which assert universal validity, are valid only with respect to themselves (hence ourselves). But, we are committed to them, and there being no contravening universally valid principles, we will act on them, even in our relations with and judgments of other cultures." As stated, the recursive use of relativism by a speaker need not derail any assertion or action based on his or her cultural principles. At this point the nonvulgar job of the relativist is done, and she must retire to her study, allowing the intercultural dialogue to unfold as it will; any further intervention is vulgar, that is, the effect of a nonrelativist, universal standard of noninterference. This is a bit like the existentialist "ethics" of authenticity: observing an attempted murder, the existentialist can admonish the agent to give up bad faith and sociocultural programming, to recognize fully his absolute freedom and total responsibility, and the true meaning, in the light of finitude, of his reasons for this act. If the prospective murderer, now fully conscious of the weight of his actions, gets back to the business of slaughter, the existentialist can only say, "Well, I tried . . ." In this sense the only effect of relativism is to modify the type of validity claimed by the agent, not to deny that validity. Trying to be more definitive and effectual leads to trouble for the relativist.

So, in what follows, let us assume a relatively powerful, troublesome yet not obviously incompetent cultural relativism that will avoid the Davidsonian and Williamsian traps and make no extravagant positive claims. To avoid cumbersome locutions I will generally refer to judgments or beliefs normed by truth as the things whose relativity must be determined, meaning these to represent as well cognitions, perspectives, theories, and even practices (where the validity of the last hangs on the truth of the beliefs they presuppose). My approach will be double-jointed, to unpack the "problem" of cultural relativism and in the process to examine what a robust cultural relativism must presuppose about culture. In effect I will be asking, Are cultures really the kind of things they would have to be for the relativity of the validity of our cognitions to them to constitute a philosophical problem?

The Problems of Cultural Relativism

"The" problem of cultural relativism is not one but three distinct, albeit related, troubles which arise in three situations, given three beliefs about what cultures are like. One arises when a policy is proposed within a polity, and some object that the policy is itself "cultural." *"That's cultural"* implies that the belief in question is "culture-bound" and thereby not potentially universal, presumably because determined by local prejudice rather than by free choice or agreement based on evidence and reasons. This epistemic debility would hold only if cultures are sufficiently unified belief systems that the objective truth of each cultural judgment is dependent on cultural presuppositions whose truth is unsupportable. The second, perhaps most famous, situation is one of intercultural evaluation. Not to put too fine a point on it, the question is: *"Are they wrong? Are they evil?"* More soberly, can *we validly* judge that their cultural practice or belief is wrong, morally or cognitively? This can only be possible if cultures overlap, if they share beliefs that make intercultural evaluation possible on a shared basis. The third situation will sound strange, since people rarely ask it in the following form, but it is nevertheless crucially bound up with the appeal, and fear, of cultural relativism. It is: *"Is my culture right?"* More completely, does the fact of my being embedded in a culture mean that I have no noncircular way to judge the validity of my own practices and beliefs? Cultural membership would present such a problem only if it were *epistemological.* I will argue that the first of these problems is what Carnap called a pseudo-problem, hence can be *dissolved* by rejecting the presupposition about culture on which it is based. The second, once we see that there is no support for its presupposition about culture, will be recognized as a contingent problem of interpretive practice, in effect a political and not a philosophical problem at all, hence one that may be practically *resolved.* And the third is a social retelling of a philosophical problem that may indeed by *unsolvable,* but has nothing particular to do with culture at all.

Can Cultural Judgments Be Valid?

The first problem is, can cultural beliefs be validly judged to be right or true? This may seem odd; certainly cultural beliefs are generally regarded as right or true by cultural members. But for that very reason we normally defer applying to such beliefs the tests we would force upon beliefs in the professions, in science, in our daily pragmatic dealings with social institutions. Are cultural beliefs beyond normative judgment, incapable of rational adjudication or universal validity, hence *merely* cultural?

The threat that the trait of "being cultural" might make a belief un-justifiable hangs on its claimed dependence on a broadly effective epis-temic context whose holistic relation to objects either cannot be validated or cannot be validated in a noncircular way. It hangs on what being "cul-turally embedded" does to a belief's chances for justification. My answer is: sometimes very little.

Suppose two women are seated at a lunch counter discussing meta-physics. One is a panpsychist, insisting that everything is a mind or a prop-erty of mind, while the other is a reductive physicalist. The panpsychist, perhaps unsure in handling solids, drops her spoon, while the physicalist, leaping to her strong suit, catches it in midair. We might imagine that on any logical reconstruction, metaphysical beliefs would be sufficiently basic and central to their respective "belief systems" that their beliefs about and dealings with the spoon ought to be significantly different. But that is not so. Despite their utterly opposed metaphysical beliefs, their interaction shows that they in fact share an uncountable list of beliefs (uncountable if for no other reason than that we have no reliable way of counting beliefs); neither tries to pass a hand through the spoon, eat it, or move it telekinetically.

The same can be applied to lunchers from different cultures. In Quine's example, the tree encountered by the native on the day before the first Western anthropologist arrives is the same tree the anthropologist hides behind the next day. Whatever the metaphysical differences between native and anthropologist, however the former may understand *gavagai* as a "moment-in-rabbit-becoming" or a "part-of-the-collective-mega-rabbit," while the latter sees an individuated physical object, they *both* include ref-erence to the same cuddly, pet-able, edible target. The alternative meta-physical schemes cannot be behaviorally discerned in this case, as Quine says. But other things *can* be discerned while metaphysics varies in the background. The meaningful tie between rabbit and metaphysics may be quite *loose* and pose little problem for the anthropologist and native in making rabbit stew. For the two can disagree, even fail to understand each other, on metaphysics, while understanding and agreeing on everything else. In fact, Quine's argument showed not the *indeterminacy* but the mere *underdeterminacy* of translation, the absence of *complete* epistemic constraint. Complete constraint would narrow the possible translations to one. Quine is right that such is unavailable. But some meanings are ruled out even in the one present speech act: by "gavagai" the pointing native cannot mean

"Don't look, nothing is happening over there." And his observed linguistic behavior over time will rule out far more possible meanings, even in the situation of "radical" translation.

For as we know, the degree of unity or coherence within the beliefs of a culture, as within any group or individual belief "system," need not be particularly high. A culture's beliefs about marriage, its death rituals, its engineering practices, and its cuisine need not express or subtend one single set of ideas, values, or images. The degree of coherence among spheres of life, institutions, practices, and so on, is itself variable among cultures. And this means that the dependence of any particular agent's act or assertion on a framework of culture prejudgments is highly variable. We must conceive of what an individual brings to the act of judgment or interaction as a loose web with many nexuses of connected interpretive patterns, memories, motivations, and so on, and not assume that every response equally implicates the entire web, or what is the same thing, a set of principles presupposed by the entire web.

The notion that there is a controlling subset within a person's or a culture's "system" of beliefs has of course a more familiar name. Since the publication of Richard Rorty's *Philosophy and the Mirror of Nature* in 1979, philosophers have become sensitive to the extent to which the metaphor of "foundations" is operative in their work. The foundationalist imagination, since Descartes, not only pictures that philosophy can demonstrate the truth of deep claims, but that we can arrange beliefs into a hierarchical system with one finite set of foundational beliefs on whose truth the truth of all others depends. This set the stage for Rorty to deny the possibility of justifying our beliefs at all, since if all depend on the foundational set of beliefs, and the latter really are foundational, then there are no beliefs that can be noncircularly used to compare the foundational set to reality. Rorty mainly aimed to show that the traditionally realist theory of truth as the "correspondence" of belief to world could never be established, but the foundationalist picture was equally entangled with another metaphor, less infamous but equally misleading, that truth is coherence of belief and thus exists within *enclosures*. If we ought not regard a finite set of beliefs held by a believer to be "founded" on deeper presuppositions, we ought to see that, absent that vertical relationship, we can no longer say what is "inside" and what is "outside" an enclosure that has been defined by that relation of dependence. For in either case what matters is that any given belief of a person or culture must be dependent upon—vertically or horizontally, founded on or enclosed in—one set of "ultimate" beliefs.

Thus I grant that "final vocabularies," as Rorty once called them, cannot be compared to reality (Rorty 1989). But my question is, *are there any?* If final vocabularies, foundations, and enclosures are bad epistemology— that is to say, unjustifiable—they are also bad logic, bad as a description of how our beliefs relate to each other and to the world. They are cases of what Karl Popper called the myth of the framework (Popper 1996). Popper objected that rational justification cannot be regarded as the discovery of an ultimate set of asserted truths that positively justify belief (although for him the underlying reason was that "justification" can only mean "not yet falsified"). The horizontal metaphor of enclosure is indeed no better than the vertical metaphor of foundations, because either way we can find no "framework" in our beliefs. We cannot identify, let along articulate, a deep structure presupposed by or implicated in every judgment made by an agent, or group of agents, even if the group is our own. This imputes too much unity to minds, judgments, and cultures, and too much dependency to the beliefs and practices we evince from day to day. Note that I do not mean we can *never* identify *any* of our beliefs, or regarding cultures, identify *any* of the beliefs that are "in" or characteristic of a culture. That would be absurd. I am claiming we cannot specify the boundaries, hence general criteria for deciding whether beliefs are in or out. *And if cultures do not provide boundaries, judgments cannot be culture-bound.* Each culture, like each mind, is a continuum in which discrete first and last elements, either temporally or logically, cannot be identified. As Charles Peirce might put it, in minds and cultures *nothing is first or last,* nothing founds all beliefs or comprehends all beliefs. If no perceptual content is identifiable as an uninterpreted datum logically prior to linguistic shaping, there are also no identifiable first principles that underlie or justify any of my beliefs (Peirce 1931b). If we have no foundations, we also have no frameworks or containers. We may put it simply: *no human being, and no culture, has a belief system at all.*

If a metaphor is required for thinking about the relations among our beliefs or meanings, then better than foundations or enclosures would be *crystals.* Our beliefs and meanings are collected in irregularly shaped and structured clumps capable of growth from any point. As in a child's construction of tinker toys, every judgment is connected to, made in reference to, some clump, none of them ever stands alone. But this does not mean each is related to *every other judgment* of the agent's mind; some hang in mid-air with only one connection to the rest. What philosophers do, among other things, is articulate the logical relations holding within and among these clumps. If you prefer, our beliefs cohere like rhizomatic plants, in Deleuze's metaphor, as in a series of mesquite bushes each member of which shares some roots with some other member of the family (Deleuze and Guattari 1987). Or, conflating two Peircean metaphors, knowledge is like seaweed. Parts of the seaweed are indeed linearly or hierarchically related, but the growth of the seaweed as a whole is not. What happens rather is the more or less simultaneous growth of each clump and the growing together of some clumps, forming a greater expanse more intricately interrelated. Regarding cultures, an indefinitely large number of clumps of my interpretive-practical repertoire can be shared with members of another culture, always open to growth or atrophy. Some of the components of some of my clumps are far from yours, and their difference is clear, but other parts are near and ill-differentiated.

Every judgment of reality by a cultural agent is culturally funded, but is no more hermetic, or more mediated, than any other human judgment. Cultures *have* arguments, they *are not* arguments. The relationship of a subsidiary belief or practice to a more "fundamental" belief or practice is not the relation of a conclusion to a premise. The "problem" of cultural relativism is one of the costs of treating cultures as if they were philosophical systems, sets of beliefs having hierarchical, logical relations, an approach the Enlightenment made possible. In this sense cultural relativism is the child of the misguided philosophy of universalism it seeks to oppose.

Is Their Culture Wrong?

The existence of intercultural comparison and judgment is not at issue. We judge and compare all the time. The issue is rather, can such judgments be *interculturally valid,* legitimate, true, or rational, which implies, can they satisfy a criterion that does not, by being internal to one of the compared cultures and not the other, beg the question of their validity? This is perhaps the most typically compelling issue raised by those who accept that cultural relativism is a problem. For there is indeed no such thing as a justification across ultimate or absolute difference, meaning difference that is

foundational, logically prior to all other beliefs, subtended by no commonality, just as we cannot make sense of a demand that we know things while
abstracting from *our entire way* of knowing. But this formulation already
hints at the path to, if not a solution, then a resolution of this problem.

At the most mundane level, in the interpretation and judgment of fellow humans we always presuppose a common species and natural environment. We dwell on the same earth, have similar biological needs, presuppose
a common set of cognitive and perceptual abilities revealing a commonly
available physical reality, and exhibit a rather small set of overlapping practices and techniques for social organization and the acquisition of the
necessities of life. Geography varies, but none of the humanly habitable
environs on earth fail to exhibit climate, causality, sky above, and earth
below. Food, water, shelter, clothing, sexual reproduction, care of young,
communication, and group decision-making must be secured, however
they are secured. Cultures thus concern a metaphysically common set of
objects on the same planet and a common set of human processes. Not
that *all* their objects were, or are, common. A polytheist and animist society
believes in the existence of things that a secular society does not; writing
exists in literate but not illiterate societies. Nevertheless, we respond to and
express the rudimentary universal pragmatic demands of the human species
(food, water, etc.), including some virtually universal social institutions
(family, property, status, warfare, religion, and so on). All this, of course,
underdetermines the constitution of any surviving culture.

Further, internal diversity of all larger cultures is such that external diversity is not of a *wholly* different order. As noted, we should never overestimate
the internal uniformity of preindustrial cultures. There uniformity existed
only at the most local of levels. In agrarian civilizations internal caste differences have far greater importance than many intercultural differences.
Minimally put, there is no reason to think cultural group differences are necessarily the greatest of all group differences. And if individuals are familiar
with greater differences that must be negotiated within their own cultures
or societies, this means cross-cultural differences are not the "most different"
differences. Historical consciousness also has a place here, for the present
generation's awareness of its temporal distinction from ancestors likewise
brings an awareness of how to negotiate difference. Certainly we have record
of the fact that cultures have interacted. Wherever this interaction implied
some sort of mutual intelligibility, there was something in common. This

does not mean that interaction cannot increase difference; it can. But it must simultaneously increase mutual understanding, even if it also increases misunderstanding.

Indeed, among what cultures pass from generation to generation is knowledge of *other* cultures. In some cases this knowledge emerged in response to episodic interactions. In other cases, it was continuous, as in the great imperial trading cities of the premodern world, whose knowledge of other cultures could be very sophisticated. In that sense multiculturalism and cosmopolitanism are not new. Add to this the various forms of "duplex" cultural housing that resulted from migration and conquest, in which communities that regarded themselves as culturally distinct lived side by side, perhaps rarely interacting but nevertheless acquiring the knowledge of, and skills for dealing with, the other. One must imagine that such knowledge alters the understanding of one's own folkways as well. Cultures need not regard themselves as superior to other cultures in *every* way; they can decide that a foreign culture is in some respects superior. If post-Wittgenstein philosophy has recognized that a solipsistic *individual,* that is, one with a private language, is logically impossible, how much less plausible is a solipsistic *culture,* given that any culture already contains far more diversity, as well as the communicative resources for negotiating differences, than any individual? The notion that cultures cannot understand each other in principle is no more plausible than the skeptical claim that persons who seem to be understanding each other *might* in fact be using their terms in systematically different hence undiscoverable ways.

Certainly the diversity within cultures makes the relation to outer diversity more intelligible. But that aside, any sophisticated culture is itself aware of cultural difference and seeks ways to deal with it. For example, cultures often make their own internal distinction between the universally valid and the culturally particular. Any historical culture that is used to welcoming strangers (for example, in its trading centers) must distinguish among its own beliefs and practices a subset to which visitors or resident aliens are not to be held to account, and other beliefs and practices which they regard as universally binding or *anthropine,* normative for human beings *per se.* A culture that cannot bracket the former cannot tolerate visitors at all. That bracketing indicates an awareness not only of its members' own peculiarities, but of levels of validity or normative necessity. Modern cultures have no monopoly on the ability to imagine the perspective of the stranger or the visitor, or on the ability to distinguish one's countrymen from human beings *per se*. And this distinction is common to different cultures, although of course each may construe the anthropine norms differently.

More conceptually, it is often possible to ascribe second-order commonalities to peoples as a way of rendering their differences intelligible. In *The Silent Language* Edward Hall tells the story of a Southwestern American town, predominantly Mexican, where the local motorcycle policeman was in the habit of enforcing the 15 mph speed limit on Anglos traveling through town with precise efficiency, handing out fines for anyone exceeding the speed limit by so much as one mile per hour (Hall 1973). Among the Spanish population, Hall suggests, the habit was for the policeman to enforce the law to the smallest technicality, then judges would negate or reduce the fine in the court system, often based on personal and familial ties. The Anglos were accustomed to the opposite, lax enforcement but stringent and bureaucratic legal processing. Frustrated, they responded by repeatedly beating the policeman. Hall's account relies on the homeostatic notion that in both Anglo and Mexican culture a balance is struck in a zero-sum game between the extremes of rigid conformity and chaotic looseness, but in different places. The Anglos could not, for example, alter their ways by abandoning laxity in enforcement while retaining technical legal process; there would be too much pressure with no safety value, no room for judgment and exceptions. The Mexicans could not abandon strict enforcement while retaining informal adjudication, for there would be vehicular chaos. Thus Hall renders the distinctive practices intelligible by assuming that each must attain a balance—restraining speeders without fining too many people too much money—but they do so through different distributions of laxity and discipline.

Now, the point of these observations is not to sing a few stanzas of "We are the world..." in celebration of universal understanding. It is that a visitor from an alien planet would be as taken by the sameness among cultures as by the differences. The burden of proof is on those who claim that the differences "go all the way down," which is to say, are so fundamental that they prevent the sharing required for communication and mutual understanding, that each culture is so holistic, so highly integrated that none of its practices, beliefs, or signs can function similarly outside its whole. Still, we may wonder how to conceive of valid comparative evaluation, "rational" evaluation if you will, across cultures? For this we can turn to three contemporary writers who ply a common theme, that the answer to cross-cultural rationality lies not in *going around culture* to a noncultural rationality, but in *going through cultures* to discover ways that rational debate can flourish through these very differences.

We begin with the most long-standing contributor to this discussion among living philosophers. In his books *After Virtue: A Study in Moral Theory* (1981) and *Whose Justice? Which Rationality?* (1988) Alasdair MacIntyre claimed that all argument, and rationality itself, is tradition- or culture-specific; rationality is literally "rationality-in-a-tradition" (MacIntyre 1988). There is no reasoning outside a culture with its "canonical texts," ultimate ends, and inherited practices. This would appear to dive right into relativism of the worst sort. But MacIntyre argues that except in a very narrow range of circumstances, no social actor is ever justified in asserting, as relativism does, the identity of "is true" and "seems true to us."

MacIntyre limits relativism by arguing along two tracks. On the one hand, he provides an *immanent* criterion of rationality universally applicable to each tradition. Within a tradition there are inherited vocabularies and problems; progress occurs whenever recognized problems are resolved, usually through a reinterpretation of canonical texts and practices. A rationally superior view is able to solve problems earlier versions could not solve, and to explain why they could not, in the sense that Einsteinian physics solves problems that Newtonian physics could not but incorporates the latter as a special case, explaining where Newton was right and wrong (MacIntyre 1989). The rationally superior view thus writes a superior history of the tradition and its problems. Now, within such "living" (meaning pluralistic and contested) traditions, there can never be a reason to fuse "true" and "seems true to x" as long as there remain such immanent rational criteria for cognitive progress. Even in radical moments of "epistemological crisis" when cultures exhaust their resources, they can judge the resources of another tradition to be superior according to their *own* criteria and import the former. In the process MacIntyre makes the important point that untranslatability does *not* entail incomprehensibility. Indeed, it is only the truly bilingual individual who can say comprehendingly, "That phrase is untranslatable."

Now, it is the bilingual person and this person alone who can, under special circumstances, face a situation in which there is no rational alternative to relativism (MacIntyre 1989). This arises in what MacIntyre calls "boundary situations," where two "incommensurable" traditions compete. For example, after a conquest by a culturally incommensurable power, conquered individuals may be confronted with two competing languages and cultures. Simply saying the name of a town can then be a political act. Most will identify with their historical or descent culture. Only those who are bicultural and bilingual, who can understand each competing tradition on its own terms, will face a dilemma. In some of these cases bilinguals may have access to a third language, one which is rich enough to produce a description of each and that does not presuppose the validity of the essential resources of either of the competing traditions. But absent a third language the bilinguals will indeed be in a relativistic position, forced to make a criterion-less choice between incommensurables. Otherwise, there is never a reason to assert relativism.

Samuel Fleishacker's *The Ethics of Culture* (1994) argues that while ethical universalism is bankrupt, ethics has little to fear from culture, for a form of cultural relativism can be accommodated to ethics. Culture he defines as *authoritative tradition,* where authority is allegiance-deserving judgment, and tradition is a set of unquestionably compelling texts, practices, and standards presented to each new generation by a particular society. Deep ethical choices, he asserts, occur in situations of risk where reason by itself cannot decide. Hence moral reasoning needs cultural traditions, which are based in faith and not reason. These posit ultimate goods which cannot be reduced to rational rules; traditions are "incarnations" of the ultimate good in a "specific way of life." Fleischacker asserts that to speak of tradition is to speak of "submission" (Fleischacker 1994: 78). Authority without tradition is dangerous, since then there is no canonical good to which the authority is beholden, before which he/she must be humble. But when ensconced in tradition, authority embodies *phronēsis,* practical wisdom, whose judgments apply a canonical narrative about the ultimate and obscure good to a particular case. Regarding the problem of normatively judging other cultures, Fleischacker argues for cross-cultural understanding through the interaction of each culture's narratives without reverting to a non- or supracultural standpoint.

The upshot of this approach is that the proof is in the pudding. The demonstration of the plausibility of intercultural communication and evaluation can only be established in actual cases where the participants in intercultural dialogue find an interpretive *modus vivendi.* Fleischacker rightly recognizes that theoretical reason cannot establish these paths; they are the product of judgment. Thus he writes, "Between universalism and relativism, between authority and reason, between a culture as a unified moral self and cultures as impermanent nodes in the flux of universal human interaction, between the specific way of life that we know we should not impose on anyone else and the general conditions which that way of life and all others ought to meet, there lies nothing but judgment" (Fleischacker 1994: 150). Only in judgment, practical wisdom, which applies generals to individual cases and hence cannot itself be reconstructed as rule-governed, can reasoning across cultures occur. Fleischacker presents fascinating examples of how cultures in seemingly fundamental disagreements may find points of commonality in their traditions' unofficial, sometimes recessive, narratives. In this he mirrors the work of Bhikhu Parekh in political theory.

We may add to MacIntyre's and Fleischacker's approaches other resources, in particular Martha Nussbaum's notion of "thick but vague" universal norms and Michael Walzer's notion of a "thin" layer of a culture's values (Nussbaum 1990; Walzer 1994). There are moral notions, which, if interpreted minimally or vaguely, in Nussbaum's sense, are shared by many cultures. David Wong and Lawrence Becker have separately claimed this for reciprocity, and one could make similar arguments for notions like justice, indebtedness, humanity-compassion-generosity, virtue, and reasoning (Wong 1995; Becker 1986). Now, no one is sufficiently polycultural to say with confidence that *all* existing cultures share those, or other, crucial notions, not to mention all past cultures. But strong arguments can be made that a number of large, complex, very different civilizations have shared these concepts. Walzer argues that in order to deal with and understand other cultures, traditions "thin" some of their concepts and norms to be capable of more universal employment and so to inform their interaction with foreigners. That the full, thick, or precise versions of a culture's practices, artifacts, and narratives fail to overlap with another culture does not prevent employment of thinned versions.

Following MacIntyre's lead, a generalized version of his narrative criterion of an explanation's rational superiority, which bears comparison both to W. W. Hartley's "comprehensive critical rationality" and to Popper's falsificationism, might be accepted as normative for a variety of cultures in some contexts. If we say that validity means comparative cognitive superiority, then the theory that is valid or superior at this moment is one that can explain or consistently account for everything competitor theories account for while avoiding or answering the problems of those competitors, *and* can explain why those competitors seemed under various conditions to be right. The standard of validity here is essentially progressive (we accept the account that improves our understanding), falsificationist (the winning

account is superior because it has not been shown inferior yet), and ab-
ductive (the point of any account is to best give reasons why things are the
way they are). Other things being equal, the criterion of rationality claims
that theories which explain something are superior to theories that don't.
The question would then be whether this criterion, where sufficiently thin,
can be accepted by otherwise recalcitrant cultures.

Last, even where cultures do not already contain, or have not had to
evolve, procedures of justification or thin/vague normative terms that bear
easy comparison to those of other cultures, two cultures that face each
other may be able to evolve a *bilateral* comparative language. How they can
do so is addressed by Lorenzo Simpson in his *Unfinished Project: Toward a
Postmetaphysical Humanism* (2001). In this work Simpson presents a Gadamer-
ian account of intercultural understanding, which he labels situated cosmopolitanism, a cosmopolitanism nevertheless characterized by communal
identification. Simpson wants to explain the possibility of a non-"invidious"
appreciation of the perspective of the other that still avoids adopting the
other's perspective, hence maintains the resources for "critical rejoinders."
He rightly points out that even to say that "your culture is not mine" presumes an ability to represent each as a perspective on a common object.
He writes, "Identifying contrasts presupposes the identification of a *Sache*
(fact), an 'X', a fundamental concern. A contrast can only be properly understood as the condition of there being two (or more) ways of addressing X"
(Simpson 2001: 84). Simpson recognizes that this identification, not the
importation of "foreign" standards, is the core difficulty of intercultural
dialogue. For identifying what X *they* are talking about is tantamount to
deciding in what register, under what description, the X in question functions in their sociocultural life, hence in what kind of "game" it is located.
We must ascertain "In what game of theirs is X an intelligible move?" To
do this is in effect to open the question, "What would I be doing/saying in
doing/saying what they are doing/saying?" Hence understanding *them*
makes a claim on *us*. This presumes a "second-order" principle of charity,
analogically "modeling [their doing/saying] upon what can be logical spaces
or dimensions of experience for us" (Simpson 2001: 90).

We may add to Simpson's analysis that one major axis of comparison in
deciding what *they* are doing is the distinction, or lack thereof, they make
between cognitive and aesthetic-practical projects, which is to say, the degree
of multifunctionality in Gellner's sense—and how this relates to the same
question about what *we* are doing. Wong suggests that for non-Western,

and especially Chinese, ways of inquiry and advanced thought, the goal is less often knowledge of the world *per se* than "attunement" to the world, which leads him to distinguish the "epistemic warrant" of a belief from the "rationality of holding" it (Wong 1989). Attunement is multifunctional, including cognitive, practical, and aesthetic elements; and rationality, if understood broadly as reason-giving, can be as well. Multifunctionality, I may hasten to add, does not by itself imply primitivism or underdevelopment. The West has its own multifunctional norms, "wisdom" being the most prominent for philosophers. But different cultures have given multifunctional norms different roles in their activities. Today's Western philosopher, carrying with her our utter divorce of cognitive from other values, in the end often finds the non-Western philosopher naive, while the non-Westerner wonders why the Westerner, if the results of her work are so irrelevant to the conduct of life or the improvement of society, bothers at all.

Simpson accepts that rationality is universal, but very thin. As he writes, "Every form of life can be understood to make the following validity claim: its practices are the best way for it to flourish; that is to say, they represent the best way for it to address the *Sachen*" (Simpson 2001: 94). Consequently, in determining whether a belief or practice enhances or is consistent with such flourishing, cultural members must occasionally debate the former.

> The form or rationality that I have implicitly referred to here is a form of rationality that I take to have transcultural, or cross-cultural, or culturally invariant standing. It is what I would call a "second-order rationality" that we are entitled to impute to everyone—that is, an inclination to reforms one's practices in the direction of more rationality when one's lack of rationality is pointed out to one in terms with which one is conversant. (Simpson 2001: 96)

Consequently, we may discover that their practices of justification—as they may discover about ours—are "arbitrary and/or untrustworthy," that is, "not . . . truth-tracking or truth-sensitive in the way that members of a given community thought they were." The result of this interpretation-that-inevitably-becomes-dialogue is "a newly forged common language" which transforms both agent and alter. Each language is transformed, stretched, by the addition of the dialogically formed metalanguage it must evolve. The metalanguage permits a shared noninvidious representation of each position in which the explicit or implicit contest between the two is reframed through "redescriptions" acceptable to each. Echoing but modifying Richard Rorty's ethnocentrism, Simpson's interpreters become "hermeneutically self-aware ethnocentrists." The point is that cultures change, can rise to occasions of interaction, and develop the resources for mutual understanding. There is at least as much evidence of that in the human past as ethnic cleansing or uncomprehending slaughter of the other.

In summary, the denial of the possibility of the intercultural validity of cross-cultural claims bears a very high burden that it cannot meet. It must presume a cultural unity, rigidity, and obstinacy that is hard to find in the real world. It must ignore intracultural diversity, change, and procedures of rational adjudication. The relativist may respond that shifting the burden of proof onto her shoulders does little to prove intercultural validity. That is true, but it is a truth that indicates a more basic point, suggested earlier: *not around but through*. We can only establish intercultural validity through the hermeneutic work of exploring and relating cultures, not by third-person philosophical arguments. But this means that the problem of the validity of cross-cultural judgment, while a real problem, is *not a philosophical one*. It is a contingent, imaginative problem of practical wisdom, of finding resources internal to cultures that make mutual judgment valid. It is no more a philosophical problem than a contract negotiation between union and management, research into the relation of Old English words to German, or the interpretation of the Qur'an. It is a *political* problem open to neither conceptual dissolution nor philosophical solution, but case-by-case hermeneutic-practical *resolution*.

Is My Culture Right?

This question may seem an odd one. People rarely ask it out loud, unless they have advanced degrees in the social sciences. One may argue that this very doubt is itself characteristic of some contemporary cultures, namely the postmodern West. But it can arise in a variety of cultures and contexts. Concerns about avoiding cross-cultural judgment, both characteristic of multiculturalism and, one might say, political correctness are, while not ubiquitous, a common enough phenomenon. At any rate, "Is my culture right?" does seem to be an at least implicitly postmodern question. Where does it come from historically?

We have seen that culture as a problem emerged in the eighteenth and early nineteenth centuries in the West. The Enlightenment, in a remarkably productive fit of ambivalence, on the one hand, eschewed cultural particularity, declaring that truth is universal and cognized only when tradition is loosened, making culture important as something to be rooted out, surpassed, cleansed from the "mirror of nature" or experience or cognition. On the other hand, the Enlightenment recognized the importance and distinctiveness of cultures as equal, fundamental, Leibnizian monads of apperception. In each case it made culture *deep,* the collection of concepts, beliefs, and assumptions shared by a society. Notice the modern egalitarianism implied: in the ancient and medieval traditions the philosopher rarely assumes that he or she shares concepts with nonphilosophers, that the prejudices of the uneducated may well skew her own inquiry. For the first time, Enlightenment philosophers begin to understand cultures as philosophically important, as *collective foundational premises.* So, if we are to follow Socrates in the examined life, we must reflect on our own culture and its validity, since that culture underlies our philosophical beliefs. In other words, the "problem of cultural relativism" assumes that cultures are to be identified and questioned much like philosophies, as if they were articulable systems of belief striving to be true, or at least cognitively founded and dependent on certain basic propositions. Cultural relativism presupposes a *social-political problem become philosophical.* It only arises where philosophy invades our naive life in the world, where we assume that the everyday, shared life of our people (whoever they are) hangs on a system of concepts and propositions open to philosophical evaluation. Once this happens, the educated class within a people may get to wondering if its own culture is "just another culture," a strange enough thought-event, which may get attached not only to any dealings with other cultures but also to internal matters of iconoclasm, liberty, and minority cultures. The philosophical discovery of culture is the *philosophicization of* culture.

Under this interpretation, to ask if my culture is right is to ask if my fundamental way of understanding the world is right. "Is my culture right?" is no more or less than the question with which Descartes started modern philosophy: "Are all my beliefs, especially my most fundamental beliefs, true? What if they are all wrong? How can I know they aren't?" The only difference is its intersubjective character: rather than a solitary Descartes doubting his beliefs in his study, it is now our shared beliefs that are suspended in disbelief. We then become *social Cartesians.* Thus this third problem of cultural relativism is not merely *a* philosophical problem, it is *the* philosophical problem *par excellence,* the problem of knowledge, the problem of whether human judgment can be known to be valid or not, albeit here collectivized. *The problem of cultural relativism is what the problem of knowledge sounds like once you accept that human cognition is social and historical.* As such, "Is my culture right?" has no solution if the problem of knowledge has no solution. Some antirealists, postmodernists, and evolutionary epistemologists, of course, think that there is no philosophical problem of knowledge at all, that to imagine such a problem is to assume foundationalism. Whether they are right or not is a story for another time, but certainly their rightness would only further undermine any epistemic problem posed by culture. The problem is the philosophical one of answering skepticism, a problem neither created nor exacerbated by embedding cognition in culture.

Cultural Knowing

Even if the foregoing negative argument against relativism holds, without a positive account of knowledge that is both cultural and realist its claim may still seem dubious. Now, by no means can we afford a major foray into epistemology here. Time, energy, and wood pulp are limited. But a suggestion such as what follows does, I think, at least render plausible as an avenue for further inquiry the proposition that an epistemology which accepts the cultural embedded-ness of cognition need not break with a chastened, minimal realism.

Twentieth-century epistemology is a series of footnotes to Hume, in spirit even when the footnotes serve to correct Hume's letter. A long list of critiques from Wittgenstein to Derrida have wakened us from any dogmatic slumbering we might have hoped to do. With much of this revisionism we can agree. Yes, all judgments have mediated relations to their objects, hence cannot claim "privilege" or "immediacy" or a grasp of "presence"; are fallible and open to revision, hence devoid of certainty; never cognize an objectivity devoid of traces of the cognizer, leaving no "immaculate perception"; are perspectival, linguistified, historicized products of particular cultures, not grasped in a "view from nowhere"; always presuppose unanalyzed conceptual and political commitments open to deconstruction and genealogical critique; and cannot hope to be given a noncircular philo-sophical justification, whether by foundationalism, coherentism, or as Susan Haack puts it, "foundherentism." All this is, if not true, at least presump-tively valid. We must accept the burden that these critiques place squarely on the shoulders of any would-be realism.

But these shoulders, if not broad, are yet strong enough. Realism mini-mally requires that the validity of our judgments be constituted by their validity *with respect to* what they judge, that the truth of the assertion is decisively constituted by a relation to *what* is judged rather than to charac-teristics of the judge or the act of judgment. Such is unavoidably impli-cated by three homely facts that, I would argue, can hardly be dismissed. First, "true" implies true *of* something. That is, assertive judgment is inten-tional, and truth is an object-relational property of such judgment. Second, *what* is truly judged, as *a* what, cannot be truly judged by judgments that contradict each other. Something, call it A, cannot be q and ~q at the same time in the same respect and remain A. This holds whether A is a physical object, a phenomenal quality, a process, a network of signs, or a thought. Last, the relevant character of that *what,* of which the judgment is true, must obtain independently of our judgment of it. The judging cannot *make* it true. Saying shares with making and doing the status of being human judg-ments, but unlike making and doing, assertive judgment is in a crucial sense reactive or representative. That is inherent in the desire to be "true of." Whether we parse this through the metaphor of correspondence or fit or being "made true" by objects is an important but derivative question, as is the issue of what cognitive unit the realistically judged object must be independent (such as proposition, perspective, theory, or culture). As I have argued elsewhere, we cannot make sense of any notion of "knowledge" or "truth," or of judgments being "true" that rejects these three homely param-eters, nor can we identify a society whose repertoire of semiotic practices can consistently dispense with the quoted terms (Cahoone 2002b). Not that all judgments, or all uses of signs, are assertive hence normed by truth. They are not. But those that are are indispensable. The deflationary attempt to disavow truth always contradicts itself, as where postmodernists and antirealists *claim* to avoid truth as if their claim were *true.* Whether philoso-phy can prove my realist parameters, can justify realism, is another question. Failure to reach the bar does not by itself invalidate where the bar is set.

If this account seems anachronistic, well, things will now get far worse, for with minimal realism go two other doctrines.

First, we cannot give up the *unity of truth*. As said, the rules by which we methodically investigate truth cannot accept that contrary judgments be true of the same thing at the same time. But this only means that *all truth-claims must be consistent*. If that were false, then contradiction in truth-governed inquiry should not motivate further inquiry, should not be a problem, any more than you and I singing different songs or marrying different persons is a problem. In inquiry, however, whether in a laboratory, a Senate subcommittee, or an Easter-egg hunt, contradictory truth-claims *are* a problem. Relativism, then, as a theory about what is true, cannot make sense of our actual behavior. We cannot give up the logic of realism and the unity of truth without, at the very least, giving up inquiry as we understand it.

Second, along with realism and the unity of truth goes the notion that cognitive advance implies a *linear* relation of objects-as-judged across differing or changed but intertranslatable semiotic nets, hence the rejection of incommensurability. This rejection is justified every day by bilingual individuals, whether fluent in Armenian and Russian or Newtonian and Einsteinian. That is, if we accept a realist interpretation of inquiry, then we have no choice but to deny that incommensurability is ever more than an artifact of contingently chosen incompatible languages, to be resolved through translation via a more comprehensive or "neutral" language. "Neutral" here means, of course, locally neutral, neutral with respect to the languages in question. No language is neutral universally or *per se*. But none is needed.

Thus we are led to an admittedly Neanderthal epistemology. What lies behind my insouciance are two convictions. One is that many contemporary revisionists are in the habit of conflating a long series of alleged bugaboos—foundationalism, the "view from nowhere," essentialism, logocentrism, a "God's eye view," the imperialism of reason, and so on—which need a careful analysis. Some of the things listed, or some of the things those terms connote, are indeed indefensible, wrong, or even bad. But they are different, and between those differences lie narrow trails we can realistically walk. Second, nobody can do without truth as understood in a realist sense in their aesthetic and practical activity. For quite some time after September 11, 2001, many in the Arab world believed that the World Trade Center was bombed by Zionists—Jews having been warned, it was claimed, not to go to work in the towers on that day—in order to discredit Muslims. This belief is *either* true *or* false, not both (I pray the reader does not wonder which). It is valid either everywhere or nowhere, not invalid in Manhattan but valid in Cairo. Without an at least minimal realism we are left in a moral, legal, and political never-never land of alternate universes, in some of which African slavery never happened, the Holocaust was a clerical error, and Stalin the Russian George Washington. Saying this does not justify realism's truth, of course. It merely indicates the price of rejecting it.

How then are we to understand a realist yet culturally embedded, mediated, historical, interested, fallible, decidedly nonimmaculate human knowing? Our cognition first has parameters dictated by the perceptual-affective-cognitive-motor capacities liberally distributed among modern *Homo sapiens*. Following Joseph Margolis we can accept that, *contra* Aristotle, these capacities evolved and are perhaps evolving, and that, *contra* Kant, no complete or *a priori* inventory of them is available (Margolis 2000). An indeterminately large module of that cognitive medium is historical, cultural, linguistic, or most broadly, semiotic. Our perception, interpretation, and knowledge are thus biocultural. The experiences, or better, saliences that cognition must explain are limited and structured, even if we cannot say completely what those limits are. Perception, as a biologically prepared receptive appropriation whose modality at some level is uncontrollable and unconscious, is both passive and mediated, intertwined with motor activity, affectivity, and semiosis. Margolis is certainly right to summarize much epistemic revisionism with the claim that language and world are *symbiotic* (Margolis 2000). We never face an un-languaged world or an un-worlded language, never confront objectivity uncolored by our cognitive means nor a perfect synopsis of our cognitive means uncluttered by reference to bits of the world.

But I claim that symbiosis is *graded*. That the adverbial means of judgment and what is judged are *ultimately* inseparable does not mean they are not *incrementally* separable. Experienced and judged objects are tied to background perspectives, methods, worldviews, and cultures, but are they *all tied to all those media in the same way and to the same degree?* It would be rather serendipitous if they were. On the contrary, not every fact or belief is as embedded as every other; degree of entanglement varies with degree of control of our own terms of judgment. That we can abstract from particulars of each makes cognitive advance and communication across nets of beliefs possible. It is not true, as some holists imply, that given disconfirmatory evidence *any* component of our worldview is *equally* up for rejection. Neither scientist nor cabbie behaves that way. The mind being at least as complex as sneakers, regarding theory- or culture- or perspective-embeddedness there is no reason to assume that one size fits all. A minimally realist notion of truth, knowledge, and the world is entirely coherent with the adverbial nature of the "media" of knowing (judgments, concepts, worldviews, cultures, and so on), the denial of "presence" or "privilege" (the claim that we have cognitions that are immediate to their objects, hence irrefragable), and the assertion of objective indeterminacy (that not every possible proposition is or must be either true or false of real things, because the latter, like our propositions, vary in their determinateness, no object being either utterly determinate or utterly indeterminate).

None of this is tantamount to that view which is arguably the dominant theme of recent revisionist epistemology, namely constructivism. Constructivism is untenable. It is far too simplistic a metaphor. Constructing is *building,* which implies making and control. If it were true that we cognitively make the world, we would presumably have done a better job, for example, have left out pain, misery, and death. The idea of a self-creating human sphere, unconstrained by anything real outside its sculpturing, fails. For while it is plausible that our perceptual-affective-cognitive-motor apparatus, with its historico-cultural variants, *shapes* the world-as-we-know-it, it is equally true that such shaping, like all other processes, has *constraints.* If it did not, then it would be a creation *ex nihilo;* presumably not even constructivists wish to deify themselves. The world, even the world-for-us, is not simply the product of our construction; indeed, to claim that it is the product of a single process of *any* kind is a metaphysical assertion of a high order. Rather than constructed it is *shaped, refracted,* or *selected,* or any other of a host of less than Promethean figures. And it should be noted that constructivism's inadequacy does not hang on the now-anachronistic notion of an *agent* of construction, which has been discredited by post-Wittgensteinian and post-Heideggerian philosophy. Construction without an agent or subject *doing* the constructing is still construction, and still untenable. Wherever the agent-less construction of postmodernism has its strongest innings, the materiality of the world and the manifold constraints on the process of "construction," which are doubted by almost no one, go strangely unmentioned. Constructivism's apparent tenability is maintained only where it implicitly accepts a distinction between "meaning" and "being," denying that it has to answer questions about the latter, about what is independent of human appropriation. Like many intellectual movements, its success depends on allowing it to make up the exam it then has to pass.

At any rate, from perception of the object through description to conceptualization and theorization runs a continuum from largely universal-thin-uncontrollable-minimally informed to historically particular-thick-controllable-maximally informed levels of appropriation. Realism and the unity of knowledge do not then imply a "God's eye" view; we cannot claim to have *the* true representation of the one real world. But we can claim *a* true representation of the one real world in our cognitive medium, other media of representation being *possibly* possible (that is, how "possible" as in plausible, how adequate and free from troubles, remains to be seen). What we know is the *one and only real world as it systematically affects and is interpreted through* the human perceptual-affective-cognitive-motor apparatus in its historical, cultural modalities. True representations in different media must then have a systematic, lawful relation, just as the common sense or brute fact must have a linear relation to the scientific fact, the earlier cognized fact must have to the cognized fact subsequent to cognitive progress, and the fact as known by one culture must have to the fact as known by another. And the account of those linear relations must itself be internal to the description of reality thereby achieved.

The relation of any particular act of knowing and its object is best pictured as a kind of genetically deformed daisy in which the center of the flower is simultaneously encircled by nested elliptically shaped petals of different sizes. Each ellipsis contains, or "knows," the center, which is the object. But the ellipses vary in how large they are, hence how much of the center and how much else they include. Our judgments each reveal the object in their own ways. We must just remember one misleading feature of the picture: we can never discern the precise difference in enclosed area between the target and the ellipse that targets it, since all we have to make such a discernment is the set of elliptical petals that *are* the known object for us. Borrowing from earlier discussions, we can use the distinction between "thick," hence particular, and "thin," hence common or universal but vague, components of any society's moral code (Walzer 1994; Nussbaum 1990). When particular, historically laden societies deal with each other, they employ a "thinned" version of their values and rules. So, members of different cultures can agree on the importance of "Justice" or "Democracy" or "Rights." Of course, when they do so they must be *vague;*

how to apply or specify justice or rights can only occur in their own thick particular moral worldview.

Applying these metaphors to our epistemic question, we can say that our networks of judgments overlap around portions of our perception that are least controllable, hence most thin and universal, albeit subject to diverse subsequent interpretation. That they overlap means that some portions of our world are minimally interpreted, least embedded, least open to cultural or other cognitive reformulation. The thicker and more particular, the more the judged or known object is colored by interconnections with diverse other judgments. The thinner and more universal, the more the judgment of the object abstracts from the particularities of other cultural judgments. For we can now see that "thinning" means first of all the *abandonment of multifunctional judgment*. In the case of assertive judgment or propositional knowledge, modern science is the *thinnest* form of cultural cognition yet created. It is not utterly thin; that would imply presuppositionless-ness or complete transparency, which is unattainable. But it is, as Cassirer argued, the most transparent of our symbolic forms, the most unconstrained in its handling of its symbols, the most fully differentiated from other modes of judgment (Cassirer 1965, vol. 3). The good news is that science is thus most capable of cross-cultural travel; the bad news is that it must fail to support the thicker needs and narratives of any culture, including the cultures that birthed it.

Nevertheless, the antifoundationalists, postmodernists, and constructivists are right about one thing: there is *no possibility of a noncircular justification of all I have just said*. Realism and the unity of truth are indispensable but cannot be ultimately shown to be true. Once we have gone down the open-ended road of validating propositions via inquiry rather than faith, social and pragmatic demands, aesthetic appeal, or private intuition, we are stuck both with realism *and* with the search for realism's validation, knowledge's "foundations," a search that *cannot* be consummated. Inquiry has its own constitutive features which inevitably exclude other modes of handling the world. What lies within these borders cannot justify itself by its own rules, any more than it can lift itself by its own beard. As I have argued elsewhere, we cannot maximize the methodological sophistication of our individual modes of appropriating the world—like inquiry—while at the same time integrating them (Cahoone 2002c). Nevertheless, we are not at liberty to reject progress. In short, once we have eaten of the fruit of the

Tree of Knowledge, there can be for us no cognitive Paradise of certainty, rest, or completion, only the endless toil of inquiry to which we have been condemned. Such, at any rate, is the legacy of realism.

Conclusion

There is then no specific epistemological problem attached to the recognition that human cognition is cultural. That is, *there is no philosophical problem of cultural relativism*. There might be if it made sense to say that human belief occurs in systems, that all our beliefs are founded on identifiable subsets of beliefs or enclosed in conceptual containers, and that cultures are such containers. But it doesn't and they aren't. There might be, if cultures did not overlap, exhibit commonalities, or have the resources for comparison. But they do. There might be if there were no such thing as the problem of knowledge, if the philosophical justification of human knowing *independent* of culture were apparent. But it isn't. None of this implies that culture is not a cognitive problem, that a culture's beliefs or values can be definitively and noncircularly justified. It only means that the fact of the location of beliefs and values in culture adds no additional barrier that the subject must escape to contact objectivity. The philosophical problem is the same, with or without culture.

8 WHAT IS THE OPPOSITE OF *JIHAD?*

As if in a horror film where some greedy developer, heedless of warnings, breeches ancient burial sites thereby releasing underworld ghosts bent on vengeance, our postmodern polities, hell-bent on the global explosion of new technology, seem to have awakened threatening primordial spirits from the past. But unlike the usually lumbering cinematic ghouls, the real spirits are very clever and move very fast. Religious fundamentalism, nationalism, ethnocentrism, nativism—whatever their differences, a seemingly very old set of foes are back. To this point ethnic nationalism, especially in the former Yugoslavia and Rwanda, has extracted the most hideous human cost, although the worldwide rise of fundamentalism has not shirked before violence, most famously in its Islamic version. But fundamentalism is an equal-opportunity killer; Hindu extremists have matched their Muslim counterparts in blood, while Sikh, Jewish, and even Buddhist militants have assassinated heads of state (respectively, India's Indira Gandhi, Israel's Rabin, and Sri Lanka's Bandaranaike, the last killed by a monk). The Cold War confrontation of communism versus capitalism has been replaced by the battle Benjamin Barber called Jihad vs. McWorld. In response to the steady international gale of postmodern, capitalist, service-knowledge-and-entertainment-oriented economies, "infotainment telesectors," devoid of communal identity and metanarrative, blowing *Baywatch* and burgers through the Earth's globalized villages, retribalized polities erect primordial walls of identity while their nonstate brothers try to blow up the wind machine (Barber 1995). Certainly liberal modernity has had bigger problems; from 1933 (Hitler's chancellorship) to 1953 (the death of Stalin) it was fighting for its life, and for almost forty more years it lived under a nuclear guillotine. But the widespread collectivist movements in the names of ethnicity and religion raise the possibility that the battle with ideological communism was a momentary aberration in a longer-term struggle between civic-liberal rule and more primordial and transcendental sources of community. Can the current revivalisms successfully challenge a liberal capitalist modernity that overcame fascism and communism? Are *jihadis* and ethnic cleansers merely the last gasp of a *revanche* or harbingers of an enduring geopolitical split? And what does their current resurgence say about our postmodern version of Western modernity?

As plausible, and inevitable, as our question is, we must be wary of lumping revivalist phenomena together into an undifferentiated wave of anti-Western antimodernism. The revivalists are younger than they look, often modernist youngsters sporting antique fashions. They are part of the modern world's confrontation with its own novel realities. And their ethnic and religious variants are distinct. To be sure, they sometimes fuse; as Mark Juergensmeyer has argued, there is such a thing as "religious nationalism" (Juergensmeyer 1993). Nevertheless, philosophically and politically they pull in different directions. Intellectually, most of the religions in question are intrinsically supranational, transcending all ethnicities and political units (the exceptions being militant Judaism and Hinduism). In political terms there is a continuum of religious-nationalist interweaving. In some conflicts religion is simply a defining characteristic of cultural communities at war over nonreligious issues (Northern Ireland until recently, and Beirut in the 1980s civil war). In others religion is the principled basis for criticism and reform of a state seen as corrupt and immoral (perhaps Turkey in recent years). Sometimes an irreligious state is the enemy, the imagined solution being establishment and protection of a majority religion that still tolerates minority religions (as in Iran—except for its treatment of Baha'is—and the stated goals of the Bharatiya Janata Party in India). For others secular nationalism is the hated doctrine; their goal is to remake their national state along theocentric lines. In the most extreme cases, they seek a religious suprastate (for example, the Islamist thinker Sayyid Qutb). Structurally, it makes sense to regard religious revivalism and nationalism, ethnic or not, as providing a basis of legitimacy, and a source of solidarity, for postcolonial peoples seeking to order their affairs under a centralized government left behind by colonial powers (Geertz 1961). Each is a way to organize power in the transition from local, clan-dominated communities to modern, centralized societies.

Last, we must be wary of narrating revivalist movements as reactionary. As the story goes, the global advance of liberal capitalism and its mostly American mass culture puts people through an introductory course of dislocation, poverty, and culture shock, a misery addressed by advanced seminars in the *madrassas* (Islamic schools for high-school through college-age students) from which pupils matriculate to al-Qaeda for graduate study. This is indeed partly true. But, as Samuel Huntington and Giles Keppel separately point out, it is the educated, middle-class youth of developing countries, especially students of science and engineering, not the disenfranchised poor, who seem most drawn to religious revival (Huntington 1996; Keppel 1994). As Roxanne Euben has argued, the reactionary theory implies that Western modernization is the only proactive force in the world, as if no other civilization were motivated by internal developments (Euben 1999). Now, all the movements in question are indeed *partially* reactions—as are a number of countermodernizing movements inside Western countries and Japan—but what constitutes the motivation and character of each reaction is a question that can be answered only from *their* side, in terms of their internal dynamics.

Islam and Modernity

The conflict of Islam with the West is not new. The intensity of the current phase has arguably revolved around the issue of Palestine, hence can be dated to the Israeli occupation of the West Bank and Gaza in 1967, the Suez Crisis of 1956, or the establishment of Israel in 1948. But this phase is part of more than a century of response both to Western imperialism and Western support for corrupt regimes in the Islamic world. It is during this period, since the late nineteenth century, that Islamic revivalism emerged, both in its "modernist" and fundamentalist forms. And of course one could go further back to the Crusades and a millennium of Christian-Islamic competition in the Iberian peninsula, the Balkans, and the holy land. But we ought not be slaves to history; Euro-American countries today enjoy relatively pacific relations with a variety of former colonies and bloody enemies. The current animosity between the West and Islam is not explained by historical interactions alone, but by a present which keeps that past alive. So we must understand the historical impulses internal to Islamic civilization that feed the moment. Certainly there can be no question here of summarizing a family of cultures that cover one-fifth of the Earth's population and have played a pivotal role in world history for fourteen centuries. But we must have some background in that tradition of which Islamic militancy claims to be a revival.

If we were to return to the early caliphate, after the death of Muhammad in 632 C.E. (all dates will be in the Christian calendar), and visit the center of the Abbasid empire at Baghdad at its height, then drop in on Cordoba in the early twelfth century, and finally travel to Ottoman Istanbul in the fifteenth century, it would be hard to escape the conclusion that Islam constitutes one of the three great, still living, largely sovereign old world civilizations over the last millennium, the others being India and China (the Byzantine and West European, however deserving of mention, having been conquered too early or arisen too late to qualify). In learning, trade, law, military prowess, theology, political justice, architecture, and other areas Islam represents a large part of what the human race has accomplished. Islamic civilization absorbed ancient civilizations along a front from Gibraltar to Western China, digesting, altering, and transmitting ancient Greek, Hebrew, Persian, and Hindu traditions to late medieval and modern societies. One can argue that Islam for the most part avoided some of the aspects of Christianity of which contemporary Christians are not so proud. Thus in Islam knowledge and reason have almost never been seen as enemies of religion. Islam did not regard nature or material life or the body as evil or dangerous. While militant Islamists may obsess over sex and fear pollution-by-woman, unlike Christianity traditional Islam counseled restraint, not avoidance; mainstream Islam has no monastic tradition, conceiving the spiritual as fully embodied in familial and social life (the Prophet himself having been both husband and father). Philosophically Islam is what it has always claimed to be: the most purified form of monotheism, with a strict but minimal set of basic beliefs, whose concerns were the individual's submission to God, followed by prayer and moral righteousness, as well as a commitment to charity and social equality. This is not to say that its confessors were always consistent practitioners. They certainly were not, which is to say, they were certainly human.

Some in the West complain that Islam never had a "Reformation," never replaced its medieval authoritarian tradition (in the Western analogy, Roman Catholicism), with an individualistic, rationalist version (like Protestantism) that promoted tolerance. This argument has little to recommend it. First, the motivating idea is suspect. Remember that the birth of Protestantism led to a century and a half of continuous religious warfare in Europe. Western religious toleration emerged less from the rise of Protestantism than from the *defeat* of its militant form, English Puritanism. So early

Protestantism in itself was not particularly tolerant. Second, far from being "Catholic" we must say that Islam is remarkably reformed. Sunni Islam is a scriptural, scribal, rational religion, devoid of miracles, magic, sacrament, saints, and clergy. Its religious elites are prayer-leading *imams* and Qur'anic scholars, not vehicles of divine grace. It is a religion of the cities, of the educated, however much it historically fed off the purifying simplicity of warlike nomads and the country-dwellers they rule, as Ibn Khaldun argued long ago (Ibn Khaldun 1967). Indeed, Islam's virtual *raison d'être* was the destruction of local polytheism and magic in Arabia, in contrast to Southern Europe and the Americas where Catholicism made continual, if unofficial, hybrids with "pagan" rites. In this sense, regarding mainstream Islam, we might say that Islam was Protestant long before Luther. Turning to the extreme, both Islam and Protestantism have tended periodically to produce evangelical and other "purifying" revivals. In this sense as well, radical Islam has been compared to radical Protestantism; M. J. Gohari refers to the eighteenth-century protofundamentalist sect, the Wahhabis, as "Muslim Calvinists" (Gohari 1999: 40).

A more plausible charge is that the militant Islam evident since the 1970s is caused by a yet unmodernized Islam's confrontation with Western modernity. And as noted, such a reaction is evident almost everywhere to some degree. But the Islamic world is not just *now* confronting modernity. Industrial, political, and cultural modernization have been occurring at many points along the Islamic world since the nineteenth century. Indeed, some Muslim writers have referred to the current revival as *postmodern:* Fazlur Rahman characterizes recent developments as "postmodernist fundamentalism," and Akbar Ahmed sees hope in the "postmodern" condition of the Islamic world (Rahman 1982: 136; Ahmed 1992). Such claims are less intriguing than they sound, hanging as they do on defining modernism as Western imperialism, so that "postmodern" here simply means postcolonial. Nevertheless, the point is that Islam is remarkably modern. As Hodgson puts it, the Islamic project is "one of the most thoroughgoing attempts in history to build a world-wide human community as if from scratch on the basis of an explicitly worked out idea," its early form having borrowed little from either local Arab culture or from Greco-Latin or Persian civilizations (Hodgson 1974, 1:98). In the West, the notion of building a society "as if from scratch" is characteristic of the political revolutions of the eighteenth through twentieth centuries and their "natural rights" and "state of nature." Just as the modern West rooted republicanism in a "rational" or "natural" theology, Islam sees its final revelation as providing the natural, rational, cosmopolitan, postethnic, and antinationalist religion of all mankind.

Four major roads have been trod by intellectuals in the Islamic world during the past hundred years. It was in the late nineteenth century that Islamic "modernism," the attempt to reconcile Islam with modern Western thought, emerged among intellectuals as a way to revitalize the Islamic world in response to imperialism and perceived decay. Modernism encouraged a tolerant, cosmopolitan approach. Later fundamentalism, hostile not only to the West but to homegrown secular nationalism, insisted on its version of original and literal scriptural meaning, and throughout the twentieth century became increasingly intolerant and violent. Traditionalism is an attempt, in response to modernism and fundamentalism, to reassert the complex Islamic tradition and its scriptural hermeneutics (e.g., Seyyed Hossein Nasr 1987). Last is the nonreligious option of nationalism. Our focus will be fundamentalism, although its relation to modernism and nationalism will be relevant as well

We should remember that "fundamentalism" is an American term that emerged in early twentieth-century Protestantism Evangelism. For Evangelicals the individual's salvation was assured, not by baptism or maturation as part of an established church, but by an adult act of renewal, of being "born again." The label "fundamental*ist*" came to be used for a subset of the Evangelicals opposed to modern "degradations" of Christianity, the term deriving from a series of religious essays edited and published by A. C. Dixon in 1910–15 under the title "The Fundamentals." Fundamentalists accepted the utter "inerrancy" of scripture and a premillennialist eschatology as tests of faith. Inerrancy forced fundamentalist thinkers, like A. A. Hodge and B. B. Warfield, to reject the doctrine of the merely "spiritual" truth of scripture as distinct from "rational" or "empirical" truth (Ammerman 1991). Truth is one, therefore scripture is not only spiritually but also empirically true. Their refusal to compromise with social vicissitudes led them to separate their communities not only from secular America but from the mainstream Protestant churches. However much fundamentalists oppose and threaten those outside the faith, their primary conflict is with the "official," mainstream churches and their traditional compromises with the state.

Westerners must keep in mind that Islamic fundamentalism is not related to mainstream Islam as Christian fundamentalism is to mainstream Christianity. The analogy fails. First, unlike the Bible the Qur'an is understood to be literally the word of God, dictated by Allah and merely transcribed by the Prophet Muhammad. Even moderate Muslims accept the truth or inerrancy of all statements in the Qur'an. Their meaning is, of course, subject to interpretation, but scriptural hermeneutics in Islam cannot, as in Jewish and Christian exegesis, exploit the alleged imperfections, motivations, and historical contingencies of a human writer. Second, we cannot distinguish militant from mainstream Islam by referring to the former as "political Islam." For mainstream Islam is *already* political. Some use the term "Islamism" for Islamic fundamentalism. This is plausible if "ism" is supposed to indicate a political ideology comparable to nationalism, capitalism, or communism. But then its opposite, Islam without the "ism," is not an *a*political religion divorced from law and social management. "Islamism" is better used for any attempt to base a political program on Islam. The best terms for violent Muslim radicalism are *militant* and *fundamentalist* Islam, the former emphasizing the political radicalism and violence, the latter the uncompromising dogma that shuns traditionalist Islam.

Dār al-Islām and *Dār Al-Harb*

Some Muslims and their supporters have argued that Islam is not an inherently intolerant or expansionist religion, that its track record on women's rights and social justice is far better than most non-Muslims believe, that terrorism is the perversion of Islam by the few. If the jingoist haters of Islam are utterly wrong (and they are), if the paranoids who call the FBI whenever a middle-aged man kneels to pray in a Detroit Walmart are wrong (and they are), so are those who claim there is *nothing* unique to Islam that makes it a likely opponent of liberal modernity. For Islam in principle repudiates the distinction that has been the modern West's most crucial bulwark of tolerance and civility with respect to religion, namely, the distinction between public political authority and "private" religious-cultural life.

Now, some may object to this sweeping generalization. First, as in all great civilizations, the realities of managing Islamic states and empires generated prudential compromises throughout its history. By no means have predominantly Muslim states conducted themselves consistently as Islamist states. Clearly Muslims living in predominantly non-Muslim countries accept a divorce between religion and ultimate public authority, in practice and perhaps in belief. Second, Muslim states have often been tolerant of minority religious communities, following Qur'an 2.256: "There shall be no coercion in matters of faith."★ The tradition holds that forced conversion makes no sense, true religion being an internal matter. This is precisely John Locke's argument in his 1689 *Letter Concerning Toleration;* on this issue Islam preceded the godfather of Western liberalism by a thousand years. Third, as the revivalists emphasize, Islam makes no distinction among peoples. *Anyone* who asserts the oneness of God (the *tawhid*), submits to Him, and accepts the prophecy of Muhammed is a Muslim (indeed, as we will see, some Muslim thinkers dispense with the last requirement). Islam is explicit in subordinating questions of group membership and identity to the universal demands of God, hence its opposition to nationalism. As Said Halim Pasha, the Ottoman prime minister, declared: "As there is no English Mathematics, German Astronomy or French chemistry, so there is no Turkish, Arabian, Persian or Indian Islam" (Iqbāl 1998: 259). This extends even to religious differences. The Qur'an upbraids Jews and Christians for their sectarianism: "And they claim: 'None shall ever enter Paradise unless he be a Jew'—or, 'a Christian.' Such are their wishful beliefs! . . . Yea, indeed: everyone who surrenders his whole being unto God, and is a doer of Good withal, shall have his reward with his Sustainer" (Qur'an 2.111–12). Thus, "Say: 'We believe in God . . . and that which has been bestowed upon Abraham and Isma'il and Isaac and Jacob and their descendants, and that which has been vouchsafed to Moses and Jesus. . . . we make no distinction between any of them" (Qur'an 2.136). Last, contrary to common judgment, Islam does not endorse theocracy. Theocracy, government by clerics, is a very rare condition. Even today's Iran is not literally a theocracy, since the clerics do not constitute the administration but a juridical trump to state actions that—in their view—violate Islamic law within an otherwise republican constitution (Juergensmeyer 1993: 176–77). Islam does reject *sectarian* power or any worldly church. Davutoglu argues that this is a direct consequence of Islam's utter separation of the divine from the worldly: only *shari'a* is divine, not governmental authority (Davutoglu 1994). In traditional Islamic states the caliph has, according to the late Malcolm Kerr, "no special religious inspiration or powers of interpretation," his only religious

---

★All quotations of the Qur'an are from Muhammad Asad's 1980 translation, *The Message of the "Qur'an."* Note that throughout this chapter transliterated Arabic terms and names now familiar in English (Qur'an, *jihad, Shiite,* Ayatollah Khomeini, Hamas) appear without full diacritical marks.

responsibility being the "protection of the generally recognized tenets of the faith," not their legal administration (Kerr 1966: 150–51). The caliphate's responsibility to protect Islam no more makes it an ecclesiastical office than the responsibility to protect the Church of England so makes the British Crown (Kerr 1966: 27).

Nevertheless, the sticking point remains that Islamic civilization has never undergone a Western-style secularization of political authority or law. From the very beginning, with the Prophet's migration to Medina, Islam has understood itself as a political community *(umma)* of believers, as a space or territory of righteous belief. The early Islamic state saw expansion as its religious duty. As we shall see, even the nineteenth-century modernists who sought reconciliation with modern Western thought rejected secularization. The Christian distinction from Matthew 22:21, give to Caesar's what is Caesar's and to God what is God's, cannot apply to Islam. Islam has never allowed itself to be *privatized,* as did Christianity in the West. Certainly political realities led Islam to evolve compromise measures to live with other states. But the early fervor, to which some revivalists wish to return, aimed to reform the entire world. To this day, in Islam *all* legitimacy is *religious* legitimacy.

Regarding that concept most fearsome to non-Muslims, believers are quick to point out that *jihad* does not primarily refer to warfare. The term means "exertion" or "struggle," in the sense of the believer's struggle to follow the path of God. Classically, there are four kinds of *jihad,* that of the heart, hand, tongue, and sword. *Jihad* means, above all, the moral struggle of righting one's own heart, expressed in works and speech, and only lastly the willingness to risk one's life in combat. In the *hadith* (sayings of the Prophet) Muhammad tells followers returning from battle that they must now turn from the "lesser" to the "greater" *jihad,* from fighting to the struggle against one's base impulses (Johnson 2001: 35). Even in international relations the *jihad* of the sword has been understood by some Muslim writers as statecraft and just governance, not as war against non-Muslims.

Nevertheless, as Khadduri makes clear, the "classical" doctrine in Islamic history dictated a normal state of war with non-Muslim states. As John Kelsay notes, in the history of warfare involving Muslim countries it is *secular* war that is dubious and needful of special justification. The only patently legitimate reason for war is defense of Islamic rule (Kelsay 1993: 48). Islamic fighters accepted as well that to die in battle for Islam guaranteed entrance to Paradise. The Islamic law of international relations "was designed for temporary purposes, on the assumption that the Islamic state was capable of absorbing the whole of mankind" (Khadduri 2002: 5). The aim was not forced conversion, however. Early Muslims aimed to extend the *dār al-islām*, the territory of peace, justice, and moral order under submission to God. The outer world is the *dār al-ḥārb*, the territory of "war." *Harbis* live in a Hobbesian state of nature. Extending Islam was thus a war to establish peace. For the polytheists unwilling to abandon their ways, the Qur'an counsels, "Slay those who ascribe divinity to aught beside God wherever you may come upon them" (9.5). *Dhimmis,* Jews and Christians, fellow "People of the Book," were exempt from such treatment as long as they accepted Islamic authority. All communities were "invited" to acknowledge Islamic rule and law by paying tribute *(jizyah),* which would permit their local religious practices, so long as those were not offensive to God (in other words, idolatrous or immoral). This made the gap between defensive and offensive war easy to cross, for the offensive war that followed a refusal to accept Islamic rule could be understood as a willful rejection of God's law, a rejection taken to imply that acts abominable to God would continue in the others' territory. Thus, as Khadduri notes, "the classical doctrine of the jihad made no distinction between defensive and offensive war." Certainly such wars did have to be authorized by the caliph. Hence in Shia Islam since the disappearance of the Twelfth Imam — the absence of an heir upon Hasan al-'Askarī's death in 873 C.E. — there was no recognized leader capable of such authorization, so only defensive, not offensive *jihad,* is accepted.

After the initial period of expansion, the dominant view softened. The Hanafī juristic school held that although the non-Muslim world is a world of unrighteousness and conflict, war against it is justified only if it threatens Islamic territory. Others, like the Shāfi'ī school, maintained the stricter view of *jihad* as the duty of every believer to war on all unbelievers simply because of their unbelief. But subsequently the Shāfi'ī argued for a middling possibility, the *dār al-sulh* or sphere of "peaceful arrangements" or coexistence with non-Muslim states, territories which the Hanafi regarded as simply part of the *dār al-islām* (Khadduri 1966: 12–13). But contracts and treaties were recognized to be temporary, not to exceed ten years. This softening made sense in a Muslim world that was already huge, and for which, as its power declined and it was threatened by fragmentation from within and Christian crusaders and Asian nomads from without, maintenance became a more sensible aim than expansion (in this sense resembling the doctrine of "socialism in one country" that the Soviets were forced to accept after the revolution failed to spread). The great medieval jurist Ibn Taymīya interpreted *jihad* of the sword as a binding duty only in defense, denying that war on unbelievers merely because of their unbelief was legitimate (Khadduri 1966: 59). Thus did the Muslim world accommodate itself to the exigencies of power, forming what we can call traditional Islam.

From Modernism to Fundamentalism

The intellectual roots and historical precedents of today's Islamic revival arguably go far back in time. Said Amir Arjomand suggests that the fundamentalist form of "violent purity" harkens back to the Khārijīs (seceders), who left Ali ibn Abi Talib's camp during the First Civil War (656–61 C.E.) over the issue of succession to the murdered third caliph. The Khārijīs killed Ali in 661, initiating the split between what would become Sunni and Shia Islam. More directly, modern fundamentalism can be traced to two groups, the Wahhabis and the Deoband movement.

Muhammed Ibn 'Abd al-Wahhab (1703–92) opposed the encroachment of un-Islamic folk practices, like shrines for saints, ultimately aiming to excise all "innovations" allowed by Islamic teachers and jurists, and return to guidance by the Qur'an and the *hadith*. He emphasized the importance of *ijtihad*, independent rational judgment, as a counterweight to established authority. Having converted the head of the ruling Saud clan, his views have remained strong in Saudi Arabia ever since. Similarly, the Deoband movement emerged from central India in the wake of the ill-fated Muslim-led revolt against the British in 1857. Founded by Mohammed Zasim Nanautawi (1833–77) and Rashid Ahmed Gangohi (1829–1905), it set up madrassas in India, Afghanistan, and Pakistan. Maulana Abdul Haw, a movement leader, the most prominent at Deoband, formed the hugely popular Haqqania madrassa in Pakistan in 1947. Indefatigable regulators of personal conduct, in the twentieth century alone the Deobandis "issued almost a quarter of a million *fatwa* on the minutiae of every life" (Griffith 2001: 60).

Simultaneous with the founding of the Deobandis, the Islamic revival against imperialism began in earnest with the late nineteenth-century modernists. Most famous among them was Sayyid Jamāl al-Din (1833–97), called "al-Afghāni." Probably of Iranian origin, and certainly influenced by the Persian intellectual climate—in which, unlike the Sunni countries, Sufism and medieval Arabic *falsafa* (Greek-inspired philosophy) continued to play a role—he was a charismatic, complex figure of intrigue who practiced *taqiyya* or "precautionary dissimulation," sometimes speaking as a Westernizing promoter of science and reason, sometimes as a revivalist of Islam. This ambiguity is particularly evident in the juxtaposition of his famously religious "Refutation of the Materialists" and his secular "Response to Renan" (Keddie 1968). What we can say is that al-Afghāni began the process of making Islam the core idea of a modern political and anti-imperial movement, an alternative to secularism, nationalism, and communism. His most prominent disciple, Muhammad 'Abduh (1849–1905), crafted a more straightforward message in service of the same aim. 'Abduh's *Theology of Unity* is founded on the *tawhīd,* the unity of God, from which he derives a remarkable set of conclusions, most prominently that Islam is utterly compatible with modern science and technology. 'Abduh insists that reason is the heart of Islam. He argued not only that the Qur'an permits minority religious freedom, but that Islam is *never* spread by the sword. Islamic expansion is achieved only by example ('Abduh 1966: 147).

While the modernists have had great intellectual impact, with the exception of their descendent Muhammad Iqbāl, who played an important role in Pakistan, their legacy was politically ineffectual. The twentieth century would see two other movements vying to lead Islamic revival: fundamentalism and nationalism. Nationalism emerged in Egypt after the First World War, led by the Wafd party of Sa'd Zaghloul, which had unsuccessfully sought to overturn British rule. But each time nationalism failed to produce results, progressively more militant forms of Islam asserted themselves. As Giles Keppel points out, re-Islamization proceeded along two tracks, "from below" and "from above." The former refers to local groups that would "honeycomb" civil society, working in hospitals, schools, and various charitable organizations. Perhaps the most prominent was the Jama'at al Tabligh (Society for the Propagation of Islam), founded in India in 1927 by Muhammad Ilyas. Promoting a "scrupulous mimicry" of the Prophet's life in every detail, the Tabligh became a widespread international movement recruiting mostly from pools of disappointed rural immigrants to the cities. In contrast, re-Islamization "from above" refers to intellectual-political movements designed to reform or take over dominant social institutions. These typically drew from the modernizing, educated sectors of society, especially technocrats and scientists in training. The most famous of these was Egypt's Muslim Brotherhood, founded by Hasan al-Bannā (1906–49) in 1929.

Al-Bannā followed many of modernism's themes. Islam is the source of reason and the pinnacle of civilization, but its recent decadence makes it easy prey for Western colonialism. The way back is through scripture, not the "blind traditionalism" of the *ulama* or community of scholars (al-Bannā 1978: 88). But unlike the modernists al-Bannā starkly defends military *jihad*. It is not merely struggle, but *fighting,* not merely defensive, but *offensive* too. All Muslims must "prepare their equipment" and get ready until the "time is ripe." He writes, "The men of learning . . . agree unanimously that *jihad* is a communal obligation imposed upon the Islamic *umma* in order to broadcast the summons . . . and that it is an individual obligation to repulse the attack of unbelievers upon it" (al-Bannā 1978: 150). The "stigma" of Islam as a militaristic religion is false, he argues, because the aim of *jihad* is the universal peace that will reign when Islam is unchallenged. Those who consider violence the "lesser *jihad*" are defying original Islam. "Some of them try," he continues, "to divert people from the importance of fighting," but "nothing . . . confers on the advocate the supreme martyrdom and the reward of the strivers in *Jihad,* unless he slays or is slain in the way of God" (al-Bannā 1978: 155). Despite this view al-Bannā's political method of choice remained *da'wa,* the calling to social activism, hence his establishment of mosques, schools, hospitals, and sporting clubs. Within the movement his discipline was authoritarian, but aimed at building Islamist community from the ground up.

Two midcentury thinkers then provided the ideological basis for completing the turn of revivalism from modernism to militancy. First was Maulana Sayyid Abul Ala Mawdudi (1903–79), who in 1941 founded Jamaat-i-Islami, which was to become Pakistan's most prominent fundamentalist group. Like the modernists Mawdudi remained a defender of reason and science. He explicitly criticized those whose opposition to the culture of the West led them to reject scientific or material progress. They are merely "safeguarding the antiques" (Mawdudi 1980: 35). Likewise, he declared that "to cover the books of the writers of the early ages with new coatings of commentaries and footnotes" serves no purpose. Science is common to all mankind, so the Muslim may without heterodoxy learn from Western science. Indeed, Islam is the ultimate source of scientific rationality, not to mention justice, equality, freedom, and hence true civilization; its current status is due to imperialism from without and decay from within. Unlike all other religions, Islam is nonsectarian and devoid of national or geographical ties; the very meaning of *islām* is simple submission to God. Thus for Mawdudi even those who submitted to God before the revelation to Muhammad were Muslims! Sivan reports the "Maudoodi dictum, often quoted by Arab fundamentalists," that "instead of claiming that Islam is truly reasonable, one should hold that the true reason is Islamic" (Sivan 1985: 67). A follower of the true cosmopolitan religion, the Muslim "does not regard anything in the world as a stranger to himself. He looks upon everything in the universe as belonging to the same Lord Whom he himself belongs to. He is not partisan in his thinking and behaviour. His sympathy, love and service do not remain confined to any particular sphere or group. His vision is enlarged, his intellectual horizon widens" (Mawdudi 1974: 98). Indeed, sounding remarkably like John Stuart Mill, Mawdudi argues that as long as one's interpretation of the Qur'an is not self-serving, disagreement over its meaning "is a stimulus to improvement and the very soul of a healthy society. Differences of this kind are found in every society whose members are endowed with intelligence and reason. Their existence is a sign of life" (Mawdudi 1990: 46).

At the same time, Mawdudi makes Islam a totalistic, universally valid, and utopian way of life. Islam is a complete system; the task of the Muslim is "to try to make the whole of Islam supreme over the whole of life" (Marty and Appleby 1995, 1:487). While he continues the older tradition of understanding *jihad* as primarily defensive, he promotes it to the status of the Five Pillars: "*Jihad* is as much a primary duty of the Muslims as are prayer and fasting" (Mawdudi 1974: 141). Every Muslim is obligated to engage in violent struggle against "those who perpetrate oppression as enemies of Islam." As Mawdudi repeats again and again, the *tawhīd* implies that no person should bow to anyone but God. Sovereignty belongs to God alone. Recognition of that fact, and the rejection of any other authority, guarantees human equality and freedom. Clan elders, tribal leaders, nationalist presidents, priests, popes—all are usurpers of God's authority and violators of human justice. The "root of all evil" is "acceptance of supremacy and overlordship other then [*sic*] that of Allah" (Mawdudi 1980: 93). Geopolitically, communism is evil, liberal capitalism is cruel and licentious, nationalism is contrary to God's will. The communist and Western powers threaten to blow up the world. Only Islam can save it. Likewise the economic problems of humanity can only be solved by "Islamic economics." The rejection of usury and conspicuous accumulation of wealth, along with the *zakat* or obligatory donation to the poor, will produce collective prosperity without the evils of Western inequality or communist oppression. Echoing the utopianism of Marx, the morally ideal society will simultaneously achieve the highest prosperity, the greatest quantity of leisure, and complete economic justice and equality. Under Islam,

> every branch of economic activity will expand and flourish. Islam roots out all these evils through the institution of *Zakat* and the agency of the public exchequer is always available to you as a helper. You need not take thought for the morrow. Whenever you are in need you can go to the public exchequer and obtain your rightful due. There is no necessity of keeping deposits in banks and of having insurance policies. You can leave this world without any anxiety for the future of your children, the exchequer of the community will be responsible for them afterwards. (Mawdudi 1992: 40)

The ideal world will result. Thus, "The objective of Islamic Jihad is to put an end to the dominance of the un-Islamic systems of government and replace them with Islamic rule. Islam intends to bring about this revolution not in one country or in a few countries but in the entire world" (Mawdudi 1980: 142).

While Muslim fundamentalist groups multiplied in Arab countries during midcentury, they were briefly outshone by secular nationalism, which reached its high point in the 1950s and 1960s during the reign of Egyptian president Gamal Abdel Nasser. Following the Nasserite model, fundamentalism was commonly suppressed in the Islamic world by newly postcolonial states. Thus the jails became the new *madrassas* for a growing extremism. The fundamentalism of the 1970s was then an explicit reaction against the perceived corruption, and the very real repression, of Nasser's regime. But the humiliation of Arab governments by Israel in the 1967 Six Day War, and their less devastating defeat in 1973, tarred nationalism beyond redemption. Then came OPEC and the rise in oil prices which flooded the oil-rich states with cash, in particular, Saudi Arabia, the home both of Islam's most sacred sites and Wahhabism.

One of those imprisoned Egyptian Islamists, Sayyid Qutb, laid the intellectual foundations for the most militant form of fundamentalism. Arrested three years after a personal conversion that led him to join the Muslim Brotherhood, he sat in prison for a decade, was released in 1964, then arrested again and hanged in 1966. Qutb followed much of Mawdudi's line. Islam is the natural human religion, recognizing no differences of ritual, ethnicity, race, or tribe. All people who have faithfully submitted to God are Muslims. Islam can absorb modern science, since "the experimental method" was invented by Islam and copied by the West (Qutb 1990: 94). Civilized society is one in which the laws of God are the law of the land, hence Allah alone is sovereign, human authorities being mere "viceregents." The only truly human community is a "community of belief." In an almost Rousseauian turn, human governance is slavery of one man to another, but in submitting to God one submits to no man, hence remains free.

Chastened by his prison experience, Qutb took the radical step of explicitly branding all existing Islamic societies as part of *jahiliyya*. Literally unbelief or ignorance, the term originally referred to those unaware of the Prophet's message, who lived before Islam or outside its spread, thus carrying as well the sense of "barbarism." Qutb regarded contemporary *jahiliyya* as "rebellion" against God, insisting that Muslims must identify, judge, and overcome unbelievers. *Jahiliyya* is for Qutb the entire world; current Islamic states are no better than Western ones. Only the Qur'an and the *hadith* are legitimate sources of social and political guidance; traditional jurists, priests, and men of theory are not to be trusted. But Qutb approved of *ijtihad,* thinking for oneself, since he believed it discredited traditional Islamic authorities and supported militancy. His attention turned from the community-building of al-Bannā to revolution; society must be remade now by direct attack on the state. This was an implicit critique of the Muslim Brotherhood; as the Sudanese Islamist Hassan al-Turabi later put it, "Look at the Brotherhood; they don't change society at all, they never detribalize society, they promote a traditional, sectarian Islam against a progressive Islam" (Shadid 2001: 62). Giles Keppel remarks, "Qutb's wish to break with the world was very singular. It was contrary to the position adopted by... even most of the Muslim Brothers—during the 1960s. They held that there could be no breaking with a society which was, however imperfectly, Islamic.... Qutb, on the other hand, thought that Nasser's 'barbarism' had reached a point of no return" (Keppel 1994: 20).

When Nasser's successor Anwar Sadat lifted the ban on fundamentalism, the children of Qutb emerged from jail with radicalized views. Some called for an internal withdrawal of believers into separatist Islamic communities, given the utter unacceptability of existing majority-Muslim societies. But Muhammed 'Abd al-Salam Faraj, a member of the militant group al-Jihād, rejected that approach. Like Qutb he insisted that "the Rulers of this age . . . were raised at the tables of imperialism, be it Crusaderism, or Communism, or Zionism. They carry nothing from Islam but their names" (Jansen 1986: 169). Faraj took the logically final step toward holy war in his *Al-Farīdah al-Ghā'ibah* (The Neglected Duty). For centuries corrupt rulers and traditional scholars have purposely suppressed the Islamic duty of offensive *jihad* espoused by the Prophet and the early caliphate: "Neglecting jihad is the cause of the lowness, humiliation, division and fragmentation in which Muslims live today" (Jansen 1986: 205). True Islam is a violent transformation of the real by the ideal, the takeover of all Islamic states by force of arms, an Islam "spread by the sword" (Jansen 1986: 193). Faraj makes *jihad* the essence of Islamic commitment. This militancy achieved its greatest success when on October 6, 1981, one of Faraj's associates assassinated President Sadat, stating afterward, "I have killed Pharaoh."

Islamic militancy thus reached the historical plateau from which September 11, 2001, can be understood. But in the almost exactly twenty years that intervened, we must also recognize the unique role of Afghanistan. After the Soviet invasion of 1979 the Afghan war became, as Anthony Shadid insightfully puts it, the Spanish Civil War for Islamists, generating an "Islamic International" of mostly Arab fighters available to travel to virtually any Islamic conflict (Shadid 2001: 79ff.). These itinerant warriors have been, however, largely devoid of a detailed ideology or political program, their purely military, pan-Islamic militancy largely unconnected to the regional and local Islamist movements they join. As Olivier Roy described the new breed of Islamic terrorists, referring to the man who would later mastermind the September 11 attacks,

> Their distinctive feature is their internationalism and lack of territorial base. . . . They are thus disconnected not only from existing states . . . but also from the large Islamist movements, which have disowned their offspring. [Those] movements, such as the Muslim Brotherhood, the FIS [Algeria], Refah in Turkey and Hamas in Palestine, place their struggles in a national framework and claim full recognition as protagonists in the political process. This approach,

which is shared by Iran, might appropriately be described as Islamic nationalism. It is a far cry from the imaginary *umma* which Bin Ladin and his associates invoke . . . without a genuine political project. (Roy 1998: 8)

According to Shadid even Hassan al-Turabi regarded bin Laden as "nothing but a foot soldier," a heroic *mujahīd* but without a political program.

We will turn to an overall evaluation of Islamic fundamentalism presently. First, let us draw some tentative conclusions from our brief survey.

Islamic fundamentalism is not, or not primarily, antimodernist, primitive, primordial, or irrational. We may say that fundamentalism is antimodernist, if we understand "modernism" in the Western sense as the attempt of mainstream denominations to relax standards and to interpret scripture more loosely and metaphorically in order to make religion workable in the modern world. In the Islamic world that relaxed interpretive style is characteristic of *traditionalism* (although the modernism of Afghani and 'Abduh produced its own version). The crucial point is that from the first emergence of fundamentalism by name in Protestant America, to its Islamist version, fundamentalists have been highly rationalist, concerned to apply a careful, if stilted, analysis of scripture as consistently as possible across all social areas of life, refusing to accept *ad hoc* pragmatic trade-offs that cannot be justified on scriptural grounds. Neither is it right to say that fundamentalists are "traditionalists." While they regard themselves as returning to original teachings, they reject all more recent traditions of interpretation, the accumulated practices of the era intervening between the time of revelation and the present. Their opposition to the elite authorities of the mainstream makes them, in their eyes, *anti-authoritarian,* alone training a harsh, critical light on mainstream scriptural hermeneutics. Fundamentalism is not what sociologist Edward Shils called "primordial," even if it trades on primordial feelings. It is not determined by history, it is not ethnic or nationalist. Fundamentalists of all kinds worship The Book, not ancestors. Most important, as we shall see, the fundamentalisms that we are familiar with are almost by definition political. They accept the modern *politicization of culture.* As Geertz argued regarding the ethnic nationalism of the postcolonial states that emerged after World War II, fundamentalism is motivated by the presence of a modern, centralized state, a "valuable new prize over which to fight and a frightening new force with which to contend"

(Geertz 1961: 22). Like nationalists, fundamentalists want to capture the state and its mass culture, not dismantle them.

Here the relationship between the fundamentalist and modernist wings of the Islamic revival is instructive. While the modernists are often considered synthesizers who sought to bridge Western and Islamic thought, hence a pole away from the militants, this is a bit misleading. Mawdudi is no less ardent in his defense of science and reason than is 'Abduh. The modernists were not suggesting a secular, non-Islamic society (although al-Afghani suggested almost everything at one time or another), and they specifically rejected the Western division of religion and politics. It was not for nothing that 'Abduh's followers called themselves Salafiyyah, devotees of the *salaf* or "pious ancestors." Certainly the fundamentalists invoke a militant understanding of *jihad,* justifying a violence that the modernists rejected. But the key difference, I think, hence the *sine qua non* of fundamentalism, goes beyond this specific doctrine. What makes militant Islam militant is not merely the doctrine of *jihad,* nor heightened intolerance, nor violence, nor traditionalism, nor fear of modernity, nor an angry response to imperialism. Its novelty is more profound than that.

Anticulture, Taliban-style

Taliban means student, and was used in southern Afghanistan in the late twentieth century to refer to religious students at a *madrassa* who, after several years of instruction, could be qualified as village *mullah* or scriptural authority. During the war against the Soviet occupation Mohammad Nabi Mohammadi's Islamist group, Harakat-I Inquilab-I Islami, drew many of its soldiers from such *taliban.* In 1994 two teenage girls near the Khandahari village of Sang Hesar were kidnapped and raped by a group of *mujahedin.* Mohammad Omar, who had been a Harakat commander but retired to study in the *madrassa,* recruited thirty students and rescued the girls. As Omar later said, "We were fighting against Muslims who had gone wrong" (Griffin 2001: 35). This was the beginning of the transformation of *taliban,* students, into *the* Taliban, revolutionary party. By late in the year Omar had fifteen hundred men.

Upon taking power the Taliban had the reputation of restraint and decency, refusing the temptations of theft and rape. This reputation was not long in losing its luster. The Taliban's religious orientation is a Deobandi radicalization of the Wahhabi line. M. J. Gohari reports that on a trip to Saudi Arabia in the 1980s he had seen what he assumed were Saudi guards preventing some elderly Iranians from kissing the Prophet's tomb, a folk-polytheist departure from *tawhīd*. He was surprised by the guards' vehemence in making an issue of this minor sign of fealty, but was more surprised to discover that they were not Saudis but Afghans. One said he was delighted to be studying "true Islam," which must have meant Wahhabism. It is this perspective that the Taliban, after ten years of brutal warfare, were now able to impose on a diverse but largely Persianate Afghanistan. Once in power they "made it clear they proposed to rewrite Afghan history" (Sinha 1997: 45). Their ideological radicalism, reminiscent of the style if not the genocidal results of the Khmer Rouge, is by now well known: virtually no music, no nonreligious books or bookstores, no visual representation, no uncontrolled television or radio, and of course no non-Islamic statuary, as seen in their gratuitous destruction of the giant Buddhas of Bamiyan, an ancient religious site posing no threat to the dominance of Islam in the region. The restriction of women reached a crescendo, barring their public education as well as travel in public alone, even though covered from toe to scalp. Sex was clearly a special concern. But Taliban doctrine evidently still permitted some forms of humor: regarding adultery, Mullah Moham-mad Hassan of Khandahar quipped, "We have a dilemma on this. One group of scholars believes you should take these people to the highest building in the city and hurl them to their deaths. [The other] recommends you dig a pit near a wall somewhere, put these people in it, then topple the wall so that they are buried alive" (Griffin 2001: 61).

We may note two brief portraits by John Sifton, a humanitarian aid worker in Taliban-controlled Afghanistan during 2000–2001. In Jozjan province, at a Soviet-era hotel used by the Taliban to house foreigners, he came across a landscape painting that included several animals. The heads of the animals had been carefully cut out by Taliban police. "This left a decapitated deer standing by a pond and a headless beaver sitting on a tree stump. . . . A terrible painting . . . done entirely with two shades of green and one shade of brown and then vandalized by the Taliban police trying to ensure its innocence before God without destroying it altogether. In its own way, I thought, it is a post-postmodern masterpiece." Later, in sum-ming up his experience, he writes, "We are off the grid. . . . There are no telephones outside the cities. There is no television reception. We have no access to 'entertainment.' There are no theaters, films, galleries or circuses. The Taliban has even banned music. . . . Sometimes it feels as if we have been brought back not just to a time before modern entertainment but to a time before art . . . a time without images and ideas and representations, only actual events" (Sifton 2001). Here the Taliban form the best, if most extreme, example of a virtually *anticultural* religious practice. Most of Afghan culture was literally eliminated or suppressed—artifacts, music, narratives, styles of dress. It is not that they eliminated decadent Western culture or secular Afghan culture. They eliminated culture *per se*. This may seem an odd formulation, since religion is itself a part of culture. But we already know that one part of culture—for example, political ideology— can tyrannize the rest. So can Church, Temple, or Mosque. In the Taliban and the post-Qutb forms of Islamic militancy generally, we see the complete condemnation of existing society, the requirement for a wholesale reconstruction of culture in strict accordance with a single dogma by a revolutionary vanguard who alone can tell its literal meaning. The enemy here is historical culture itself.

As this implies, and as Roxanne Euben notes of Islamic fundamentalism in general, the Taliban exhibited a Marxist-Leninist analogy (Euben 1999). For the militants the crumbling of extant world systems—capitalism, communism, nationalism—is inevitable. The ideal social order is possible, if the right ideology is accepted, and all can accept it, because it is the final fulfillment of human civilization, transcending any of the older human divisions of nation, caste, or class. Once accomplished, all of life, economic, social, political, intellectual, and cultural, will be different. Only truly Islamic rule, either by making all humanity Muslims or forcing other monotheists to accept Muslim authority, will allow humanity to be truly human. And the key to this transformation is held by an educated elite who understand the inner truths. Mawdudi even called for a "permanent *jihad*," echoing Trotsky's notion of permanent revolution. But not only is leftist utopianism thereby invoked. The Taliban scoured the semiotic landscape of all other religious and cultural inheritances, an obsession not unlike the Nazi determination to root out that last shopkeeper hiding in an attic, to render the homeland *judenrein*. Of course Islamic fundamentalism has a very long way to go to complete that analogy. In terms of totalitarian slaughter the West remains unchallenged, its ideological children, fascist-nationalism and

Russian communism, being hard to beat (even if Chinese and Cambodian communists made a strong showing). Militant Islam will undoubtedly never catch up. But it will not be for lack of the right spirit.

How Many Modernities?

What marks the special nature of Islamic fundamentalism, as other commentators have noted, is its *modernism*. It entails a closeted form of the Western modernism that it so publicly claims to oppose. If Islam was always political in the sense that it sought to establish a righteous monotheistic community, for Islamists the *whole* point and method of Islam becomes political. Personal confession and virtue matter less than the inauguration of a new order. As Arjomand points out,

> The Principle of Qutb's neo-Kharijite sectarianism is this: the profession of faith according to the canonical formula and the belief in the Five Pillars are not the defining mark of a Muslim believer. The believer must in addition reject all man-made laws and governments, which are the foundations of the new paganism. The true believers, the elect, must organize themselves into vanguard groups apart from the new society of ignorance and repeat the original pattern of the establishment of Islam through withdrawal/ migration, jihad, and conquest of power. (Marty and Appleby 1995, 5:184)

As Olivier Roy explains of twentieth-century Islamists, "Far from having emerged from the clergy or traditional circles, they are to be found within the modern institutions of society (colleges, faculties of science, and in general in the urban environment)" (Roy 1986: 6). Islamist leaders discovered themselves as modern people in barely modernized societies suffering from economic underdevelopment, geopolitical inferiority, and political infantilization under autocratic leaders. Exposed to the West, often educated in it, they sought the source of their home society's inadequacy with Western tools. Knowing the modern West better than their own religious tradition, Hamid Dabashi argues, "They recognize a heightened state of ideological self-awareness on the part of 'the West' that they identify as the source and cause of its achievements." They bend Islam to fill the role of an ideological alternative to secularism, capitalism, nationalism, and communism, "to create from Islam a political model capable of competing with the great ideologies of the Western world" (Roy 1986: 6). Repulsed by "backward and superstitious" Islam, the traditional Islam of their birth communities, the militant seeks "'the True Islam,' which he imagines as socially active and politically progressive," that is, as fulfilling the function of ideology in the postreligious West (Dabashi 1993: 326–27). The acceptance of the modern state left behind by retreating Western imperialists as the ultimate prize, the free decision to break with given social norms to join an elite vanguard, the rationalist planning that hopes, through novel methods and technologies, to win the prize, and the utopian reconstruction according to intellectual principles it hopes to carry out—these are the fruit of modern secularism, not the religious tradition.

In this, militant Islam is neither orthodox nor traditional. Its heterodoxy lies not only in the use of violence by terrorists, which when it kills women and children, violates the *hadith*. The ideologically hidden violation of tradition is deeper and more essential. For society can only be remade by militants if they organize as a modern, Western-style political party and seize control of a modern, Western-style, centralized state: "Instead of wishing, like the *'ulama,* to manage civil society, their ambition is to reconstruct society, starting with the state" (Roy 1986: 6). In doing so they must eliminate the power of traditional Islamic authorities. As Ann Mayer explains, "Islamic law was applied for over a millennium without there having been recourse to legislative measures by governments to bring it into force," rather merely by local juristic interpretation and application (Mayer 1990: 182). To be legislated, Islamic law had to be, for the first time, codified. The Ayatollah Khomeini himself ordered in 1988 that the Iranian government be free to "prevent any matter, be it spiritual or material, that poses a threat to its interests," hence that "for Islam, the requirements of government supersede every tenet, including even those of prayer, fasting and pilgrimage to Mecca"! (Pipes 2002: 82). Last and most blatant, the very idea of constructing a worldly utopia, as called for by Mawdudi and Qutb, is heterodox, for like Christianity, Islam posits paradise in the next world, not this one.

The militants' merger of government and legal administration is reminiscent of that nadir of modern Western legal practice, totalitarianism. And this is precisely the conclusion of S. N. Eisenstadt: militant Islam is the religious version of twentieth-century totalitarianism, thus a kind of *religious Jacobinism* (Eisenstadt 1999). The Jacobins, utopian radicals of the French Revolution, were certainly not antimodernist, nor premodern. Their movement was a *kind of* modernism, a perennial option within modernity, a collectivist, rationalist, utopian reorganization of society by a centralized state claiming to represent a democratic egalitarian social order, in which civil society, individualism, and pluralism are repressed. Such reorganization was attempted in the past century by a mythic-primordialist nationalism in Italy, Germany, and Japan, and by a mythic-progressive communism in Russia, China, and elsewhere. The Islamic militants have devised their own version.

How then can we understand the differences between contemporary Islamic civilization, with its revivalism, and Western modernity? First, the Islamic world never nationalized in any thorough way. In the West nationalism provided the supralocal, culturally unified context for modernization, breaking traditional hierarchy, localism, and clan politics. But in the Islamic world, while nationalism has been the slogan for various secular anti-imperialists, most famously Nasser, it never remade social loyalty among the masses. With rare exceptions, in terms of political identification, Islamic peoples have gone from local, tribal, ethnic identity directly to pan-Islamic identity with little in between. In the Islamic world it is religion, not nation, that has provided the modernist trump to community and locale. Second, this suggests that majority Islamic societies find themselves to be based in Islam in a way that Western societies are not based in Christianity. The relation of Western civilization to Christianity now appears to have been more mediated, enabling the West to *culturalize* Christianity, to sublimate its otherworldly, doctrinal, and liturgical aims into cultural ideas. In contrast, a call to Islam in Islamic societies is a call to identity and ideality, to the true self and the righteous social order. However much they may reject the intolerance and violence tied to it, even mainstream Muslims seem ill at ease with the prospect of rejecting such revivalism. Third, in the West-Islam conflict we may witness the unique historical confrontation of the two most aggressive forms of moral universalism the world has yet seen. Islam's belief in its own natural, rational, universal, transethnic validity, coupled with its expansionist past, mirrors the modern West's secular universalism, embodied in imperialism and its current geopolitical primacy. No other civilization of the past two millennia has coupled its belief that it represented the best of humanity—a common enough view—with the claim that all others *can and ought* accept its uniquely culture-transcending ways.*

Fourth and most basically, Islam and even Islamism are not less rational than Western modernism or postmodernism, they are *more* rational. Islam's refusal to draw a hard line between religion and political authority is more, not less, intellectually and normatively consistent than the Western duality. If the ultimate truth is what is given by religion in the form of discursively available norms that citizens endorse, why should the *polis* operate on any other basis? The modern West's largely instrumentalist rationality cannot answer that question. It refuses to rationalize all the way down, to make all contexts of life consistent. Ernest Gellner's unappealing term for the necessary mental substructure of modern Western civil society is *hypocritization.* That society does not require that we be agnostics or atheists, as the Marxist version of modern secularism did. Liberal secularism allows, even encourages, people to have religious worldviews, but requires that they abandon them at key points in public life with only a pragmatic explanation of why that should be (namely, to avoid social conflict). Strikingly, in her unique definition of liberalism, *Ordinary Vices,* the late political theorist Judith Sklar makes Gellner's point: in order to restrict power and respect rights—hence to make *cruelty* the worst vice—liberalism had to invoke a rigid private-public distinction that in effect permitted and even encouraged *hypocrisy.* Liberal toleration is not that of a philosophical system that justifies toleration as one of its theorems; it is the toleration of one who is willing to doff his or her philosophical system because of contextual judgments, later to don it again. What I have called the differentiation of spheres and modes of judgment, and the powerful advantages it gives us, are more dear than the attempt at a synthetic, integrative metanarrative.

Islamic consistency need not, however, be incompatible with other features of liberal republican politics. Democracy is not difficult to imagine in Islam. It exists in fact in today's Turkey, more or less in Pakistan, and in another sense in Iran. Muhammad Khalaf-Allah in fact argues that Islam *requires* democracy (Kurzman 1998). Here one can invoke the concept of *shura,* or consultation; the Muslim community is described as one "whose rule [in all matters of common concern] is consultation among themselves" (Qur'an 42:38). Further, as noted, Islamic rule does have a tradition of tol-

---

*As was suggested to me by Mark Ryan.

eration of minority religious communities. Michael Walzer has shown that the American style of largely culturally neutral government permitting maximum individual liberty is only one "regime of toleration" among several (Walzer 1997). In particular, the "millet" system, most recently embodied in the Ottoman Empire, traditionally allowed local religious or national autonomy under an imperial government. Davutoglu argues that the millet system is characteristically Islamic (Davutoglu 1994). The bigger problem is domestic liberalism, the restriction of governmental and majoritarian power to respect individual liberties. Nevertheless, even here a number of Islamic writers have argued for a "liberal Islam" that employs Islamic sources to justify toleration. As Kurzman recounts, this has come in three distinct but overlapping forms: the argument that the Qur'an and *shari'a* themselves demand toleration of other groups, most famously proposed by Ali Bulaç; the claim of 'Ali 'Abd al-Raziq and Muhammad Sa'id al-'Ashmawi that the *shari'a* is a religious code not meant to be codified into a positive legal system; and a hermeneutic toleration of varieties of interpretation of Islam based in the notion of *ijtihad,* that believers are to use their own reasoning to understand the word of God, as suggested by Muhammad Asad, Yusef al-Qaradawi, and Mohammed Arkoun (Kurzman 1998). Whatever option is exercised, we must imagine that the continued modernization of majority Islamic societies will presumably bar any return to a "customary" Islamic world informally tolerant of local deviations. For that is just what modernization cannot abide. If toleration is to be reliably practiced in Islamic countries, it must become an explicit policy. Nor can we imagine a literal return to the millet system of the Ottomans. Absent a sheer resort to empire, we are not going to see every land from Algiers to Jakarta ruled by a single sovereign entity. But multiple Islamist sovereignties embodying a variety of traditionalist, capacious interpretations of the *shari'a* might well be plausible.

In all this we must be careful not to impose our black-and-white Western, and especially American, choice between a putatively modern "wall" of separation of church and state and a "theocratic" merger. For we must acknowledge that there are many ways of *managing the relation of the sacred and the profane.* One mode is secularization *simpliciter,* a sheer demise of religious fervor, commitment, and institutional significance. Another is the segregation of religious feeling to nonpublic, nonpolitical life, except in its vaguest, most ecumenical form. A third would be the presence or evolution of a form of religion that can endorse, or even redirect spiritual enthusiasm into, modernity. A fourth, resembling but distinct from the second and third, is the presence or evolution of a religious tradition valid across all spheres of life but for which modern activities are either spiritually irrelevant or, what amounts to the same thing, pose no special problem of religious vetting.

Arguably the level of religious intensity, focused on properly religious aims and objects, was indeed lessened in the West by modernity. But the remarkable fact about the West is the unique combination of the second and third strategies. While the West achieved a privatization of religion, at the same time, as Weber argued, it evolved a form of Christianity that endorsed and even fueled key parts of the modernist project, namely, Protestantism. Its radical, militant form (Puritanism), after its political defeat, helped to inspire a modern economy, especially the—in Weber's term—"this-worldly asceticism" of profit accumulation, while its private-public distinction made possible modern liberal democratic politics. The fourth strategy seems to have been the case in East Asia, both in Japan and in the Confucian societies of Hong Kong, Taiwan, Singapore, and South Korea, allowing them to evolve a more communitarian but still pragmatic capitalism in league with gradually increasing democratization, without any showdown with religious tradition at all. In the case of Islamic societies it would also seem the fourth is the most promising, perhaps helped by a dollop of the third, that is, some combination of a scientific-economic-bureaucratic modernization that has no anti-Islamic implications, with a yet-to-evolve strain of Islamic interpretation that finds scriptural justification for endorsing constitutional democratic politics. At any rate, the achievement of political stability and tolerant democracy in the Islamic world will likely hang on the internal development of moderate Islamism, that is, a revivalist Islam which accepts the non-neutrality of government toward Islam (versus the Western model), but nevertheless finds within itself the resources for tolerating minority communities, allowing a scope for individual intellectual and political expression (if still lesser than the Western model), and which generates loyalty to, and legitimacy of, normalized, legalistic states, without either secular nationalism or autocrats whose pretense of Islamism serves only to bolster their power by deflecting criticism.

In conclusion, while some think liberalization and democratization would eventually lead Islamic societies to a more Western-looking modernization path, just as some—perhaps the same "some"—assume that China's attempt to modernize economically but not politically must fail, leading, again, to a more Westerly route, most of the evidence points in the opposite direction. More Islamic democracy probably means more Islamism. And there is little reason to believe this is merely a short-term phenomenon. It may well be that today's Islamic revivalism represents yet another form of modernism, one that largely abandons the Western liberal independence of state from religion. It may be that a sizable chunk of the great swath of humanity living from Morocco to Indonesia may modernize *not* through secularizing or developing a strong public/private distinction or abandoning official meta-narratives, but by being economically and technologically sophisticated Wahhabis. In twenty years the present spate of militant Islamic violence might end if tolerable solutions are reached in Kashmir and the West Bank, with stable moderate Islamist regimes in Afghanistan and Iraq (as well as Turkey), allowing the U.S. military presence on Arab land and Afghanistan to be reduced to a minimum. Many ifs to be sure, but a viable status quo that isolates the militants is not inconceivable. My point is that even such a pacific future would not mean Islamic imitation of the West, or the discontinuation of its own inner struggles with modernity, or a future devoid of ever more clashes around the borders of modernization. What we see in the Islamic world, not the terrorism of the extremists but widespread official and public endorsement of Islam with a strong pan-Islamic identification, *may well be what a modernized Islamic civilization looks like.* Pan-Islamic revival may be a late analogue of Western nationalism, the centralization and politicization of high culture as the idiom of social life. But unlike earlier Western nationalism, the high culture in question is far more cosmopolitan and may be capable of long-term economic, techno-logical, and even democratic progress. If so, we may have to admit a new, if not long-term then at least middling-term option for modernization, just as scholars have recognized a non-individualistic, more communitarian or corporate modernization in the vibrant East Asian economies. If we in the West, familiar with our own individualist, capitalist, agonistic or *competitive* modernity, have watched the failure of *communist* modernity, and recog-nized the apparent success of *communitarian* modernity, we may now have to admit as well the viability of a *congregational* modernity.

CONCLUSION: CULTURE'S REASONS

From one perspective, the central philosophical problem raised by locating human being in culture is *the autonomy of reason*. Is our faculty and method of inquiry and deliberation self-grounding, does it provide its own justification? The dominant modern Western tradition thinks reason is indeed autonomous, not dependent upon or justified by anything outside itself. This is a normative statement, of course, not descriptive. No contemporary philosophers believe that there is a metaphysical Reason subsisting in itself, that if there were no neurons and no signs in the world, Reason would yet persist. Reason is something about the mind, or something about the way signs and concepts are ordered in human speech and writing. Nevertheless, we commonly conceive reason as something whose validity is not drawn from pragmatic consequences, divine utterances, emotional cathexes, survival probabilities, or social conventions, but from itself.

Already in the Enlightenment, however, that autonomy was in question, particularly among thinkers on the periphery of the eighteenth-century English flame, simultaneously drawn to the most advanced country on earth and a bit wary of being burned. For the Scotsmen Thomas Reid, Adam Smith, and David Hume and the Irishman Edmund Burke, the realm of legitimate belief extended beyond what reason can ground. They held that reason *per se* is inadequate to life, in particular to practical-ethical (hence political) life, there being beliefs we inevitably or legitimately hold which reason nevertheless cannot know to be true. Hume did this most negatively, implying that such beliefs are irrational, but dictated by our natural constitution. The others agreed that reason is limited and grounded in something outside itself, either common sense (Reid), social tradition (Burke), or social identification (Smith). But for them, that-on-which reason is founded is not irrational or contradictory to reason: reason is continuous with practical-ethical life and its necessary commitments. Thus they prefigured many radical twentieth-century critiques of reason, although in a nonapocalyptic way.

That reason is not autonomous implies no collapse into chaos or barbarism, just a demystifying acceptance of its sociocultural location.

It will come as no surprise to the reader if, with the thinkers mentioned, I deny the autonomy of reason. *Reason is emergent from or supervenient upon culture.* It is culture operating at a sufficiently complex and responsible level of interrogation. Reason can be defined as *methodical metajudgment,* the methodical adjudication of conflict among human judgments. Given a range of multiple or competing judgments of any kind, reason is the capacity to decide among them validly, that is, validly by contemporary criteria. It is thus an intrinsically normative and interrogative concept. We must imagine that humans have engaged in reason at least since the development of "symbolic culture" in the Upper Paleolithic age, and perhaps earlier, since the maturation of relatively complex natural languages. Perhaps we could follow Bateson in saying that once humans could reflexively refer to discursive-practical contexts, situations of linguistically mediated shared activity, reason was present. But what matters here is less its lineage than its commonality to segmentary, agroliterate, and modern societies. Implicit in this claim is that it makes little sense to restrict reason to naturalistic, nonreligious, postmythical cultural forms, to claim that reason somehow was born in ancient Greek natural philosophy, fell asleep for a millennium or two, then awakened for good in Europe's "Age of Reason." Modernity is not more rational than other eras. It is *differently* rational.

The Three Reasons

Gellner distinguished what he called "Durkheimian" from "Weberian" rationality. The former was for him the rationality of embodiment and instantiation, the participation of instances in socially shared ideal forms. The latter, which emerges only in modernity, is the piecemeal logical and instrumental rationality by which acts or claims are shown to be implicated by, or consistent with, each other. Oddly enough, this bivalent notion of reason does not correspond to Gellner's own tripartite historical scheme. Nevertheless, his instinct was, I think, sound. We do not find in history and prehistory a transition from the non- or prerational to the rational. Lucien Levy-Bruhl's notion of the prelogical mentality has been rightly criticized. Rather, we find a transition among different *modes of rationality or reason.*

This becomes plausible once we accept a broad notion of reason as methodical metajudgment. Segmentary societies engage in such adjudication, just as agrarian and industrial societies do. The absence of reason would mean the absence of the articulation of *reasons,* of social validation or justification. But such is barely conceivable, given complex natural languages and cultures. We do not know of societies in which fully competent members do not steer among values in polynormative and novel situations, weighing competing rules and giving reasons for their decisions. We know of no societies in which members do not *explain* themselves.

But we need to expand Gellner's scheme by separating out two modes of rationality he conflated under the "Durkheimian." I suggest that ritual-segmentary, stratified–axial, and modern–industrial society each have their own characteristic mode of reason. Thus there are three "reasons," Durkheimian, Jasperian, and Weberian. No argument will be mounted here to show that reason is historically divided into *only* these three types. The claim is rather that what we refer to as reason or methodical metajudgment is a complex notion that can abide division, and that at least three types of reason can be distinguished across history and prehistory. Which is to say that, all told, the attribution of variant forms of reason to historical and pre-historical periods is preferable to asserting the sameness of reason, hence the unreasonableness or irrationality of the earlier periods. Last, this developmental scheme does *not* mean that the earlier forms are unavailable in the later, that Durkheimian and Jasperian rationality are absent in modern society. In this as in many other cases, development implies the emergence of a new capacity having priority over retained but demoted older capacities. The leading form of rationality, as embodied not only in speech but in practices and institutions, is characteristic of an age's dealings with what it regards as its chief interests and problems, the others playing subaltern roles, but available either to challenge the dominant form or fill in its gaps.

For Durkheimian rationality meaning is embodied in the structures of social life, to which there can be no rational objection. One may, of course, object to a way of interpreting those structures, or a way of dealing with their conflict. Simply put, in segmentary life society is everything, a condition made easier by the fact that society exists in harmony with its natural environment, with a minimum of artifice and manipulation, divine characters multiplying along the border between the two. Signs and referents are not *systematically* distinguished; they are commonly distinguished—none of the Narragansetts whose folkways Roger Williams chronicled in the seventeenth-century ever believed that *ewáchim-neash,* their word for corn, could make a good meal—but there are cases where the word is efficacious, has physical power (Williams 1971: 100). Beliefs and words are indiscriminately events or things, following the same social norms as actions and constructions. To be a "wise" man or woman is then to interpret narrative tradition, to reason from a variety of validities expressed in practices, usually via analogy to paradigmatic cases, in order to adjudicate current disagreements or problems. It is to understand the function of reason as handling communal problems against the background of a tradition that exhausts intelligibility and normativity.

While the agroliterate age is roughly ten thousand years old, cities only emerged around 3,000 B.C.E. Thus the new mentality of the age may well have taken a long time in developing. Its full expression is certainly on display by the time of Jaspers's Axial revolution. Starting then, and through the history of Agraria, rationality came to be understood as the embodiment of or participation in a transcendent ideal, or the attempt to demonstrate such participation, verbally expressed in a logical hierarchy of principles. Socrates' attempt at universal definition of each norm, with his Pythagorean-Orphic belief in the soul, the Hebrew Prophets' condemnation of contemporary society by transcendent standards, the Upanishads' turn from Vedic ritual to contemplation, and Gautama's assertion of the unreality of the world—or, equivalently, the superiority of logic to common experience—all express the new view. Validation is participation in, emulation, embodiment, or instantiation of what is beyond sensory experience and social convention. One might say in a Derridean vein that this Jasperian or Axial rationality is the full exploitation of the implicit possibilities of *writing,* itself definitive of the agroliterate age. For now, just as ancient writings can be used to show that contemporary society has declined, that it fails to be true to its normative documents, the religious genius and the philosopher can announce that the real is *not* ideal. Society is no longer everything; it is now merely *almost* everything. The dualism of ideal and real matches the cosmic, metaphysical dualism of God and world, or truth and appearance, and the hierarchy of elite (almost always two-headed, warrior-aristocracy and literate scribes) versus commoners (peasants plus merchants). Gellner is right to see Plato's *Republic* as a marvelous expression of this world, with its perfectly coordinated hierarchy of classes (philosophers-guardians-moneymakers), levels of education, modes of cognition, the cardinal virtues, and types of political regimes.

Weberian rationality is but a couple of centuries old, which is to say that only in the last two centuries has its implicit form been made explicit and differentiated from the Durkheimian and Jasperian. It is the functional or instrumental rationality by which practices and claims achieve justification in the context of aims and explicit premises. Hence efficiency in achievement or logicality of procedure rationalizes any particular act or claim. It is highly differentiated, or as Gellner says, "modular." Truth, goodness, beauty, salvation, and pragmatic norms like efficiency are utterly separable. Incommensurability of norms then permits commensurable judgments *within* the discourse of each norm. As Weber saw, this makes it impossible to project an integrated factual-moral world. But since in most respects human historical development combines rather than replaces earlier forms, it would make sense to say that Jasperian rationality retains the Durkheimian, and we modern Weberians retain the other two. Thus we move among the three. While our leading form of rationality cannot project an omnivalent whole, our vestigial, subaltern, contextually employed Jasperian and Durkheimian rationalities can continue to do so. This is not to suggest that we integrate, reconcile, or unify the three reasons. We cannot. For the Weberian the third moment is not a Hegelian sublimation of the other two, but as Peirce claimed of his Thirdness, or Relation, it is merely a more complex dimension of a totality it does not exhaust (Peirce 1955: 266–67).

Each of these modes of reason has a distinct relation to culture. Durkheimian reason is reason *undifferentiated* from culture, or more precisely, the capacity to judge other judgments in an environment where modes of judgmental validity are not distinguished from cultural norms. It takes the form of weighing a variety of considerations regarding which we moderns would accuse the reasoner of continual category mistakes. It is the reason of the implicit or unarticulated whole. I am tempted to say that, to this very day, this is what constitutes being "reasonable" in our everyday English sense of the word. Reasonableness, as opposed to reason or rationality, implies that no one consideration is either foundational or overwhelming, no one part of the whole determines all others, that one must take plural saliences into consideration, rather than appeal to a logical hierarchy of principles. It may sound odd to connect a modern person's "reasonableness" with ritualistic, segmentary versions of "reason," but that is because we reject other components of segmentary thinking, for example, the ontological continuity of signs and things. Still for us today, Bernard Shaw's quip holds, that the reasonable man [*sic*] adapts to society while the unreasonable man demands that society adapt to himself, hence history is made by the unreasonable man. Reasonableness takes pluralistic current considerations as its guide, while the unreasonable refer to some narrower norm that trumps all others. "Be reasonable" is a plea to honor the normal pluralism, hence balanced inconsistency, of social criteria rather than force one criterion above all. This socially pluralistic form of reason was *the* human form of reason for the vast majority of human existence.

Jasperian reason is the capacity to evaluate judgments in terms of society-and-culture-transcending norms. The model of validity is Platonic or Alexandrian or mathematical. The particular, the decision, or the action in question is valid because it embodies or participates in an ideal or transcendent model. Reasoning must operate by relating worldly events and possibilities to rules independent of the processes or events in question. This is the reason of the explicit or articulated whole. The normative models can only be known by those with special knowledge, that is, literacy. They carry high culture, now distinct for the first time from low or folk culture. This form of reason is always dogged by the need to debate and clarify what those transcendent rules are, hence the sticky problem of what can justify a transcendent rule. But wherever this problem is ignored or solved, the hierarchy of reason can nicely match the hierarchy of caste, virtue, and power.

Weberian reason is the reason of a culture split into progressive spheres. Each context is made rational by formulating its premises, or goals, which then dictate what means are rational. The task of understanding the world is distinguished from social fealty, status, moral duty, aesthetic satisfaction, and salvation. Certainly one might, having completed a bout of research, then evaluate that research in terms of these other values. But no one can claim cognitive legitimacy, truth, for a result *because* it would be good to believe it, will make society operate better, or is more beautiful. As Weber rightly said in his classic essay "Science as a Vocation," we modernists are "polytheists," our version of reason having discovered that the connective tissue linking goodness, truth, and beauty—which Jasperian rationality had no trouble finding in God—is unavailable (Weber 1972). Reason can only move among given concepts, premises, and rules within the normative contexts they define. One might say that while modernity saw the rise of Weberian or instrumental reason, our current period of modernity, the postmodern, is defined by the discovery of the incompatibility of Weberian and Jasperian reason, the gradual disentangling of Weberian reasoning from its anachronistic Axial parentage.

Given this, what did the notion of the autonomy of Reason, floated by the ancient Greeks but actualized only in the Enlightenment, mean? I suggest it was nothing more than the *differentiation* of inquiry into truth from other forms of human judgment, speech, activity, and production. Modernity is based in the rejection of omnivalence, which is to say, the rejection of the Durkheimian or "natural" condition of humankind. The inability to project a whole is precisely the deep modern problem of the relation of human values or norms to the material, putatively value-less, undesigned universe achieved by modern, truth-governed science. Modernity is then, as Weberian, radically contextual; each social endeavor generates its own norms and "constructs" its own environment. Niklas Luhmann would say that this is a permanent condition, in which modern or postmodern society has worked out alternative modes of social and intellectual organization which cannot tolerate and do not need Durkheimian or omnivalent unity (Luhmann 1982). Postmodern society is, as he says, "a whole that is less than the sum of its parts." Ominivalence remains of course in the supracontextual zones of decision in which we variously abandon Weberian rationality, going by our "instincts," "sensibility," "experience," "practical wisdom," and so on.

Now certainly these disentangled spheres are still the constructions of a culture and characteristic of the people that employ them. They serve the ends of the culture. They do so, however, *through* this disentanglement and unifunctionality. Carried far away by the wind, the seed better serves its parent plant. But in doing so it takes the species to unanticipated realms, opening it to novel changes. The progress of the unifunctional spheres develops unimaginable cultural resources but in the process reconstitutes the culture, again and again.

The Bend of History

At the outset of our study we noted Francis Fukuyama's famous argument that global politics in a postcommunist era experiences "the end of history" (Fukuyama 1989). That thesis is at odds with, on the one hand, Benjamin

Barber's claim that the world is dividing along a new bipolarity between premodern *jihad* and postmodern "McWorld" (Barber 1992) and on the other, Samuel Huntington's "clash of civilizations" thesis, which anticipates a pluralistic world of permanently conflicted cultural units (Huntington 1993). Certainly the plausibility of Fukuyama's thesis has suffered in the last decade; most of the phenomena treated by the present study have added fuel to the polycultural thesis.

But Fukuyama's view is not *all* wrong. What we mean by modernity is an environment based in certain kinds of progress, which, once achieved, are relatively self-sustaining and hard to do without. Whatever else is true of the contemporary world, it has created a direction, a cognitive, technological, economic, and—at least in terms of the public control of the modern state through democracy and universal education—political standard for the rest of the world to meet. Virtually all societies and major parties acknowledge these goals, hence everyone accepts a roughly equivalent meaning of "development." Disapproval of Western modernization concerns the cost of these achievements or what may accompany them, but no peoples or national elites are today in favor of less science, worse health care, and fewer economic opportunities. If we can say that there is no such thing as complete modernization—since every society and culture retains elements that are relatively unreformed by progress, including the United States—we can also say that today there is no such thing as complete or full antimodernism, no true attempts to return to the premodern era *simpliciter.* For such a return would have to mean abandonment of social and legal equality, a return to caste distinctions, aristocratic or royal ownership of land or the means of production, abandonment of modern science and technological progress, the social primacy of kin and locale, and hence the weakness of central government. There are *no* such movements in the world today, for a "movement" requires centralization, politicization, rationalist organization, and modern technology. Or if there are such, they occur only in situations of crisis that fulfill no culture's normative criteria, during the collapse of the state into warlord-ism or a reversion to tribal and clan social organization. Modernization rules out some forms of cognition, culture, and social organization.

Nevertheless, there is nothing in the impressive recent spread of global capitalism, the information revolution, and liberal republicanism which together spell the end of ethnic, religious, or nationalistic modes of social organization, either now or soon or *ever.* Reports of identity's demise have

been greatly exaggerated. The reason for the persistence of primordial versions of identity and affiliation is not only the enduring need for them, but
as well the very flexibility of modernity and its technologies, which can be
exploited and channeled in different ways by all sorts of polities. We do not
know what aspects of human culture will be dispensed with by the various
experiments in modernization now under way.

Thus it appears that expansion of the modernized areas of the globe will
mean *more and more different ways to be modern*. We face not one but *many*
globalizations (Berger and Huntington 2002). An earlier round of modernization and its discontents produced fascism and communism, direct threats
against liberal capitalist modernity. The first was destroyed, the second, in
its own phrase, "withered away." But the newer round of discontents is
more amorphous and arguably more creative. One does not have to accept
former Singapore president Lee Kuan Yew's promotion of "Asian values"
against Western-style individual rights to recognize that the modernized
Pacific Rim nations have their own model of capitalism, a communitarian
rather than individualist model. Will South Africa and Nigeria lead a novel
African modernity in the next half century? What kind of society will China
become by the time it takes the lead in East Asia? And how different will
the *least modernized* countries look from those countries exhibiting the *least
Western* forms of modernization? What we see as a failure to modernize
may in fact be a novel non-Western form of modernization. I think it
likely that this spiral goes on indefinitely, with convergence not on a single
model but around certain constraints that the various extant models must
share, such as, for example, mastery of the technological-scientific developments of the day. For if there is a lesson of postmodern society, it is not that
things fall apart when the center does not hold, but that some things can
function quite well without a center.

That is what is really disturbing to the fundamentalist mind, not secularization, but the combination of claimed religious identity *with* secularization, embodied most of all by the United States. For we can now say that
the Islamic revival is *Axial* or *Jasperian*. That is its distinction. Even in its fundamentalist expressions it is a highly rational form of moral-Platonic thinking, divorced from ultimately segmentary-ethnic-kin-local ties, thing the
particular always in terms of the transcendent universal. Militants elevate
this into a utopian scheme through a politicized modernity that accepts
modern science, technological innovation, industrialism, and commercialism
(not full capitalism, given the Islamic rejection of usury). This is instructive.

Islam today represents unambiguous Axial reason, particularly as the militants seek to denude Islamic society of its Durkheimian substructures, its social traditionalism. It is its Axial nature that makes the Islamic revival most frustrating to the West, in that it exhibits what is, for the postmodern West, a hyperrational (which is to say, modernized) version of its own Axial past.

Regarding those postmodern societies we can offer a tentative and surprising suggestion: as *Jaspers recedes, Durkheim returns.* To say that Reason is *not* autonomous is to say that it remains irreducibly Durkheimian, hence social. That form of reason has been present for as long as human beings could adjudicate disagreement. Axial or Jasperian reason discovered the advantages of a detour *away from* social life *for* social life, and Weberian reason did it one better, bestowing massive power and prosperity on societies that renounced the substantive dependence of cognition and production on culture. But the Rortyan resocialization of reason is a return to Durkheimian reason after the withdrawal of Jaspers. The Axial age metanarratives cease to be central to the human societies that have evolved modernity on the terms described herein, however they ornament our discourse. Still, in the central societal processes of the most advanced societies the socialized cognition and segmentary rationality that is forever the fallback position of human beings remain. For oddly enough, if Durkheim's notion of collective consciousness fits any society, it fits contemporary postmodern mass culture. Thus Weber and Durkheim ambiguously join hands. That is our unique situation. Our culture is fragmented, ironic, open, volatile, hence unlike any earlier culture. That is its Weberian content. But that content functions as a formidable social whole bearing the echoes of centralized nationalism, subtended by a common context-free culture that is inculcated by electronic mass media, all to form a very powerful We-World. Our behavior is composed of piecemeal but serviceable Weberian roles, contexts, and calculations, which nevertheless grow and spread into Durkheimian functions, strategically retaining Jasperian fig leaves. Flanking the great agroliterate period of 5,000 B.C.E. to 1900 C.E., the source of our normative civilizations, the modern Weberian and the segmentary Durkheimian forms of reason meet in our postmodern era. To what end, or to what new beginning, remains to be seen.

REFERENCES

'Abduh, Muhammed. 1966. *The Theology of Unity.* Trans. Ishaq Musa'ad and Kenneth Cragg. London: Allen & Unwin.

Ahmad, Mumtaz. 1991. "Islamic Fundamentalism in South Asia: The Jamaat-I-Islami and the Tablighi Jamat." In *Fundamentalisms Observed,* ed. Martin Marty and R. Scott Appleby, vol. 1. Chicago: University of Chicago Press.

Ahmed, Akbar S. 1992. *Postmodernism and Islam: Predicament and Promise.* New York: Routledge.

Ammerman, Nancy. 1991. "North American Protestant Fundamentalism." In *Fundamentalisms Observed,* ed. Martin Marty and R. Scott Appleby, vol. 1. Chicago: University of Chicago Press.

Anderson, Benedict. 1991. *Imagined Communities: Reflections on the Origin and Spread of Nationalism.* London: Verso.

Appiah, Kwame Anthony. 1992. *My Father's House: Africa in the Philosophy of Culture.* New York: Oxford University Press.

———. 1994. "Identity, Authenticity, Survival: Multicultural Societies and Social Reproduction." In *Multiculturalism: Examining the Politics of Recognition,* ed. Amy Gutmann. Princeton: Princeton University Press.

———. 1996. "Race, Culture, Identity: Misunderstood Connections." In *Color Conscious: The Political Morality of Race,* ed. Kwame Anthony Appiah and Amy Gutmann. Princeton: Princeton University Press.

———. 1997. "The Multiculturalist Misunderstanding." *New York Review of Books,* October 9.

Arendt, Hannah. 1958. *The Human Condition.* Chicago: University of Chicago Press.

Arjomand, Said Amir. 1995. "Unity and Diversity in Islamic Fundamentalism." In *Fundamentalisms Comprehended,* ed. Martin Marty and R. Scott Appleby, vol. 5. Chicago: University of Chicago Press.

Asad, Muhammad. 1980. *The Message of the Qur'an.* Trans. Muhammad Asad. Gibraltar: Dar al-Andalus.

Atlas, James. 2000. *Bellow.* New York: Random House.

Bachelard, Gaston. 1964. *The Poetics of Space.* Trans. M. Jolas. New York: Orion Press.

Baeten, Elizabeth. 1996. *The Magic Mirror: Myth's Abiding Power.* Albany: SUNY Press.

Bannā, Hasan al-. 1978. *Five Tracts of Hasan al-Bannā.* Trans. Charles Wendell. Berkeley and Los Angeles: University of California Press.

Barber, Benjamin. 1992. "Jihad vs. McWorld." *Atlantic Monthly,* March.

———. 1995. *Jihad vs. McWorld: How Globalism and Tribalism Are Reshaping the World.* New York: Ballantine Books.

Barry, Brian. 1990. "How Not to Defend Liberal Institutions." In *Liberalism and the Good,* ed. R. Bruce Douglass et al. New York: Routledge.

————. 2001. *Culture and Equality: An Egalitarian Critique of Multiculturalism.* Cambridge: Harvard University Press.

Barth, Fredrick. 1969. *Ethnic Groups and Boundaries.* Boston: Little, Brown.

Bartley, W. W., III. 1987. "Theories of Rationality." In *Evolutionary Epistemology, Rationality, and the Sociology of Knowledge,* ed. Gerrard Radnitzky and W. W. Bartley III. LaSalle, Ill.: Open Court.

Bateson, Gregory. 2000. "A Theory of Play and Fantasy." In *Steps Toward an Ecology of Mind: Collected Essays in Anthropology, Psychiatry, Evolution, and Epistemology.* Chicago: University of Chicago Press.

Becker, Lawrence C. 1986. *Reciprocity.* London: Routledge & Kegan Paul.

Bell, Daniel. 1976. *The Coming of Post-Industrial Society.* New York: Basic Books.

Berger, Peter, Brigitte Berger, and Hansfried Kellner. 1973. *The Homeless Mind: Modernization and Consciousness.* New York: Random House.

Berger, Peter, and Samuel Huntington. 2002. *Many Globalizations: Cultural Diversity in the Contemporary World.* New York: Oxford University Press.

Bourdieu, Pierre. 1990. *The Logic of Practice.* Trans. Richard Nice. Stanford: Stanford University Press.

Braudel, Ferdinand. 1993. *A History of Civilizations.* Trans. Richard Mayne. New York: Penguin Books.

Brightman, Robert. 1995. "Forget Culture: Replacement, Transcendence, Relexification." *Cultural Anthropology* 10, no. 4.

Brooks, David. 2001. *Bobos in Paradise: The New Upper Class and How They Got There.* Thorndike, Maine: Thorndike Press.

Buchanan, Allen. 1995. "The Morality of Secession." In *The Rights of Minority Cultures,* ed. Will Kymlicka. Oxford: Oxford University Press.

Buchler, Justus. 1955. *Nature and Judgment.* New York: Columbia University Press.

Burke, William. 1987. *Reflections on the Revolution in France.* Indianapolis: Hackett.

Cahoone, Lawrence. 1988. *The Dilemma of Modernity: Philosophy, Culture, and Anticulture.* Albany: SUNY Press.

————. 1989. "Buchler on Habermas on Modernity." *Southern Journal of Philosophy* 27, no. 4 (winter).

————. 2002a. *Civil Society: The Conservative Meanings of Liberal Politics.* Oxford: Blackwell Publishers.

————. 2002b. *The Ends of Philosophy: Pragmatism, Foundationalism, and Postmodernism.* Oxford: Blackwell Publishers.

————. 2002c. "Margoline Relativism." *Idealistic Studies* 32, no. 1.

————. 2003. *From Modernism to Postmodernism: An Anthology.* Oxford: Blackwell Publishers.

Callois, Roger. 2001. *Man, Play and Games.* Trans. Meyer Barash. Urbana: University of Illinois Press.

Carr, David. 1986. *Time, Narrative and History.* Bloomington: Indiana University Press.

Casey, Edward. 1995. *Getting Back into Place: Toward a Renewed Understanding of the Place World.* Berkeley and Los Angeles: University of California Press.

————. 1999. *The Fate of Place: A Philosophical History.* Berkeley and Los Angeles: University of California Press.

Cassirer, Ernst. 1944. *An Essay on Man: An Introduction to a Philosophy of Human Culture.* Trans. Charles Hendel. New Haven: Yale University Press.

————. 1965. *The Philosophy of Symbolic Forms.* Three volumes. Trans. Ralph Mannheim. New Haven: Yale University Press.

Chase, Philip. 1999. "Symbolism as Reference and Symbolism as Culture." In *The Evolution of Culture,* ed. Robin Dunbar, Chris Knight, and Camilla Power. New Brunswick: Rutgers University Press.

Cohen, Jean L., and Andrew Arato. 1997. *Civil Society and Political Theory.* Cambridge: MIT Press.

Dabashi, Hamid. 1993. *Theology of Discontent: The Ideological Foundations of the Islamic Revolution in Iran.* New York: New York University Press.

Damasio, Antonio R. 1999. *The Feeling of What Happens: Body and Emotion in the Making of Consciousness.* New York: Harcourt, Brace.

Davidson, Donald. 1984. "On the Very Idea of a Conceptual Scheme." In *Inquiries into Truth and Interpretation.* Oxford: Clarendon Press.

———. 1986. "A Coherence Theory of Truth and Knowledge." In *Truth and Interpretation: Perspectives on the Philosophy of Donald Davidson,* ed. Ernest Lepore. Oxford: Blackwell Publishers.

Davutoglu, Ahmet. 1994. *Alternative Paradigms: The Impact of Islamic and Western Weltanschauungs on Political Theory.* Lanham, Md.: University Press of America.

Deleuze, Giles, and Félix Guattari. 1987. *A Thousand Plateaus.* Trans. Brian Massumi. Minneapolis: University of Minnesota Press.

Derrida, Jacques. 1973. "Differance." *Speech and Phenomena and Other Essays on Husserl's Theory of Signs.* Trans. David Allison. Evanston: Northwestern University Press.

Dewey, John. 1944. *Democracy and Education.* New York: The Free Press.

———. 1958. *Experience and Nature.* New York: Dover Books.

———. 1979. *Freedom and Culture.* New York: Paragon Books.

Dixon, A. C. 1910–15. *The Fundamentals.* Chicago: Testimony Publishing.

Douglass, R. Bruce, Gerald Mara, and Henry Richardson, eds. 1990. *Liberalism and the Good.* New York: Routledge.

Drucker, Peter. 1995. *The End of Economic Man: The Origins of Totalitarianism.* New Brunswick, N.J.: Transaction Publishers.

Dunbar, Robin, Chris Knight, and Camilla Power, ed. 1999. *The Evolution of Culture.* New Brunswick: Rutgers University Press.

Durkheim, Emile. 2001. *The Elementary Forms of Religious Life.* Trans. Carol Cosman. New York: Oxford University Press.

Dylan, Bob. 1967. *All Along the Watchtower.* Columbia Records.

Eisenstadt, S. N. 1999. *Fundamentalism, Sectarianism, and Revolution: The Jacobin Dimension of Modernity.* Cambridge: Cambridge University Press.

Eliade, Mircea. 1954. *The Myth of the Eternal Return, Or, Cosmos and History.* Trans. Willard Trask. Princeton: Princeton University Press.

Elias, Norbert. 1994. *The Civilizing Process: The History of Manners and State Formation and Civilization.* Oxford: Blackwell Publishers.

Elshtain, Jean Bethke. 1995. *Democracy on Trial.* New York: Basic Books.

Euben, Roxanne. 1999. *The Enemy in the Mirror: Islamic Fundamentalism and the Limits of Modern Rationalism: A Work of Comparative Political Theory.* Princeton: Princeton University Press.

Fichte, Johann G. 1979. *Addresses to the German Nation.* Trans. R. F. Jones and G. H. Turnbull. Westport, Conn.: Greenwood Press.

Fleischacker, Samuel. 1994. *The Ethics of Culture.* Ithaca: Cornell University Press.

Fraser, Sir James. 1994. *The Golden Bough: A Study in Magic and Religion.* Oxford: Oxford University Press.

Freeman, Mark. 1993. *Rewriting the Self: History, Memory, Narrative*. New York: Routledge.

Friedman, Thomas. 1999. *The Lexus and the Olive Tree: Understanding Globalization*. New York: Farrar, Straus, Giroux.

Fukuyama, Francis. 1989. "The End of History." *The National Interest*, no.16 (summer).

———. 1992. *The End of History and the Last Man*. New York: The Free Press.

Gadamer, Hans-Georg. 1994. *Truth and Method*. Trans. Joel Weinsheimer and Donald Marshall. New York: Continuum.

Galston, William. 1989. "Civic Education in the Liberal State." In *Liberalism and the Moral Life*, ed. Nancy Rosenblum. Cambridge: Harvard University Press.

———. 1991. *Liberal Purposes: Goods, Virtues, and Diversity in the Liberal State*. Cambridge: Cambridge University Press.

Geertz, Clifford. 1961. *The Integrative Revolution: Primordial Sentiments and Civil Politics in the New States*. Ph.D. diss., University of Chicago. Reprinted as *Old Societies and New States* (New York: The Free Press, 1963).

———. 1989. "Anti Anti-Relativism." In *Relativism: Interpretation and Confrontation*, ed. Michael Krausz. Notre Dame: University of Notre Dame Press.

Gellner, Ernest. 1981. *Muslim Society*. Cambridge: Cambridge University Press.

———. 1983. *Nations and Nationalism*. Ithaca: Cornell University Press.

———. 1988. *Plough, Sword, and Book: The Structure of Human History*. Chicago: University of Chicago Press.

———. 1992. *Reason and Culture: The Historic Role of Rationality and Rationalism*. Oxford: Blackwell Publishers.

Gibson, James J. 1979. *The Ecological Approach to Visual Perception*. Boston: Houghton Mifflin.

Giddens, Anthony. 1990. *The Consequences of Modernity*. Stanford: Stanford University Press.

Gohari, M. J. 1999. *The Taliban: Ascent to Power*. Oxford: Oxford Logos Society.

Gouldner, Alvin. 1979. *The Future of Intellectuals and the Rise of the New Class*. New York: Seabury Press.

Greenfeld, Liah. 1992. *Nationalism: Five Roads to Modernity*. Cambridge: Harvard University Press.

Griffin, Michael. 2001. *Reaping the Whirlwind: The Taliban Movement in Afghanistan*. London: Pluto Press.

Gutmann, Amy, ed. 1994. *Multiculturalism and the Politics of Recognition*. Princeton: Princeton University Press. Originally *Multiculturalism: Examining The Politics of Recognition* (Princeton: Princeton University Press, 1992).

Habermas, Jürgen. 1984. *The Theory of Communicative Action. Volume One: Reason and the Rationalization of Society*. Trans. Thomas McCarthy. Boston: Beacon Press.

———. 1987. *The Theory of Communicative Action. Volume Two: Lifeworld and System: A Critique of Functionalist Reason*. Trans. Thomas McCarthy. Boston: Beacon Press.

———. 1989. *The Structural Transformation of the Public Sphere: An Inquiry into a Category of Bourgeois Society*. Trans. Thomas Burger, with Frederick Lawrence. Cambridge: MIT Press.

———. 1990. "Discourse Ethics: Notes on a Program of Philosophical Justification." In *Moral Consciousness and Communicative Action*. Trans. Christian Lenhardt and Shierry Weber Nicholsen. Cambridge: MIT Press.

Hall, Edward T. 1973. *The Silent Language*. New York: Anchor Books.

Heidegger, Martin. 1962. *Being and Time*. Trans. John Macquarrie and Edward Robinson. New York: Harper & Row.

Herder, Johann G. 1968. *Ideas on the Philosophy of the History of Mankind*. Trans. Frank Manuel. Chicago: University of Chicago Press.

Hodgson, Marshall. 1974. *The Venture of Islam: Conscience and History in a World Civilization*. Two volumes. Chicago: University of Chicago Press.

Hollinger, David A. 1995. *Postethnic America: Beyond Multiculturalism*. New York: Basic Books.

Holmes, Stephen. 1993. *The Anatomy of Antiliberalism*. Cambridge: Harvard University Press.

Horkheimer, Max, and Theodor Adorno. 1972. *Dialectic of Enlightenment*. Trans. John Cumming. New York: Seabury Press.

Huizinga, Johan. 1980. *Homo Ludens: A Study of the Play Element in Culture*. New York: Routledge.

Huntington, Samuel. 1993. "The Clash of Civilizations." *Foreign Affairs* 73, no. 3 (summer).

———. 1996. *The Clash of Civilizations and the Remaking of World Order*. New York: Simon & Schuster.

Ibn Khaldûn. 1967. *The Muqqaddimah: An Introduction to History*. Abridged by N. J. Dawood. Trans. Franz Rosenthal. Princeton: Princeton University Press.

Iqbāl, Muhammad. 1998. "The Principle of Movement in the Structure of Islam." In *Liberal Islam: A Sourcebook,* ed. Charles Kurzman. Oxford: Oxford University Press.

Jansen, Johannes. 1986. *The Neglected Duty: The Creed of Sadat's Assassins and the Islamic Resurgence in the Middle East*. New York: Macmillan.

Jaspers, Karl. 1953. *The Origin and Goal of History*. Trans. Michael Bullock. New Haven: Yale University Press.

Johnson, James Turner. 2001. *The Holy War Idea in Western and Islamic Traditions*. University Park: Pennsylvania State University Press.

Jonas, Hans. 1966. *The Phenomenon of Life: Toward a Philosophical Biology*. New York: Harper & Row.

Juergensmeyer, Mark. 1993. *The New Cold War? Religious Nationalism Confronts the Secular State*. Berkeley and Los Angeles: University of California Press.

Kateb, George. 1992. *The Inner Ocean: Individualism and Democratic Culture*. Ithaca: Cornell University Press.

Keddie, Nikki R. 1968. *An Islamic Response to Imperialism: Political and Religious Writings of Sayyid Jamāl ad-din "al-Afghani."* Berkeley and Los Angeles: University of California Press.

Kedourie, Elie. 1960. *Nationalism*. London: Hutchinson.

Kelsay, John. 1990. *Cross, Crescent and Sword: The Justification and Limitation of War in Western and Islamic Tradition*. Westport, Conn.: Greenwood Press.

———. 1993. *Islam and War: A Study in Comparative Ethics, the Gulf War and Beyond*. Louisville, Ky.: John Knox Press.

Keppel, Giles. 1994. *The Revenge of God: The Resurgence of Islam, Christianity, and Judaism in the Modern World*. Trans. Alan Braley. University Park: Pennsylvania State University Press.

Kerr, Malcolm. 1966. *Islamic Reform: The Political and Legal Theories of Muhammad 'Abduh and Rashīd Ridā*. Berkeley and Los Angeles: University of California Press.

Khadduri, Majid. 2002. *The Islamic Law of Nations: Shaybani's Siyar*. Baltimore: Johns Hopkins University Press.

Kitcher, Philip. 1999. "Race, Ethnicity, Biology, Culture." In *Racism,* ed. Leonard Harris. Amherst, Mass.: Humanity Books.

Kneale, William, and Martha Kneale. 1962. *The Development of Logic*. Oxford: Clarendon Press.

Knight, Chris. 1999. "Sex and Language as Pretend-Play." In *The Evolution of Culture*, ed. Robin Dunbar, Chris Knight, and Camilla Power. New Brunswick: Rutgers University Press.

Knight, Chris, Robin Dunbar, and Camilla Power, eds. 1999. "An Evolutionary Approach to Human Culture." In *The Evolution of Culture*, ed. Robin Dunbar, Chris Knight, and Camilla Power. New Brunswick: Rutgers University Press.

Koyré, Alexandre. 1957. *From the Closed World to the Infinite Universe*. Baltimore: Johns Hopkins University Press.

Krausz, Michael. 1989. *Relativism: Interpretation and Confrontation*. Notre Dame: University of Notre Dame Press.

Kroeber, A. L., and Clyde Kluckhohn. 1952. "Culture: A Critical Review of Concepts and Definitions." *Papers of the Peabody Museum of American Archaeology and Ethnology* 47, no. 1.

Kukathas, Chandran. 2003. *The Liberal Archipelago: A Theory of Diversity and Freedom*. Oxford: Oxford University Press.

Kundera, Milan. 1984a. "The Tragedy of Central Europe." *New York Review of Books*, April 25.

———. 1984b. *The Unbearable Lightness of Being*. Trans. Michael Henry Heim. New York: Harper & Row.

Kurzman, Charles. 1998. "Introduction: Liberal Islam and Its Islamic Context." In *Liberal Islam: A Sourcebook*, ed. Kurzman. Oxford: Oxford University Press.

Kymlicka, Will. 1989. *Liberalism, Community, and Culture*. Oxford: Oxford University Press.

———. 1995a. *Multicultural Citizenship: A Liberal Theory of Minority Rights*. Oxford: Oxford University Press.

———, ed. 1995b. *The Rights of Minority Cultures*. Oxford: Oxford University Press.

Lasch, Christopher. 1979. *The Culture of Narcissism*. New York: W. W. Norton.

———. 1991. *The True and Only Heaven: Progress and Its Critics*. New York: W. W. Norton.

———. 1995. *The Revolt of the Elites and the Betrayal of Democracy*. New York: W. W. Norton.

Levy, Jacob. 2000. *The Multiculturalism of Fear*. Oxford: Oxford University Press.

Levy, Marion, Jr. 1972. *Modernization: Latecomers and Survivors*. New York: Basic Books.

Lonergan, Bernard. 1957. *Insight: A Study of Human Understanding*. New York: Harper & Row.

Loury, Glenn C. 1995. "Second Thoughts on First Principles." In Loury, *One by one from the inside out; essays and reviews on race and responsibility in America*. New York: The Free Press.

Luhmann, Niklas. 1982. *The Differentiation of Society*. Trans. Stephen Holmes and Charles Larmore. New York: Columbia University Press.

———. 2003. "The Cognitive Program of Constructivism and a Reality Which Remains Unknown." In *From Modernism to Postmodernism: An Anthology*, ed. Lawrence Cahoone. Oxford: Blackwell Publishers.

Lyotard, Jean-François. 1984. *The Postmodern Condition: A Report on Knowledge*. Trans. Brian Massumi and Geoff Bennington. Minneapolis: University of Minnesota Press.

Macedo, Stephen. 1991. *Liberal Virtues: Citizenship, Virtue, and Community in Liberal Constitutionalism*. Oxford: Oxford University Press.

MacIntyre, Alasdair. 1981. *After Virtue: A Study in Moral Theory*. Notre Dame: University of Notre Dame Press.

———. 1988. *Whose Justice? Which Rationality?* Notre Dame: University of Notre Dame Press.

———. 1989. "Relativism, Power, and Philosophy." In *Relativism: Interpretation and Confrontation*, ed. Michael Krausz. Notre Dame: University of Notre Dame Press.

Margalit, Avishai, and Joseph Raz. 1995. "National Self-Determination." In *The Rights of Minority Cultures*, ed. Will Kymlicka. Oxford: Oxford University Press.

Margolis, Joseph. 2000. *Historied Thought, Constructed World: A Conceptual Primer for the Turn of the Millennium*. Berkeley and Los Angeles: University of California Press.

———. 2001. *Selves and Other Texts: The Case for Cultural Realism*. University Park: Pennsylvania State University Press.

Marsden, Gary. 1980. *Fundamentalism and American Culture: The Shaping of Twentieth Century Evangelicalism, 1870–1925*. New York: Oxford University Press.

Marty, Martin E., and R. Scott Appleby, eds. 1991. *Fundamentalisms Observed*. Volume 1. Chicago: University of Chicago Press.

———. 1995. *Fundamentalisms Comprehended*. Volume 5. Chicago: University of Chicago Press.

Marx, Karl. 1973. *Grundrisse: Foundations of the Critique of Political Economy*. Trans. Martin Nicolaus. Harmondsworth, U.K.: Penguin Books.

Maturana, Humberto, and Francisco Varela. 1980. *Autopoeisis and Cognition*. Boston: D. Reidel Publishing.

Mawdudi, Sayyid Abul A'Lā. 1974. *Towards Understanding Islam*. Trans. Khurshid Ahmad. Lahore: Idara Tarjuman-ul-Qur'an.

———. 1979. *The Process of Islamic Revolution*. Lahore: Islamic Publications.

———. 1980. *Come Let Us Change the World*. Trans. Kaukab Siddique. Singapore: Thinker's Library.

———. 1990. *An Introduction to Understanding the Qur'an*. Trans. Zafar Ishaq Ansari. Riyadh: World Assembly of Muslim Youth.

———. 1992. *The Economic Problem of Man and its Islamic Solution*. Lahore: Islamic Publications.

Mayer, Ann. 1990. "The *Shari'ah*: A Methodology or a Body of Substantives Rules?" In *Islamic Law and Jurisprudence: Studies in Honor of Farhat J. Ziadeh*, ed. Nicholas Heer. Seattle: University of Washington Press.

Mead, George Herbert. 1974. *Mind, Self, and Society from the Standpoint of a Social Behaviorist*. Chicago: University of Chicago Press.

Merleau-Ponty, Maurice. 1968. "The Intertwining—the Chiasm." In *The Visible and the Invisible*. Trans. Alphonso Lingis. Evanston: Northwestern University Press.

Mill, John Stuart. 1978. *On Liberty*. Indianapolis: Hackett Publishing.

Miller, David. 1997. *On Nationality*. New York: Oxford University Press.

Nanda, Meera. 1997. "The Science Wars in India." *Dissent* 44, no. 1 (winter).

Nasr, Seyyed Hossein. 1987. *Traditional Islam in the Modern World*. London: KPI.

Nietzsche, Friedrich. 1956. *The Birth of Tragedy and The Genealogy of Morals*. Trans. Francis Golffing. Garden City, N.Y.: Doubleday.

Nisbet, Robert. 1990. *The Quest for Community: A Study in the Ethics of Order and Freedom*. Oakland, Calif.: ICS Press.

Nussbaum, Martha. 1990. "Aristotelian Social Democracy." In *Liberalism and the Good*, ed. R. Bruce Douglass et al. New York: Routledge.

Oakeshott, Michael. 1975. *On Human Conduct*. Oxford: Clarendon Press.

———. 1991. *Rationalism in Politics and Other Essays*. Indianapolis: Liberty Fund.

Oren, Michael B. 2002. *Six Days of War: June 1967 and the Making of the Modern Middle East*. New York: Oxford University Press.

Ortega y Gasset, José. 1972. *Meditations on Hunting*. New York: Scribner's.

Parekh, Bhikhu. 1991. "British Citizenship and Cultural Difference." In *Citizenship*, ed. Geoff Andrews. London: Lawrence & Wishart.

———. 1995a. "Ethnocentricity of the Nationalist Discourse." *Nations and Nationalism* 1, no. 1.

———. 1995b. "The Rushdie Affair: Research Agenda for Political Philosophy." In *The Rights of Minority Cultures*, ed. Will Kymlicka. Oxford: Oxford University Press.

———. 1998. "Integrating Minorities." In *Race Relations in Britain*, ed. Tesse Blackstone et al. London: Routledge.

———. 2000. *Rethinking Multiculturalism: Cultural Diversity and Political Theory*. Houndmills, Basingstoke, Hampshire: Macmillan.

Peirce, Charles S. 1931a. *Collected Papers of Charles Sanders Peirce*. Edited by Charles Hartshorne and Paul Weiss. Volume 1. Cambridge: Harvard University Press.

———. 1931b. "Questions Concerning Certain Faculties Claimed for Man." In *Collected Papers of Charles Sanders Peirce*, ed. Charles Hartshorne and Paul Weiss, vol. 5. Cambridge: Harvard University Press.

———. 1955. *Philosophical Writings of Peirce*. Edited by Justus Buchler. New York: Dover Books.

Pipes, Daniel. 2002. *Militant Islam Reaches America*. New York: W. W. Norton.

Pocock, J.G.A. 1975. *The Machiavellian Moment: Florentine Political Thought and the Atlantic Republican Tradition*. Princeton: Princeton University Press.

Polanyi, Karl. 1957. *The Great Transformation: The Political and Economic Origins of Our Time*. Boston: Beacon Press.

Popper, Sir Karl. 1996. *The Myth of the Framework: A Defense of Science and Rationality*. New York: Routledge.

Putnam, Robert. 1995. "Bowling Alone: America's Declining Social Capital." *Journal of Democracy* 6, no. 1 (January).

———. 2000. *Bowling Alone: The Collapse and Revival of American Community*. New York: Simon & Schuster.

Quigley, Carroll. 1979. *The Evolution of Civilizations: An Introduction to Historical Analysis*. Indianapolis: Liberty Fund.

Qutb, Sayyid. 1990. *Milestones*. Trans. Ma'alimfi al-Tariq. Indianapolis: American Trust Publications.

Quine, W.V.O. 1960. "Translation and Meaning." *Word and Object*. Cambridge: MIT Press.

———. 1969. "Ontological Relativity." *Ontological Relativity and Other Essays*. New York: Columbia University Press.

Rahman, Fazlur. 1982. *Islam and Modernity: Transformation of an Intellectual Tradition*. Chicago: University of Chicago Press.

Rashid, Ahmen. 2000. *Taliban: Militant Islam, Oil and Fundamentalism in Central Asia*. New Haven: Yale University Press.

Rawls, John. 1993. *Political Liberalism*. New York: Columbia University Press.

Rodriguez, Richard. 1982. *Hunger of Memory: An Autobiography. The Education of Richard Rodriguez*. New York: Bantam Books.

Rorty, Richard. 1979. *Philosophy and the Mirror of Nature*. Princeton: Princeton University Press.

———. 1989. *Contingency, Irony, and Solidarity*. Cambridge: Cambridge University Press.

———. 1991a. "Habermas and Lyotard on Postmodernity." In *Essays on Heidegger and Others*. Cambridge: Cambridge University Press.

———. 1991b. "Solidarity or Objectivity?" In *Objectivity, Relativism, and Truth*. Cambridge: Cambridge University Press.

———. 1998. "Hilary Putnam and the Relativist Menace." In *Truth and Progress: Philosophical Papers, Volume Three*. Cambridge: Cambridge University Press.

Rose, Margaret. 1991. *The Post-Modern and the Post-Industrial: A Critical Analysis*. Cambridge: Cambridge University Press.

Roy, Olivier. 1986. *Islam and Resistance in Afghanistan*. Trans. Cambridge University Press. Cambridge: Cambridge University Press.

———. 1998. "Fundamentalists without a Common Cause." *Le Monde Diplomatique*, October 2. http://mondediplo.com/1998/10/04/afghan

Royce, Josiah. 1967. "Provincialism." In *Race Questions, Provincialism, and Other American Problems*. Freeport, N.Y.: Books for Libraries Press.

Sandel, Michael. 1996. *Democracy's Discontents: America in Search of a Public Philosophy*. Cambridge: Harvard University Press.

Schiller, Friedrich. 1965. *On the Aesthetic Education of Man in a Series of Letters*. Trans. Reginald Snell. New York: Frederick Ungar Publishing.

Schmitt, Carl. 1996. *The Concept of the Political*. Trans. George Schwab. Chicago: University of Chicago Press.

Sennett, Richard. 1978. *The Fall of Public Man: On the Social Psychology of Capitalism*. New York: Vintage Books.

Shadid, Anthony. 2001. *Legacy of the Prophet: Despots, Democrats, and the New Politics of Islam*. Boulder, Colo.: Westview Press.

Shils, Edward. 1957. "Primordial, Personal, Sacred, and Civil Ties." *British Journal of Sociology* 8 (June).

———. 1997. *The Virtue of Civility: Selected Essays on Liberalism, Tradition, and Civil Society*, ed. Steven Grosby. Indianapolis: Liberty Fund.

Shapiro, Ian, and Will Kymlicka. 1997. *Ethnicity and Group Rights*. New York: New York University Press.

Shklar, Judith. 1984. *Ordinary Vices*. Cambridge: Harvard University Press.

Simpson, Lorenzo. 2001. *The Unfinished Project: Toward a Postmetaphysical Humanism*. New York: Routledge.

Sinha, Rakesh. 1997. "Taliban as I Saw it." In *Taliban and the Afghan Turmoil: The Role of the USA, Pakistan, Iran, and China*, ed. Sreedhar. New Delhi: Himalayan Books.

Sifton, John. 2001. "Temporal Vertigo: A Last Road Trip Through Premodern, Postmodern Afghanistan." *New York Times Magazine*, September 30.

Sivan, Emmanuel. 1985. *Radical Islam: Medieval Theology and Modern Politics*. New Haven: Yale University Press.

Spencer Brown, G. 1969. *Laws of Form*. London: Allen & Unwin.

Spengler, Oswald. 1926–28. *Decline of the West*. Trans. Charles F. Atkinson. New York: A. A. Knopf.

Tamir, Yael. 1993. *Liberal Nationalism*. Princeton: Princeton University Press.

Taylor, Charles. 1992. "The Politics of Recognition." In *Multiculturalism and the Politics of Recognition*, ed. Amy Gutmann. Princeton: Princeton University Press.

Tönnies, Ferdinand. 1957. *Community and Society*. Trans. Charles Loomis. Lansing: Michigan State University Press.

Touraine, Alaine. 1971. *The Post-Industrial Society*. Trans. Leonard Mayhew. New York: Random House.

Toynbee, Arnold. 1961. *A Study of History.* Volume 12, *Reconsiderations.* London: Oxford University Press.

Tucker, Robert C. 1978. *The Marx-Engels Reader.* New York: W. W. Norton.

Turnbull, Colin. 1972. *The Mountain People.* New York: Simon & Schuster.

Von Laue, Theodore. 1987. *The World Revolution of Westernization: The Twentieth Century in Historical Perspective.* New York: Oxford University Press.

Von Uexküll, Jakob. 1926. *Theoretical Biology.* Trans. D. L. MacKinnon. New York: Harcourt, Brace.

Walzer, Michael. 1983. *Spheres of Justice: A Defense of Pluralism and Equality.* New York: Basic Books.

———. 1994. *Thick and Thin: Moral Argument at Home and Abroad.* Notre Dame: University of Notre Dame Press.

———. 1997. *On Toleration.* New Haven: Yale University Press.

Watts, Ian. 1999. "The Origin of Symbolic Culture." In *The Evolution of Culture,* ed. Robin Dunbar, Chris Knight, and Camilla Power. New Brunswick: Rutgers University Press.

Waugh, Evelyn. 1964. *Brideshead Revisited: The Sacred and Profane Memories of Captain Charles Ryder.* London: Chapman & Hall.

Weber, Max. 1972. "Science as a Vocation." In *From Max Weber: Essays in Sociology,* translated and edited by H. H. Gerth and C. Wright Mills. New York: Oxford University Press.

Weinberg, Steven. 1977. *The First Three Minutes: A Modern View of the Origin of the Universe.* Toronto: Bantam Books.

West, Cornell. 1994. *Race Matters.* New York: Vintage Books.

Williams, Bernard. 1981. "The Truth in Relativism." In *Moral Luck: Philosophical Papers, 1973–1980.* Cambridge: Cambridge University Press.

Williams, Roger. 1971. *A Key into the Language of America; Or, An Help to the Language of the Natives in that Part of America, Called New-England* (1643). Menston, U.K.: Scolar Press.

Wilson, Bryan R. 1970. *Rationality.* New York: Harper & Row.

Winch, Peter. 1970. "Understanding a Primitive Society." In *Rationality,* ed. Bryan Wilson. New York: Harper & Row.

Winnicott, D. W. 1965. "The Capacity to Be Alone." In *The Maturational Processes and the Facilitating Environment.* Madison: International Universities Press.

———. 1999. *Playing and Reality.* London: Routledge.

Wong, David B. 1984. *Moral Relativity.* Berkeley and Los Angeles: University of California Press.

———. 1989. "Three Kinds of Incommensurability." In *Relativism: Interpretation and Confrontation,* ed. Michael Krausz. Notre Dame: University of Notre Dame Press.

———. 1995. "Pluralistic Relativism." *Midwest Studies in Philosophy* 20: 378–99.

Young, Iris Marion. 1990. *Justice and the Politics of Difference.* Princeton: Princeton University Press.

Zangwill, Israel. 1909. *The Melting Pot: A Drama in Four Acts.* New York: Macmillan.

INDEX